Hanging Between Heaven and Earth

Hanging Between Heaven and Earth

Capital Crime, Execution Preaching, and Theology in Early New England

SCOTT D. SEAY

Northern Illinois University Press

Published by the Northern Illinois University Press, DeKalb, Illinois 60115

Printed in Canada using postconsumer-recycled, acid-free paper.

Design by Shaun Allshouse

Library of Congress Cataloging-in-Publication Data

Seay, Scott D.

Hanging between heaven and earth: capital crime, execution preaching, and theology in early New England / Scott D. Seay.

p. cm.

Includes bibliographical references and index.

ISBN 978-0-87580-402-6 (clothbound: alk. paper)

1. Execution sermons—New England—History. 2. Capital punishment—Religious aspects—Christianity—History. 3. New England—Church history. 4. New England theology. I. Title.

BV4262.S437 2009

251.00974—dc22

2009007874

In loving memory of my father,
L. David Seay, Jr.

With deepest gratitude to my mother,
Dolores A. Seay

Contents

Acknowledgments

When I ran across my first execution sermon in the spring of 1998, I had no idea that ruminating about capital crime in early New England would occupy nearly the next decade of my life. Thankfully, however, I did not ruminate in solitude. This book has benefited from helpful conversations, occasional arguments, and frequent advice from many people. Over the years I have incurred a number of debts, and I will try now to repay them with heartfelt thanks.

This book began formally as a doctoral dissertation written for the Graduate Department of Religion at Vanderbilt University. So, I extend my thanks first of all to the members of my reading committee: Kathleen Flake, Lewis Baldwin, and George Becker.

But the codirectors of my dissertation deserve special mention. Jack Fitzmier was a mentor in the best sense of the word and an inexhaustible resource for making sense of eighteenth-century New England religion and culture. I am especially grateful to him for remaining committed to this project despite his departure from Vanderbilt to become vice president at Claremont School of Theology. Overseeing my dissertation was a responsibility that would have been much easier for him to have left behind in Nashville.

Dale Johnson was my principal dissertation advisor following Jack's departure. He was an essential figure in my intellectual development throughout my studies at Vanderbilt. He was a model teacher and always insisted that my judgments stand up to the historical evidence without ever losing sight of what is really at stake for me as I engage in historical reflection. In other words, it is he who taught me how to think historically and why doing so matters at all. More importantly, he has been an incomparable pedagogical mentor. I served as his teaching assistant in at least four church history courses, during which our conversations usually focused more on broad issues of teaching than they did on the mechanics of course administration. Never coercive in any sense of the word, his pedagogical mentoring largely made me into the teacher that I am. Indeed, my student teaching evaluations at Vanderbilt Divinity School frequently mentioned the similarities between my teaching and Dale's. Not only does this attest to the great formative influence that he has had on me, but I also consider this a compliment to a superlative degree.

At this point I should express my gratitude also to the Graduate Department of Religion for providing me with a Dissertation Enhancement Grant for the academic year of 2000/01 that enabled me to travel to a number of historical societies and libraries in New England. Although my research there was not as fruitful as I had hoped, I was able at least to put to rest the nagging suspicion that I was missing something. In addition, that grant provided the financial resources for me to print hard copies of all of the execution sermons and related gallows literature that I could find in microprint format. Those twenty-six volumes have traveled with me from Nashville to upstate New York, to northeast Ohio, and now to Indianapolis. On this score I also wish to thank Susie Hanson, Director of the Special Collections at Case Western Reserve University. She helped me gain access to one last execution sermon that for some reason was excluded from both the Evans and the Shaw and Shoemaker microprint collections.

Even after my dissertation was complete, my colleagues at Hamilton College, Ashland University, and Christian Theological Seminary pressed me to continue thinking about the history and theology of capital crime in America and offered many, many opportunities to talk publicly about these issues. A very popular course resulted partly out of my research for this book—"Religious Faith and Criminal Justice in American History"—and I also owe thanks to the eager students who have taken that course over the past six years. My interactions with these colleagues and students undoubtedly have influenced my thinking on these issues in ways of which I am not fully aware.

I owe a tremendous debt of gratitude to Melody Herr and Sara Hoerdeman, my editors at Northern Illinois University Press. They both saw book potential in this project even when all I could see was a dissertation. They also have been wonderfully patient as I obsessed over every prepublication detail, withheld drafts to go over them "one more time," and fumed over the critiques of my reviewers. It is not too much to say that they have made publishing my first book an enjoyable task.

As the book project entered the home stretch, the faculty assistant at Christian Theological Seminary, Joyce Krauser, read and critiqued the entire manuscript. Fortunately for me, she has the mind of a historian and offered a number of very helpful suggestions to make this book better than it ever would have been without her help.

My parents, Dave and Dolores Seay, are the two persons to whom I owe my greatest debts. From my earliest childhood they have encouraged my own intellectual curiosity and supported my academic ambitions without wavering, even when doing so was inconvenient and expensive. Dad was a research chemist, and I always assumed that he secretly hoped that I would follow in his footsteps with a career in the natural sciences. Even though I chose a different path, he patiently encouraged me every step of the way. A man of great faith, he understood as my calling to become a teacher became clearer and supported me unconditionally as I pursued that calling. I wish that he had lived to share with me as I finished this leg of my vocational journey. Mom gave sacrificially to all of her children as we grew up, and continues to do so today. I am especially indebted to her for all of the love and care that she showed to me through a very long childhood illness. She has always been there to pick me up when I fell, to dust me off, and to set me back on my way. Her unfailing maternal commitment continues even in my adulthood: several times during the course of my doctoral studies I was ready to throw in the towel, but she refused to let me. She helped me stay my course. I can honestly say that this project—first the dissertation, then the book—would never have been completed without her encouragement and assistance.

For these reasons and a thousand others, this work is lovingly dedicated to the man and woman I am proud to call my parents.

Hanging Between Heaven and Earth

Introduction

> But ye have set at naught all my counsel,
>
> and would none of my reproof;
>
> I also will laugh at your calamity,
>
> I will mock when your fear cometh.
>
> —*Proverbs 1:25–26*

Early in the morning on September 10, 1801, four men climbed into an open carriage outside the Boston gaol. One of them, Jason Fairbanks, had been sentenced to death a month earlier for the murder of his lover, Elizabeth Fales. Authorities were transporting him back to his hometown to be hanged on the public square. With his wrists and ankles bound in irons, the prisoner sat uncomfortably beside the Suffolk County sheriff. Facing them from the other seat were a deputy sheriff and Dr. Peter Thacher, the minister of Boston's influential Brattle Street Church. It is possible only to imagine what thoughts occupied the condemned man's mind as the driver cracked his whip and the carriage began rolling through the crisp morning air.[1]

The town of Dedham, where Fairbanks soon would be hanged, was organized in 1636 and settled by about thirty yeoman farmers and their families. Among those who signed the original town covenant were Jonathan Fayerbanke and Henry Brock, the great, great, great grandfathers of both the condemned man and his sweetheart. By design, the town had remained a small and exclusive community for generations. The townsmen had signed a covenant that specifically bound them to work toward maintaining religious, social, and economic homogeneity; strangers who wished to settle in Dedham needed the approval of the town's selectmen. The census of 1790 reveals that the strategy basically worked: the agricultural community had fewer than 1,600 members, and most of them belonged to a handful of large and interconnected family systems. Throughout the eighteenth century, the community's idea of religious diversity meant that the town had three Congregationalist churches and an Episcopalian one composed mainly of former Congregationalists.[2]

By 1800, however, there were clear signs that the character of the town was changing irreversibly. Dedham was now the squire town of the newly formed Norfolk County, and this status brought with it an influx of lawyers, politicians, and other people doing county business. Those traveling from Boston southward toward Providence and westward toward Hartford often preferred taking the improved roads running through the town. Taverns were springing up along these thoroughfares, housing a transient population and providing a way to make a living in Dedham besides farming. Political parties were emerging in all levels of government, and the freemen found themselves evenly divided between Federalist and Republican. Newspapers, relatively new phenomena in country towns, were fueling partisan rancor, and social unrest was becoming alarmingly common. Finally, dissenting religious traditions—mainly Baptists—were gaining ground in some circles, and even the Congregationalist churches were feeling the rumblings of division as unitarianism and universalism became increasingly attractive to many. One thing was certain: Dedham after 1800 no longer would be the insular utopia that generations of the Fairbanks family had known.[3]

Fairbanks and his sweetheart "Betsey" Fales first noticed one another in 1796 because both were enrolled in a singing school conducted at the Third Parish Church in Dedham. He was sixteen, and she was fourteen, about the age that young people of the time were expected to begin a courtship. Soon they learned that they had much in common. Both came from respectable, well-established families. Beyond their musical talents, they shared a passion for literature and began spending hours together poring over the latest sentimental novels. They often took walks together through the Norfolk County countryside, communing with nature and with one another. They spent a great deal of time entertaining themselves in their family homes and in the homes of mutual friends. To many observers, and especially to Fairbanks himself, it appeared that the couple was falling in love and soon would be married.[4]

From another perspective, the courtship seemed different. In an agricultural community that valued industry and self-reliance, Fairbanks had developed a reputation for being idle and overly dependent on his family. Partly his physical condition was to blame: at the age of twelve, he had been inoculated against smallpox and soon thereafter developed a life-threatening case of the disease. Consistent with the medical customs of the day, doctors aggressively treated him with mercury; although the regimen saved his life, it also irreparably damaged his overall constitution. He suffered from frequent bleeding of the lungs, chronic headaches, and stiffness in his joints. In fact, his right arm was virtually immobile and became atrophied over time from disuse. This physical debility rendered him unable to help his father and four older brothers on the family farm. He briefly attended the nearby Wethersfield Academy, but his headaches prevented him from completing his course of study. He was apprenticed to a relative in the county clerk's office, but he proved unable to tolerate the tedious work of a transcriber, too. Many of the hardy country folk of Dedham showed little sympathy for the ailing youth; to them he seemed just plain lazy. It is clear that Nehemiah and Sarah Fales especially began to question whether Fairbanks offered much promise as a husband for their beloved daughter.[5]

But Fairbanks himself bore some responsibility for the souring relationship between him and his lover's family. During one of his many visits in the Fales home, he made a thoughtless comment about the suitor of Betsey's sister, and the whole family took offense. Worse still, he had penned a poem poking fun at Betsey's mother; when his bawdy verse appeared in print (probably without his permission), the whole family became his inveterate enemies. Nehemiah and Sarah Fales banned Fairbanks from their home and did all that they could to frustrate the young couple's relationship. They must have felt some relief when, after more than a year of courtship, the young couple agreed to part company until tempers cooled.[6]

Tensions between Fairbanks and his suitor's parents kept them apart for over a year. But sometime in the summer of 1800, the lovers resumed their courtship in secret: they rendezvoused twice a week in Mason's Pasture among a cluster of birch trees a short distance from the Fales farm. At other times, they met in the Fairbanks home or in the homes of mutual friends who encouraged their covert relationship. On rare occasions, they even spent the night together. Growing increasingly impatient, Fairbanks pressed Fales to run off to Wrentham with him to be married, but she consistently refused, fearing that her parents would disown her. For almost a year, the couple lived the kind of tortured love affair described on the pages of the sentimental novels that they loved to read together.[7]

The fateful day came on May 18, 1801. It is impossible to know for certain what happened when the couple met for the last time in Mason's Pasture shortly after one o'clock. All that is known for sure is that two hours later Fairbanks staggered up to the doorstep of the Fales home, covered in blood and brandishing a penknife. He frantically exclaimed that Fales had killed herself and that he had made an attempt on his own life, but his physical disability prevented him from succeeding. Not surprisingly, the story did not convince Nehemiah Fales, and he ordered one of his sons to detain the suspected murderer while he and his brother Samuel rushed to help the dying young woman. Nehemiah filled his hat with water from the nearby stream and offered it to her while her uncle covered her with her shawl and Fairbanks's greatcoat. A frantic Sarah Fales arrived twenty minutes later, just in time to see her daughter expire. Besides the ten stab wounds covering her body, the young woman's throat was slit; she had no chance of survival.[8]

Meanwhile, the remaining men of the Fales house carried Fairbanks into an upstairs bedroom and eventually called upon Dedham physician Charles Kitteridge to tend to him. He was in critical condition, with a wide gash across his throat and three deep stab wounds each in his breast, right side, thigh, and belly. For the next two days Fairbanks convalesced in the Fales home; the family's resentment of him must surely have been exceeded only by their unspeakable grief. Long before Fairbanks was brought to trial, the Fales family had drawn their own conclusion about what happened. The young woman's tombstone in the First Parish cemetery reads: "Sacred to the memory of Miss Elizabeth Fales, dau. of Mr. Nehe'h & Mrs. Sarah Fales, who was found *murdered* 18 May 1801, in the 19th year of her age."[9]

Dr. Kitteridge watched nervously as the sheriff of Norfolk County and his deputies carried Fairbanks out of the Fales house in a makeshift litter. A coroner's inquest jury determined that the young man probably was at least an accessory in Fales's death and that he should be detained until the whole thing could be sorted out. For two months the suspected murderer languished in the Dedham gaol, surviving at least one serious case of tetanus. For a short time in midsummer some newspapers even reported that he died while in custody. More damaging rumors were circulating about him, though: some were heard to say that Paine's *Age of Reason* was more important to him than his Bible; others denounced him as callously impenitent, devoid of conscience and of a sense of right and wrong. In a society that was deeply suspicious of deist infidelity and that expected a criminal to undergo a dramatic eleventh-hour conversion, these rumors were damaging indeed. It appeared that his fate was sealed before he ever came to trial.[10]

Surprisingly Fairbanks did recover and was arraigned before the Supreme Judicial Court on August 5. He pleaded "not guilty" to the charge that he "feloniously, willfully, maliciously, and of his malice aforethought" committed murder. When the trial opened early on the following morning, it became clear that the newly erected Norfolk County Court House would not be able to accommodate the crowd. Accordingly, the proceedings were moved to the First Parish meetinghouse, where curious spectators eventually overflowed into the churchyard and listened through the open windows. For the next day and a half, veteran attorney general and Republican party leader James Sullivan prosecuted the case;

two up-and-coming attorneys and Federalist party leaders—Harrison Gray Otis and John Lowell, Jr.—ably stood as Fairbanks's state-provided defense team. Presiding over the trial were four eminent Massachusetts jurists, all of them boasting of long and distinguished careers as architects of both state and federal jurisprudence. In the end, however, democracy demanded that twelve ordinary Dedham citizens would decide the fate of the accused murderer.[11]

The attorney general began by painting a damning portrait of the defendant's character: unwilling to work and too lazy to pursue an education, Fairbanks began nurturing the lustful obsession with Fales that ended in tragedy. The key prosecution witness was Dr. Nathaniel Ames, one of several physicians who examined the victim's body, and he testified with resolute certainty that Fales could not have inflicted the fatal wounds on herself. Twenty-six other prosecution witnesses were paraded before the packed meetinghouse to develop a strong circumstantial case. Members of the Fales family testified that the relationship was a figment of his imagination; others claimed that he nurtured resentment against her parents and even vowed revenge; still others revealed that on the day in question, he resolved to rape her if she again refused to marry him. In his closing argument, the prosecutor hammered away at this circumstantial evidence to prove that Fairbanks committed his crime "with malice aforethought."

His defense attorneys made a valiant effort to defend Fairbanks. They played up his physical debility, claiming that his withered right arm and his weak constitution would have made it impossible for him to overpower Fales and kill her. They called their own medical experts, whose testimony directly contradicted that of the respected Dr. Ames. In a moment of zealous representation of his client, Lowell nearly amputated one of his fingers demonstrating how it would have been possible for Fales to stab herself in the back. Fourteen additional defense witnesses were called to develop an equally strong circumstantial case in Fairbanks's defense. Some explained that Fales was an overwrought and melodramatic adolescent, whose perception of reality had been warped by the sentimental novels that she loved to read.[12] Others claimed that some of the prosecution witnesses were mentally unstable and therefore unreliable.[13]

The defense rested its case shortly after ten o'clock on Friday evening, and by eight o'clock the next morning the jury had reached a consensus. Before a packed meetinghouse, the foreman, a Revolutionary War veteran named Eliakim Adams, delivered the verdict: "guilty." After affirming the fairness of his trial and unanimous agreement of the justices with the verdict, Chief Justice Francis Dana urged Fairbanks to make profitable use of his remaining days by repenting of his crime and making atonement for the profligacy of his life. The convicted murderer pleaded with the court to challenge the testimony of two prosecution witnesses that he considered perjurious, but his request was denied. The Chief Justice then pronounced the sentence required by law: that "you, Jason Fairbanks, be carried from the gaol from whence you came, and from thence to the place of execution, and be hanged by the neck until you are dead." As was the custom, the court granted a reprieve of an unspecified duration so that Fairbanks could make his peace with God.[14]

Unsatisfied with the outcome of the trial, Fairbanks's older brother, Ebenezer, sneaked up to the Dedham gaol with at least six accomplices in the middle of the night on August 19, determined to break the condemned man out of jail. Two of those involved—Isaac Whiting and Reuben Farrington—had been witnesses for the prosecution and apparently felt that their testimony had been misrepresented at trial. However they managed to do so, they freed not only Fairbanks, but also Andrew Bartholomew, a man being held pending trial for housebreaking. Fairbanks and another of his liberators, Henry Dukeham, parted company with the others and hurried out of Dedham under cover of night.[15]

The next morning, newspaper headlines throughout the region issued an urgent appeal: "Stop the Murderer!!" Sheriff Cutler offered a reward of first $500 and then $1,000 for anyone who would capture and return the escapees. Federalist attorney and Dedham resident Fisher Ames knew the danger that the escape posed to the reputation of his hometown and drew up a statement signed by over three hundred residents. Signatories agreed to whatever measures law enforcement authorities thought would be necessary to find and apprehend the convicted murderer. Meanwhile, Fairbanks and his liberator made their way across western

Massachusetts to Worcester and Spencer, then to Hadley where they crossed the Connecticut River. They turned northward and passed through Cheshire on their way to Bennington, Vermont. After a brief stay in Arlington, they crossed over into New York and reached Skeensborough on the southernmost tip of Lake Champlain. The convicted murderer had been at large for four days, and it seemed to many that he might escape judgment.[16]

The partisan press had a field day debating the political significance of Fairbanks's escape. Boston's leading Federalist paper, the *Columbian Sentinel*, linked the jailbreak with an incident three years before in which some of the Republican citizens of Dedham had erected a liberty pole in protest against President Adams's unpopular Alien and Sedition Acts (1798). The paper claimed that Fairbanks had been liberated by "a banditti of liberty-pole gentry," a group of Jacobin malcontents looking for any opportunity to rebel against established authorities. Boston's widely read Republican paper, the *Independent Chronicle,* aggressively vindicated the reputation of the Dedham citizenry. Accusing its rival of slander, the paper assured its readers that there had been no mob action to liberate the condemned man. Locals were, in fact, cooperating fully with authorities to see that Fairbanks was apprehended as quickly as possible. Not all Republicans, they argued, were complete anarchists.[17]

On the morning of August 23, Fairbanks and his companion sat in the Skeensborough tavern where they had spent the night; they were waiting on their breakfast to be served. Dukeham had paid fifteen dollars to hire a boat to take Fairbanks up Lake Champlain to St. John's in Canada. Just then a man from Hadley named Moses Holt entered the tavern and queried whether anyone was headed to Canada. Unaware that the stranger was one of a three-man posse hired by the Norfolk County sheriff, Dukeham offered him passage aboard the vessel that he had hired. Under this ruse, Holt managed to separate the two fugitives long enough for his fellow bounty hunters—Henry Tisdale of Dover and Seth Wheelock of Medfield—to apprehend the accomplice, while Holt himself returned to the tavern to apprehend Fairbanks. Neither of the fugitives had been on his guard since crossing the Massachusetts state line; they never dreamed that anyone would pursue them as far as they had.[18]

Bound with ropes and guarded by three armed men, Fairbanks and Henry Dukeham were transported on horseback over the Massachusetts state line to Northhampton. By order of Governor Caleb Strong, the bounty hunters transferred custody to Ebenezer Mattoon, the Sheriff of Hampshire County. He and his deputies had been charged with the unpleasant task of transporting the condemned murderer and his accomplice to Boston. His hands and feet bound in irons, Fairbanks spoke freely about his trial and escape during the two-day carriage ride; but when questioned about the murder itself, he remained peculiarly silent, convincing the lawmen that he was indeed guilty. When they arrived at the Boston gaol in the late morning of August 29, they discovered that the governor had issued a warrant for Fairbanks's execution twelve days later. Rev. Thomas Thacher made repeated pastoral visits to him during his final days, at one point making a last-ditch effort to drive the prisoner to repentance. "Unhappy young man!" he began during one of these visits, "You have wandered very far from your heavenly Father . . . if you returned to him with sincere acknowledgement of your crimes, he would receive you to his house and arms. But under no other condition could you expect forgiveness."[19]

The day finally had come for Fairbanks to be executed. A crowd of ten thousand people milled around on the Dedham Commons, waiting for the condemned man to arrive and face his eternal fate. None of those gathered were likely to remember the last time the town had played host to a public execution seventy years before. Pennysheet broadsides circulated among the crowd, one of them pronouncing the condemned man's innocence, another warning parents of the dangers of interfering in the love lives of their children. A half-mile down the road, Fairbanks emerged from the Dedham gaol, accompanied by the Revs. Peter and Thomas Thacher, and began walking down his *via dolorosa* to the gallows erected on the town square. Because Fairbanks was flanked by the Roxbury troop of horses, everyone in the crowd had to strain to catch a glimpse of the dead man walking. Along the way, his two chaplains repeatedly pled with the condemned man to follow the model of the Bible's penitent thief on the cross: they urged him to especially acknowledge his crime and affirm the justice of his death sentence.[20]

As Fairbanks approached the town common, the execution ritual neared its climax. Sheriff Cutler and his men maintained a vigilant watch over the restless crowd, fearing that mob violence might break out without notice. Especially since the Revolution, the behavior of such crowds was increasingly unpredictable; sometimes conflicts arose between parties debating the guilt or innocence of the condemned; occasionally attempts were made to free the condemned person; some crowds were even known to heckle or assault civil and religious authorities out of sheer defiance. No wonder critics were arguing that the spectacle of public execution had a demoralizing effect on the public and were calling for an end to the practice.[21]

Fairbanks, Rev. Thacher, and Sheriff Cutler slowly ascended the steep stairs of the scaffold. After reaching the top of the narrow platform, the condemned man stood on display before the enormous crowd. After the minister pronounced a blessing on him and prayed for his soul, Sheriff Cutler asked the young man if he had anything to say. He shook his head slightly. Performing what must be one of the most unpleasant duties of his office, the sheriff then pulled a white linen cap over Fairbanks's head and tightened the noose around his neck. His hands were tied together behind his back, but in one of them was a handkerchief, with which he was expected to signal when he was ready to die. Almost immediately, he dropped the bright cloth. The deputies below pulled the support beam out from underneath the plank on which Fairbanks was standing; with one blinding jerk his body hanged between heaven and earth. Only those closest to the scaffold heard the creaking timbers as they watched the poor malefactor expire. After the lifeless corpse of Jason Fairbanks had swung for about twenty-five minutes, the county coroner cut it down and prepared it for burial.[22]

As New Englanders had done for generations, some undoubtedly looked to their ministers to help them make meaning of this prolonged tragedy. On the Sunday morning following the execution, Rev. Thomas Thacher stood before his congregation at Third Parish Church and preached a sermon entitled "The Danger of Despising the Divine Counsel." Basing his remarks on Proverbs 1:24–28, he made the age-old argument that the calamities of life only make sense when people are willing to learn moral lessons from them. Indeed, such divine counsels remind us that we are accountable to God for our behavior; unless we take heed of them and cultivate lives of "progressive virtue," we are likely to reap from life only misery and woe. In the Fairbanks execution specifically, he claimed that God had exhibited the consequences of being carried away by "black, impetuous passions." This was a warning from God to everyone: "Can it be possible," he asked, "[that] his sacred voice should be unheard? Are there any among us, who, from that tragical event, will not be awakened from levity and vice, to a sense of religion and virtue?" "Are there any," he concluded, "who while contemplating this melancholy event, will still go on in their profligate habits?"[23]

But Thacher apparently wanted to do more in his sermon than merely identify a moral lesson to be learned; he dedicated a large section of his sermon to defending Fairbanks against the exaggerated rumors about him that were swirling in the community. Offering neither apology nor extenuation, the minister coolly related his observations of the condemned man's behavior and urged everyone to judge for themselves according to the dictates of their consciences.

In describing his numerous prison meetings with Fairbanks throughout his ordeal, Thacher emphasized the prisoner's "calm mind" and "perfect decorum." After his trial and condemnation, he reported, the young man was embittered toward several of the witnesses; slowly his hostility eased, however, and he entered a "state of benevolence with all mankind." Most importantly for his hearers, the minister told of his efforts to lead the prisoner to a sincere and evangelical conversion experience in preparation for his death. Apparently, he had not been successful. Thacher reported that Fairbanks usually lacked the candor for discussing such matters and never really admitted his guilt or professed a hope in eternal life. Nonetheless, Fairbanks died with a kind of stoic resolve that, in any other person, might have been an admirable quality. Thacher concluded that, although he was not a model of penitence, Fairbanks certainly did not deserve the reputation of being a hardened wretch devoid of all sensibility or of being hostile to all religious instruction.[24]

Later that afternoon the minister in nearby Dorchester, Rev. Thaddeus Mason Harris, preached a second execution sermon in

Third Parish Church. Because he had not had been given "sufficient warning . . . to prepare an appropriate discourse," he chose from his manuscripts a sermon that he had preached seven years before. Drawing from Psalm 34:11–14, the Unitarian minister urged all young people to follow the "plan of life" recommended by the psalmist: fear the Lord, avoid sin by governing the passions, and do good to others. Although he did not even mention Fairbanks or Fales, near the end of the discourse, he urged young people to avoid "idle and romantic books." Almost as if he were recalling the trial testimony, he warned that they "give wrong ideas of human life, inflame the passions, delude the imagination, and corrupt the heart." The major purpose of this second sermon appears to have been conciliatory; he urged the citizens of Dedham to "forego all of those personal animosities and censorious reflections, to which the unhappy affair may have given rise." He plainly told them to "Drop the subject and all contentious disquisition upon it," and pray for a time when "harmony and quiet" again would "prevail through this perplexed and distressed vicinity."[25]

Within a week of the execution, caretakers of the cemetery at the First Parish Church erected a tombstone in the loose soil at the head of Fairbanks's grave. Ironically, his final resting place was a mere seventy feet from that of Betsey Fales. The stone reads: "Sacred to the memory of Jason Fairbanks, who departed this life 10th September, 1801. Aged 21 years." Obviously, the epitaph obscures more of the story than it reveals, and perhaps that is the point: the gravestone is not for remembering after all, but for forgetting the whole sordid affair.[26]

Rituals of public execution like this one were repeated throughout New England at least 460 times between 1623 and 1835. Though the story lines varied and the characters changed, the essential purposes of these rituals remained constant across the period: they warned of the wages of sin, reconciled the convict to both God and the community, and demonstrated the cooperative authority of church and state. The surprising frequency of New England public executions, as well as the assumption that such gruesome displays taught important moral lessons for the community, made the ritual of public execution a central plank in the platform of criminal justice administration in early New England.[27]

This book explores one element of the complex ritual of hanging day: the execution sermon. Chapter One situates the execution sermon in the larger ritual of public execution and describes its place in the developing body of early American crime literature. Contextualizing the execution sermons of early New England in this way will help illumine both their theological content and the development of this content across time.

Undertaking a sustained theological analysis of the hundred or so execution sermons preached and published in early New England, Chapters Two through Four answer two interrelated questions: how did the New England clergy make theological sense out of capital crime and justify punishing such crimes with death; and how did their theological explications of capital crime and its punishment develop across the period, especially as they relate to broader trends in New England theology? These chapters track developments in the theology of capital crime and punishment by looking at three themes in particular: human sinfulness; the economy of conversion; and the nature and function of civil government. This analysis reveals that patterns of development in execution preaching specifically mirror developments in New England theology generally. Thus, in addition to helping us see how people of the past made theological sense out of capital crime and its punishment, execution sermons also provide us with a window into a world of theological change in this broader context.

Chapter Five describes a "new moral discourse" about crime and punishment that emerged after the American Revolution. Although it arose primarily outside of New England, this new moral discourse challenged many of the cherished assumptions that had developed in generations of execution preaching. Even as New England legislators were debating the privatization of executions, this new moral discourse helped erode the intellectual support for both public executions themselves and for execution preaching until both traditions quietly disappeared.

Almost everything about the ritual of public execution in early New England seems quite distant from our time and place. The American public generally no longer thinks theologically about crime and punishment. Today executions are performed in private, with only a select few chosen to be witnesses. The authorities of church and state are sharply separated; when they talk about it at all, church authorities most often vigorously oppose capital punishment rather than support it. Nevertheless, the Conclusion will suggest that the questions with which the people of Dedham struggled over two hundred years ago are still the questions with which we struggle today: what motivates people to commit heinous crimes in the first place? What possibility—if any—exists for criminals to be reformed? What roles do the state and the church play in deciding such matters as life and death? What is the purpose of punishment, and how is that purpose best achieved?

By looking at the execution sermons of early New England, we will discover some of the compelling answers that the people of that time found to their vexing questions about crime and punishment. In so doing, perhaps we might come to greater clarity about our own answers as well.

CHAPTER ONE

The Contexts of the Execution Sermon

> And those which remain shall hear and fear, and shall henceforth commit no more any such evil among you.
>
> —*Deuteronomy 19:20*

The Fairbanks execution narrated in the previous chapter illustrates how important it is to situate the execution sermons of early New England in their ritual, literary, and historical contexts. In their oral form, execution sermons were important parts of the larger ritual of public execution. Depending on historical context, the delivery of an execution sermon contributed to the ritual by helping cleanse the land of the threat of evil, facilitating the repentance and final salvation of the condemned, or justifying theologically the cooperative authority of church and state. Because the clergy were such important public intellectuals in early New England, their role in the ritual of public execution was a critical one: until the American Revolution, virtually they alone were authorized to make meaning of the activities of hanging day.

In their written form, execution sermons were an important part of a developing body of crime literature in early New England. The execution sermon initially was the unrivalled genre in that body, but slowly other genres began to appear—criminal conversion narratives, last dying speeches, poems and broadsides, trial reports, and criminal biographies—most of which were modeled upon similar forms in England. Unique to New England, the published execution sermon nonetheless remained an explicitly theological interpretation of capital crime and its punishment. Because they were very popular reading material in early New England, they reinforced the moral and theological lessons of hanging day long after the ritual itself had concluded.

Before this study continues in subsequent chapters to explore the theological content of the execution sermons of early New England, the present chapter situates them in various contexts. After describing the ritual of public execution in early modern England and some of the crime literature associated with it, the chapter explores the place of New England execution sermons in three major contexts: Puritan, Provincial, and Early National. These labels are not used in any technical sense here; rather they intend to provide a chronological structure for this analysis and to suggest broad patterns of belief and action only. From this survey it will be clear that both the ritual of public execution in early New England and the literature related to it developed significantly over the period. Understanding these contextual developments, then, should be the first step in making sense of these unique sermons theologically.

The English Background

As early as the 1570s, those who had been condemned to death in England—almost always for murder and property crimes—sat in the dark cells of London's historic Newgate prison, awaiting either their pardon or their hanging day. The prison chaplain, known as the Ordinary, ministered to the condemned in their remaining weeks in order to prepare them spiritually for their eternal fate and to extract a confession from them. On the Sunday prior to execution day, all of the condemned crowded into the chapel at Newgate prison to hear one last sermon and to have a burial service said for them. In the chapel, they sat in the "condemned pew," a black enclosure containing a coffin situated at the foot of the pulpit. Curious Londoners often paid a small admission fee to observe the spectacle.

Early the next morning, on the day of execution itself, the condemned were led in a group from their cells to the press yard at Newgate, where a blacksmith removed the iron fetters from their hands and feet. The hangman then bound the hands of the condemned with rope and slipped halters over their heads, coiling the remaining rope around their bodies. A procession then formed, including the hangman and his assistants, a company of armed militia, the under sheriff, the Ordinary, and the condemned themselves, who rode atop their coffins in horse-drawn carts. Upon leaving the press yard, the procession met a large crowd who lined both sides of Oxford Street for the three miles leading to the gallows at Tyburn. The unruly spectators often threw objects and shouted obscenities at the condemned and their escorts, while the great bell at St. Sepulchre —rung only on execution days—pealed in the background. Sometimes the drunken crowd and the condemned together sang the "Hanging Song" based upon Psalm 51. In cases where the crowd was more calm, the procession stopped at the two taverns en route, where the condemned were treated to their last drinks.

Upon reaching Tyburn, the carts were backed under the crossbeams of the large "triple tree" gallows standing in the middle of Oxford Street. The condemned stood at the back end of the cart, and the hangman fastened the halter rope to the crossbeam. Standing in the cart, the Ordinary prayed and the condemned customarily delivered a "last dying speech" warning spectators about the dangers of sinful living and sometimes making a confession of their crimes. Afterward the hangman pulled the white linen caps over the faces of the condemned and double-checked the hanging ropes. At the hangman's signal the drivers of the carts whipped the horses, pulling the carts out from underneath the condemned, who were left suspended only inches from the ground. Sometimes the hangman, his assistants, and even members of the condemned person's family would pull on their dangling legs to hasten death. After hanging for a half an hour or so, the corpses were cut down and claimed by members of the family for burial or sold to local physicians for dissection. Though variations certainly existed, this basic ritual was repeated at Newgate and Tyburn until 1783, when executions were moved into the press yard at the prison, where fewer spectators could gather. Parliament finally abolished the practice of public execution altogether in 1868.[1]

A rich body of gallows literature developed in connection with public executions in early modern England. As early as the 1580s, murder pamphlets began flooding the streets of London and finding their way into the English countryside on the carts of traveling booksellers. These pamphlets were wildly popular because they unashamedly catered to the prurient interests of their readership: they shocked readers with graphic images of murders in progress, narrated the gruesome crimes in titillating detail, and speculated about the cosmic battle between God and the devil being played out in the crimes. Owing to the ascendancy of English Puritanism, by the 1640s criminal conversion narratives also emerged as a popular genre of crime literature. Less concerned with the crimes themselves, these narratives recounted instead the miraculous spiritual transformation of condemned criminals. Finally, in the 1680s the Ordinary of Newgate began publishing execution accounts that described the behavior of the condemned and recorded their last words at the gallows. Hundreds of these execution accounts were published in the eighteenth century, and sometimes they included a brief synopsis of the "condemned sermon" that the Ordinary preached prior to the execution. Although these genres of crime literature certainly taught important civil and religious lessons about crime and its punishment, historians agree that the main reason that they were printed was to turn a profit.[2]

Peter Lake and Michael Questier have argued that both the ritual of public execution in early modern England and the literature associated with it often were arenas of significant ideological conflict between representatives of the established Church of England, Roman Catholics, and dissenting Protestants like the Puritans and Quakers. For the purposes of this study it is important especially to discern the place of English Puritans in this conflict. Although they were nonconformists and therefore had no legal standing to be involved in the ritual, English Puritans between the 1580s and 1680s were eager participants in public executions. They often visited with the condemned in prison before their executions. They eagerly joined the crowds who lined Oxford Street and stood at the Tyburn gallows, except they regularly prayed for the condemned rather than heckled them. And they sometimes intervened at the gallows, preaching impromptu sermons in order to drive the condemned to repentance if they believed that the Ordinary had failed.[3]

The Puritan Context (1623–1700)

By the time the New England Puritans performed their first public execution in 1623, they undoubtedly were familiar with the ritual and the related literature on the other side of the Atlantic. Judging from the available evidence, public executions in New England during the first decades of settlement followed the basic patterns of the English ritual. New England Puritans retained at least the sermon and the scaffold speech, although neither genre achieved the authority of print until later in the century.

When infanticide Dorothy Talbye was executed at Boston in 1638, for example, the venerable Hugh Peter "gave an exhortation to the people" in spite of the fact that the condemned woman made quite a show of her impenitence and refused to make a gallows confession. Another infanticide named Mary Martin played the more predictable role when she was executed at Boston in 1647. At her execution John Cotton "preached a sermon on Ezek. 16. 20, 21 . . . whereof great notice was taken." Martin's comportment at the gallows was "very penitent," and she even admitted before her death that she had tried two times to kill her infant before she finally succeeded. And in 1662, John Davenport preached a sermon before the execution of a sixty-year-old man named Mr. Poster, condemned for repeated acts of bestiality. At the gallows the "bewitched beast . . . was awakened into a most unutterable and intolerable anguish of soul" and made a last dying speech in which he warned others of the danger of neglecting their lives of prayer.[4]

In the last three decades of the seventeenth century, many Puritan leaders were convinced that New England had entered a spiral of moral and religious decline that needed to be reversed. They complained that younger generations were failing to meet the strident Puritan standards of church membership; colonists were becoming more materialistic; more people flaunted social vices like drunkenness, fornication, and Sabbath-breaking; and the older social hierarchies were under more frequent attack. In their regular preaching, the Puritan clergy adopted the role of modern-day Jeremiahs who decried this declining piety and warned that God's judgment would fall upon the land if New Englanders did not repent.[5]

A more elaborate and formalized ritual of public execution emerged as a response to this perceived decline in Puritan piety and the related fear that evil was overtaking the Holy Commonwealth. Along with other rituals that developed or became more common about this time—fast days and days of humiliation, church discipline and excommunication, witch trials and clerical exorcisms—public executions helped alleviate the anxieties of New England Puritans. David Hall has argued that all of these rituals embodied the "moral allegory of repentance and renewal." Because Puritans believed so strongly that God held people accountable for their sins and punished them accordingly, their rituals functioned to "erase the taint of sin" and reaffirm "the ideal nature of the body social." Especially after 1670, public executions in New England "recapitulated the great cycle of sinning and repentance that men and women passed through as pilgrims on their way to grace."[6]

Similarly, Karen Halttunen has argued that public executions functioned in Puritan New England as a "ritual response to the problem of evil." Burdened with an acute sense of the ever-present danger of evil, Puritans developed a number of rituals, not to avert evil completely, but to find safety in the midst of it. These rituals fully acknowledged the power of evil and then transcended it "through an act of reconciliation that mended both the breach between the sinner and God and that between the sinner and the community." Thus, the cyclical movement from sin to hope, from danger to deliverance was enacted in the rituals themselves, the very dynamic that formed the core of all Puritan religious experience. By helping Puritans find security in the midst of pervasive evil, rituals like public executions calmed their anxieties about the decline of the Holy Commonwealth and relieved their fears that God's judgment was imminent.[7]

Evidence suggests that the ritual of public execution in Puritan New England after 1670 shared some characteristics with its English counterpart but that it was developing unique qualities as well. After his or her arrest, the condemned was held in the gaol of the town in which he or she allegedly committed the offense. During the two months or so of imprisonment pending trial, the accused received visits from the clergy and pious laypeople who helped him or her prepare spiritually for the trial and its consequences. After the trial, efforts to drive the condemned to credible repentance became more vigorous because the time was short. Until the turn of the eighteenth century the length of time between condemnation and execution was alarmingly brief, usually no more than ten or twelve days.[8]

One important difference between the rituals of public execution as they developed in England and New England has to do with what counted as a capital crime. In seventeenth-century England, no fewer than fifty crimes regularly were punished with death, even if many criminals escaped through the court's liberal application of "benefit of clergy." By contrast, the capital jurisdiction of Puritan New England was relatively trim. Because they sought to build a "Bible commonwealth," Puritan leaders in Massachusetts, for example, initially restricted their list of capital crimes to those for which the Bible specifically said that the offender "shall surely be put to death." Twelve crimes deserved death according to the Bay Colony's first criminal code, the *Body of Liberties* (1641). All of them found specific sanction in the Law of Moses: idolatry, witchcraft, blasphemy, murder, manslaughter, poisoning, bestiality, sodomy, kidnapping, bearing false witness, rebellion against one's parents, and striking one's parents. As the seventeenth century wore on, several other capital crimes were added to the list: arson and heresy (1652); violation by Quakers of the terms of their banishment (1658); robbery (1672); piracy and mutiny (1673); treason (1678); and service in a foreign army (1684). In actual practice, however, Massachusetts Puritans most frequently executed only those who committed murder (including infanticide), those who practiced witchcraft, and those who committed sexual crimes such as adultery, rape, incest, and bestiality. Apparently, the evil against which New England needed defense was the kind that threatened the religious and moral purity of Holy Commonwealth.[9]

Either for the Sunday before or on the day of the execution itself, a leading Puritan minister prepared a sermon to be delivered in the town meetinghouse. The more celebrated cases occasioned multiple execution sermons—either individual sermons by several ministers or a series of sermons by a single minister—and some of them were preached during the week prior to hanging day, usually the Thursday "lecture day." In front of the enormous crowd who packed into the meetinghouse, the condemned sat on the front pew below the pulpit, except on the rare occasions when he or she refused to attend the service. The ritual purpose of preaching these execution sermons was not merely to harangue the condemned about his or her crime prior to death. As succeeding chapters will demonstrate, the execution sermon in Puritan New England instead explained how public execution healed the breach in the integrity of the community by ridding the land of those who commit serious crime and thereby preventing God's judgment on the entire community. Because they were the clergy of an established church, Puritan execution preachers embodied the cooperative authority of church and state as they preached execution sermons.

According to the standards of the day, the crowds who packed into Puritan meetinghouses to hear these sermons and to gawk at the condemned were quite large. The average New England meetinghouse held no more than 750 persons, and documentary evidence suggests that when execution sermons were preached the pews usually were crammed full and additional auditors stood in the aisles, leaned against the walls, and gathered outside underneath open windows.[10]

Although it may be an exceptional case, details about the crowds gathered for the execution activities of murderer James Morgan in 1686 may be instructive. After preaching one of the three sermons occasioned by this execution on the Sunday before the hanging day, Rev. Cotton Mather mused in his diary that he "could not gett unto the Pulpit, but by climbing over Pues and Heads."

Leading Puritan jurist Samuel Sewall described the scene outside the meetinghouse on this same occasion, writing in his diary that "there was a very vast Assembly, and the street [was] full of such as could not get in." An even larger crowd assembled to witness Morgan's execution four days later. So many people crammed into Boston's sizeable Old North Church to hear Rev. Increase Mather's execution sermon that the walls of the gallery began to crack under the weight of the audience. So, the massive crowd removed to Old South Church, where Mather finished his sermon. London bookseller John Dutton was an eyewitness to the Morgan execution, and in a letter to his friend George Larkin he estimated the crowd to be nearly 5,000. The size of the crowds gathered at the Morgan execution activities is even more impressive when they are compared with the entire population of Boston at the time, which was no more than 7,000.[11]

On hanging day, the crowd poured out of the meetinghouse following the delivery of the execution sermon and joined the throng outside. If no execution sermon had begun the day's activities, the crowd gathered outside the gaol instead of the meetinghouse. Similar to their contemporaries in England, the New England Puritans lined both sides of a path leading from either the meetinghouse or the jail to the town common, where temporary gallows had been erected. The condemned walked or rode in a horse-drawn cart a short distance to "gallows hill"—usually no more than a mile—accompanied by the execution preacher or other clergymen, the town sheriff, and on rare occasions a small band of local militia.

Rev. Cotton Mather provides a glimpse of what happened as the condemned walked this *via dolorosa* in Puritan New England. He says that "a minister" (probably Mather himself) accompanied Hugh Stone to the gallows in Boston in 1689, and he provides a transcript of the "principal passages of the discourse between them." The man who murdered his wife spoke with the minister about his "ungodly life," the heinous nature of his crime, the justice of his condemnation, his repentance, and the trust that he has in the "sin-pardoning blood" of Jesus Christ. Because there is no evidence to the contrary, it is reasonable to assume that the Puritan execution crowd was more decorous than their English contemporaries, permitting this last-minute conference to go on uninterrupted.[12]

Upon arriving at the town common, the condemned made his or her last dying speech at the gallows. The condemned not only admitted guilt for the specific offense that led to the execution, but reviewed his or her past life of delinquency as a warning to others. James Morgan warned the audience at his execution, "Have a care of Drunkenness, and ill company, and mind all good instruction, and don't turn your back upon the Word of God as I have done." He concluded his speech, "O take warning by me, and beg of God to keep you from this sin which hath been my ruin!" Similarly, Hugh Stone warned others about making idle threats. "Take example by me," he said, "if you say when a person has provoked you, 'I will kill him,' 'tis a thousand to one, but the next time you will do it." With this emphasis on confession and warning, the last dying speeches in Puritan New England were virtually indistinguishable from the ones that had been delivered in England by the condemned throughout the seventeenth century.[13]

No evidence survives to describe the mechanics of the execution itself in Puritan New England, but it is probably safe to assume that they differed little from those employed by their contemporaries across the Atlantic.

In 1674, when he published the first execution sermon in New England, Rev. Samuel Danforth broke with the traditions of gallows literature that he had known in England. Rather than publishing a sensationalist description of the crime, a conversion narrative, or a report of the execution activities, he chose to publish, in full, the sermon that he delivered at the execution of Benjamin Goad, who had been condemned for bestiality. By the end of the century, a handful of other leading Puritan ministers—Increase and Cotton Mather, Joshua Moodey, Samuel Lee, Samuel Willard, and John Rogers—also had published execution sermons. As important as the oral sermons were to the ritual of public execution, published ones had more staying power. Most Puritan ministers probably agreed with Cotton Mather when he said that "Sermons *preached* are like showers of rain that water for an instant, but sermons *printed* are like snow that lies longer on the earth."[14]

Homiletically speaking, there was nothing exceptional about Puritan execution sermons themselves: they followed the Puritan "plain style." New England execution sermons of the seventeenth-century began with a scripture quotation, usually two or three verses. The preacher then expounded briefly on the context of the passage and sometimes explained its textual features. Afterward, the preacher flatly announced a "doctrine" that he believed was contained in the text or could be deduced logically from it. The bulk of the Puritan execution sermon consisted of two rhetorical movements. First, the preacher drew out implications from the text and doctrine, logical extensions of his basic point. These "proofs" usually were stated flatly point by point, each usually building upon the one before it. Second, the preacher applied the text to the specific execution. Also stated flatly, these "uses" might relate to some circumstance that aggravated the crime of the condemned person. Puritan execution sermons always concluded with brief addresses to the condemned and the audience, and these addresses emphasized the need for repentance from sin and for trusting in the grace of God to save. New England execution sermons followed this same basic pattern until the turn of the nineteenth century.[15]

In his analysis of execution sermons as a new genre of literature, Daniel Cohen notes that these sermons were as effectively marketed and distributed as any other genre of Puritan literature. Advertisements for newly released execution sermons often were included on the last page of other popular publications, but the executions themselves "were probably their best form of publicity." Rushed to press immediately after hanging day, execution sermons were made available in all of Boston's eight bookstores by the end of the seventeenth century, and many other copies were carried into the rural areas by chapmen. Although exact prices cannot be determined with certainty, execution sermons in simple pamphlet form would have been available at a fraction of a day's wage for a common laborer. Execution sermons penetrated all social ranks of Puritan society, from magistrate to slave. There is even some evidence that copies of execution sermons were provided to condemned persons while they awaited in jail for their own executions. Cohen concludes that the only serious barrier to the reading of execution sermons in Puritan New England was illiteracy.[16]

The Provincial Context (1700–1774)

By the end of the seventeenth century, the ritual of public execution in early New England was more or less established, and the Puritan execution sermon had emerged as the unrivaled genre of crime literature. Between 1700 and 1775, however, the colonies of New England were increasingly "anglicized." Their commercial ties with England strengthened, their political life became influenced more and more by developments in England, their strident Puritanism generally yielded to theological liberalism and religious pluralism, and their legal procedures were brought into line with those across the Atlantic. While it is dangerous to overstate this anglicanization, it is safe to assume that English manners and customs became increasingly important to the provinces of New England in the eighteenth century. This complex social, economic, political, and religious process had a direct bearing on the ritual of public execution in New England and on the literature related to it.[17]

In the first half of the eighteenth century the execution ritual began to focus with particular interest on the spiritual conversion —not just the confession—of the condemned. In some ways this is understandable: the religious fervor that would erupt in the Great Awakening of the 1730s and 1740s already was beginning to stir in the first few years of the eighteenth century. But this interest in conversion also suggests that the ritual itself was beginning to function in a new way. By facilitating the spiritual transformation of the condemned and opening up the possibility of their final salvation, the church and state cooperated to heal the breach in the integrity of the community caused by serious crime. The sinner-turned-saint was drawn back into the moral community, even if he or she still was put to death. Moreover, the struggle of the capital criminal for redemption represented the larger struggle of New England itself; ironically, penitent capital criminals became exemplars of the salvation toward which all pious New Englanders thought they should be pressing.[18]

The case of Esther Rodgers illustrates this new emphasis on criminal conversion with striking clarity. She spent the better part of the year 1701 languishing in the gaol at Ipswich, Massachusetts, because she had been found to be the "unnatural mother and cruel Murtherer of two spurious babes, the fruit of her own body." Although the infanticide originally had been housed in the Newbury gaol, she was conveyed to the one in Ipswich for a very deliberate purpose: the good Christians in the town had a reputation for effective ministry with capital criminals in their dying days. In Rodgers's case, they did not disappoint. Members of the Congregationalist church there "made Incessant Prayers to heaven on her behalf . . . and turn[ed] their Private Meetings into whole days of Fasting and Prayer." In addition, the minister John Rogers "took constant unwearied pains" to effect Rodgers's repentance from her heinous crimes. Over eight months later, the "Tragick Scene" was "strangely changed into a Theater of Mercy," and Rodgers herself became a "Pillar of Salt Transformed into a Monument of Free Grace." She entered the gaol a "Bloody Malefactor" but came forth "Sprinkled, Cleaned, Comforted, a Candidate of Heaven." When the infanticide's hanging day came, Rogers could preach a series of three execution sermons, holding her out as a model of repentance and salvation for all Puritans to emulate.[19]

As the Rodgers case illustrates, the average length of time between the arrest and execution of a capital criminal increased significantly in the first half of the eighteenth century. Even though the Provincial courts met with increasing frequency, those accused of capital crimes remained in prison an average of just over five months awaiting trial. Even after their condemnation, capital criminals customarily were granted a reprieve of several weeks to finish preparing themselves for execution. Theodore Ferdinand has argued that the growing bureaucracy of the Provincial criminal justice system accounts for this trend. As specially trained judicial personnel jockeyed for prominence and as trial procedure became more complex, the whole process simply took longer. But the growing concern for and expectation of the conversion of capital criminals may also account for the trend. Perhaps the ritual of public execution was extended to permit the condemned enough time to struggle for salvation with the help of pious laypeople and ministers of the Gospel.[20]

However, the condemned did not always struggle for salvation in the ways that magistrates and ministers of the early eighteenth century expected, and William Fly is a good case in point. Responsible for at least two gruesome murders, the plundering of four vessels, and holding more than fifty people hostage on his pirate ship, Fly was condemned to die with two accomplices in Boston on July 12, 1726. The condemned pirate adamantly refused to play the expected role of sinner-turned-saint, despite the best efforts of Boston's ministers, including the eminent Rev. Cotton Mather. He refused to attend the execution sermon, because he "would not have the mob gaze upon him" as he sat in irons. On the day of his execution, Rev. Benjamin Colman reported that Fly flaunted both civil and religious authority by "briskly and in a way of bravery jump[ing] into the cart" that would carry him from the gaol to gallows hill. Cotton Mather observed that Fly impudently greeted the execution crowd along the way, gesturing "with a nosegay in his hand." Even as he stood on the gallows, his surliness continued when he "reproached the hangman, for not understanding his trade" and adjusted the halter around his own neck. Mather deemed the pirate "a most uncommon and amazing instance of Impenitency and Stupidity," and Colman concluded that Fly was "the greatest instance of obdurancy that has yet been seen among all the Malefactors who have suffer'd in these parts."[21]

The impenitence and insubordination of condemned criminals threatened to subvert the moral lessons of execution day in Provincial New England and to rob the ritual of its significance. By rejecting God's gracious, last-minute offer of salvation, the impenitent prevented the ritual from healing the breach in the community caused by their crimes and guaranteed their eternal damnation. By flaunting the civil and religious authorities who presided over the ritual, the impenitent denied the God-ordained structure of the Holy Commonwealth. Concerning the ritual of public execution in the early eighteenth century, Daniel Williams comments, "By working a last minute conversion and by exhibiting the penitent sinner to the public . . . ministers could turn the event into a triumph of Christ and the Puritan way, thereby reaffirming the same values the sinner had threatened in his godless pursuits." When the criminal refused to play his or her assigned role, the ritual significance of hanging day potentially was lost.[22]

Interestingly, the executions of Fly and over fifty other pirates inspired the first genre of crime literature published independently of the execution sermon in Provincial New England. During the first three decades of the eighteenth century, colonial authorities and the royal navy were under pressure to crack down on pirates who prowled the coasts of British holdings across the globe, including those of New England. As a part of this campaign, the Royal Court of the Admiralty in London required colonial authorities to produce reports of all judicial proceedings against pirates for its approval. Initially New England printers produced these trial reports as official legal documents, but interest in such trials apparently was high, because the reports were then published for popular consumption. The first such trial report was published in 1704, and then four more in the 1710s and 1720s. Thereafter, very few trial reports would be published until after the turn of the nineteenth century.[23]

Beginning in the 1730s, Provincial printers in New England began producing a genre of crime literature that had been a staple of public executions across the Atlantic for at least two decades: the execution broadside. By far the least expensive of all crime literature, the one-page broadsides usually contained only the confession and last dying speech of the condemned. Occasionally, however, other elements were included, such as a brief criminal biography, an account of the crime, or a summary of the trial proceedings. Other broadsides contained "execution poems" probably inspired by the crime ballads so common in seventeenth-century England. Issued in the week prior to and following the execution, these execution broadsides undoubtedly were passed hand-to-hand in urban centers, hanged in public places like taverns and print shops, and sold in the countryside by chapmen. The message of the execution broadside was nearly identical to that of the execution sermon: it warned about the dangers of sin and called people to repentance lest they experience a similar fate on the gallows. The execution broadside remained an important genre of crime literature in New England well into the nineteenth century.[24]

Changing political, social, and economic circumstances in Provincial New England forced periodic revisions to its capital jurisdiction. Although each colony's death penalty laws evolved independently of one another, the developments in Massachusetts Bay are more or less representative of the whole. Between 1711 and 1761, eleven crimes were added to and nine were removed from the list of those considered to be worthy of death; generally speaking, moral and religious offenses were replaced by property crimes and other "secular" offenses. On the eve of the American Revolution, criminal law of the province treated the following thirteen crimes to be worthy of death: murder, sodomy (including bestiality), rape, piracy, treason, counterfeiting, arson, robbery, burglary, polygamy, military insubordination, plotting to assassinate the English monarch, and military service with a foreign state. It should be clear that biblical law had become less important as a source for defining the capital jurisdiction of Provincial New England and that precedent in English common law was taking its place.[25]

What is most remarkable about this "anglicanization" of the capital jurisdiction of Provincial New England actually is its *limited* scope. In England, the number of offenses deemed worthy of death ballooned from about fifty in 1700 to 220 by 1800. Draconian implementation of the "Bloody Code" naturally led to an exponential growth in actual executions as well. Historians generally argue that this crackdown aimed at protecting emergent capitalism and the increasing property holdings of the rising middle class. Although the New England colonies certainly were becoming more prosperous in the eighteenth century, their capital jurisdiction remained relatively trim, even if a greater number of "secular" offenses were now capital. Moreover, the civil authorities of Provincial New England proved more reluctant than their English contemporaries to execute when other punishments were thought to suffice.[26]

The case of Hugh Henderson clearly illustrates both the concern for the conversion of capital criminals and the way in which the evolving capital jurisdiction transformed the ritual of public execution in Provincial New England. For three days in September of 1737, Henderson went on a burglary spree in which he plundered at least three houses in Worcester County, Massachusetts. The loot that he managed to collect was rather modest, and the most valuable item probably was a keg of rum. Nonetheless, he was convicted of three counts of housebreaking, enough to qualify him as a habitual offender. Although he was imprisoned for an unusually short period of time—just under three months—at least four ministers and countless laypeople offered him assistance in finding repentance. He made the obligatory last dying speech at the gallows, but his eternal fate was uncertain. Even he admitted, "I am sorry that I have not improv'd the whole time of [my reprieve] better than I have; but I trust that it has been a Mercy to my Soul."[27]

Because the ritual itself focused more intently on driving the condemned to repentance, the criminal conversion narrative and last dying speech emerged as important genres of crime literature in Provincial New England. Prior to the turn of the eighteenth century, these narratives and speeches occasionally were published as supplementary materials included with execution sermons themselves. Rev. Increase Mather, for example, published the "Last Expressions and Solemn Warning of James Morgan" as an appendix to his sermon occasioned by the convicted murderer in 1686. Morgan's puny statement contains only the basics: regret for his life of crime, his hope in Jesus Christ for salvation, and a warning against drunkenness. After the turn of the eighteenth century, however, these criminal conversion narratives and last dying speeches became far more elaborate, like the one published by Rev. John Rogers as an appendix to his series of execution sermons occasioned by the aforementioned case of infanticide Esther Rodgers. In fact, her thirty-five-page narrative chronicles her spiritual progress from the cradle to the gallows and ends with an elaborate last dying speech that is quite moving (even if it probably is embellished).[28]

Not surprisingly, the criminal conversion narrative came into its own as a genre of crime literature published independently of execution sermons during the era of the Great Awakening. As early as 1726, the evangelical firebrand Rev. Samuel Moody led the way by publishing the first full criminal conversion narrative, the story of Native American murderer Joseph Quasson. While stationed in York, Maine, as a member of her Majesty's army, the Native American killed a fellow soldier in a drunken brawl. Moody records very little of Quasson's biography, focusing instead on his efforts toward repentance during his six-month imprisonment: praying seven or eight times a day, reading his Bible, and poring over devotional literature, especially the sermons preached in connection with the execution of sinner-turned-saint Esther Rodgers twenty-five years earlier. Moody reports how the entire village of York offered up "fervent and effectual prayer, solitary and social" on behalf of the young man. Quasson even asked for and received the prayers of a convention of Congregationalist ministers who met in York while he was in prison. His spiritual striving was interrupted by unruly cell mates, his own nagging doubts, and periods of spiritual hardening. He was accompanied to the gallows by most of the ministers of the county, who continued to encourage his repentance. When the moment of truth came, Quasson "found mercy at last." He "cheerfully ascended the ladder" and delivered his last dying speech about the dangers of strong drink. The three thousand people assembled at his execution, Moody implies, were convinced that he had found salvation. As New England entered the throes of the Great Awakening, similar narratives were published and repeatedly republished about the remarkable conversions of three other capital criminals: infanticide Patience Boston (1738), burglar Philip Kennison (1738), and murderer Elizabeth Shaw (1744).[29]

Between the Great Awakening and the American Revolution, the criminal conversion narrative underwent a significant transformation: concern for the criminal's conversion was downplayed or dropped out altogether, and the genre became more like the criminal biographies that had been popular in England since at least the 1720s. Initially, New England printers imported these "secular" criminal biographies and republished them in commercial centers like New York, Philadelphia, and Boston. By 1756, New England printers struck out on their own to produce their first homegrown criminal biography, narrating the life of celebrated counterfeiter Owen Syllavan. Thereafter, such criminal biographies appeared with regularity in New England through the middle of the nineteenth century, almost always stressing that poverty, disrupted family life, inadequate education, and other environmental factors contributed to the making of the criminal's behavior.[30]

Cohen suggests that the appearance of the criminal biography as an independent genre in New England signaled the breakdown of "ideological coherence" of the printed materials that helped the people of early New England make sense of crime. "Explanations of crime based on theological doctrines of original sin," he claims, "were increasingly supplemented by arguments involving faulty pedagogy, romantic contingency, and flawed social policy." Nonetheless, Cohen also suggests that the appearance of such alternative genres of crime literature permitted the execution sermon to remain what it was intended to be. Because trial reports and criminal biographies provided the opportunities for alternative interpretations of crime and punishment to be articulated, the execution sermon remained an explicitly theological interpretation as it had been for generations.[31]

As the population of New England grew during the eighteenth century, the size of the crowds gathered on execution days grew proportionately. Precise numbers are not available, of course, but Rev. William Shurtleff reported that a "vast concourse of people" flocked to the execution of infanticides Sarah Simpson and Penelope Kenney in Portsmouth, New Hampshire, in 1739. In New London, Connecticut, more than ten thousand spectators gathered to witness the execution of impenitent infanticide Sarah Bramble in 1753. And the local newspaper reported that twelve thousand spectators descended on Salem, Massachusetts, to attend the execution of convicted rapist Bryan Sheehan in 1772.[32]

The growing size of the crowds became a source of concern for the civil and clerical authorities who presided over the ritual of public execution in Provincial New England. Beginning about midcentury, execution preachers appeared to be most interested in making sure that solemnity and decorum prevailed. In 1754, Rev. Charles Chauncy urged his audience not to make the execution of William Wieer "a matter of vain curiosity; much less of Sport and Merriment." Immediately before the execution of sixteen-year-old "Negro Bristol" for an inexplicable murder in 1763, Rev. Sylvanus Conant warned that "all Indecencies, Rudeness, Vanity, and unbecoming Behavior" at the gallows would be "highly provoking of the holy God." Instead the crowd ought to "behave soberly and decently," praying earnestly for the young man in his final moments of life. "Let your behavior be with all decency and moderation," Rev. Moses Baldwin pleaded with the crowd gathered at the execution of murderer William Shaw in 1770. "It is not a day for rioting and vain merriment," he continued, "rather for fasting, humiliation and prayer." Judging from these warnings and many others just like them, it is reasonable to conclude that the public executions in Provincial New England were developing the carnivalesque character that long had dominated the ritual in England. Or, at least they had the potential to.[33]

One final variation in the ritual of public execution in Provincial New England deserves mentioning. Gibbeting—the act of displaying the corpse of an executed criminal in a cagelike structure—was used in New England in only two periods. Between 1700 and 1730, most of the fifty-five pirates condemned in New England were gibbeted, including the aforementioned impenitent pirate William Fly. Authorities assumed that displaying the corpses of executed pirates in busy port cities would warn others who might be prowling the New England coast. Again in the 1750s, gibbeting was briefly used to warn others against the crime of murder. In 1751, for example, convicted murderer Thomas Carter was executed in South Kingston, Rhode Island, before an enormous crowd of ten thousand. In case the spectators missed the point, authorities then coated his corpse with tar, placed it in a gibbet, and hanged it from a large pole at the very spot where he committed the murder. Executed for murdering his slave master, "Negro Mark" was gibbeted in a similar manner in 1755 in Charlestown, Massachusetts, as a warning to other slaves. The cage containing his dry bones was not taken down until just before the American Revolution, almost twenty years later. Aside from these two periods, gibbeting appears to have been virtually unknown in early New England.[34]

The ritual of public execution in Provincial New England down to the time of the American Revolution, then, was a curious mixture of both the secular and the religious. Secular crimes that threatened the security and prosperity of society—burglary, robbery, and arson—increasingly were punished with death. Nonetheless, the ritual of public execution continued to require the last-minute spiritual conversion of the capital criminal in order to be effective in demonstrating the cooperative power of church and state and in mending the breach in society caused by serious crime.

The Early National Context (1775–1835)

During the American Revolution (1775–1783), the ritual of public execution in New England was reshaped in the midst of the economic, political, and social turmoil of the times. A new nation was being forged in the crucible of a war with England, and this conflict meant that people would be executed for crimes that long had been considered capital—especially treason and army desertion—even if no one actually had been executed for those crimes before that time. But even after the war ended, the "revolution" continued for several decades as the new nation struggled to implement the ideas of democracy in actual practice. Most of the newly formed states trimmed their capital jurisdictions, and opposition to public execution—and in some cases to the death penalty itself—began to mount in some circles. Although public execution continued in New England until 1835, these and other pressures reshaped both the ritual and the literature related to it.

Of the thirty-one persons executed in New England during the American Revolution, twenty-three of them had been convicted of wartime crimes: insubordination, army desertion, treason, and espionage. In most of these cases, the accused were tried, convicted, and executed by hanging or firing squad in less than a month. Such swift justice was perceived to be necessary during a time of war; the ritual of public execution was typically suspended in these cases, and they occasioned almost no crime literature. The remaining eight executions that took place during the American Revolution, however, were carried out in the same way that they had been for generations in New England and occasioned the typical variety of crime literature.[35]

Throughout the late 1780s and early 1790s, an emphasis on state power became especially visible in the ritual of public execution in New England. In the years immediately following the American Revolution, the cost of the war saddled both the federal and state governments with debts that they would never be able to repay, and the economic collapse of the new nation seemed imminent. In rural New England civil unrest was becoming alarmingly common and threatened to overthrow the fragile government. The population of New England's major cities—especially Boston—virtually had been depleted during the British occupation, and repopulation would take two decades. Everywhere they turned, citizens of New England saw disorder, economic crises, and infidelity. In this context especially, some leaders looked to the ritual of public execution to assert the authority of government and to reestablish order where it seemed to be most threatened.[36]

The case of John Bly and Charles Rose illustrates this point clearly. Both men had been disgruntled participants in Shays's Rebellion throughout the winter of 1786 and the spring of 1787. By that summer, however, the daring pair decided to capitalize on the continuing social unrest in western Massachusetts and took to burglary and highway robbery. They laid in wait outside the village of Lanesborough, and when a stagecoach-and-six rumbled past, they shot the lead horses, causing the coach to capsize. Inside, they found a wealthy squire named Elijah Phelps, robbed him of his valuables, and beat him within an inch of his life. Phelps survived, however, and stirred up a posse to pursue the highwaymen and bring them to justice. Eventually the pair were discovered, taken into custody, tried, and condemned to death. On December 6, 1787, the two men were executed at Lenox, not for participating in Shays's Rebellion, but for highway robbery.[37]

On execution day, Rev. Stephen West, a leading voice of a conservative theological movement among New England clergy known as the "New Divinity" movement, preached an execution sermon before a packed meetinghouse. He encouraged his audience to "prize and revere [civil government] as a divine institution" and to praise God for providing a way "that the world may rid itself of those who, by their crimes of violence, have made themselves intolerable to society." Although Bly and Rose probably did not speak the exact words, in their dying speech the highwaymen directed their warning to Daniel Shays's, the officers of the rebel forces, and others "who have been instrumental in raising the Opposition to the Government of this Commonwealth." With little equivocation, the point was made: "Our fate is a loud and solemn lesson to you who have excited the people to rise against the Government." The two men may have been executed for highway robbery, but it is clear that their execution day ritual aimed at demonstrating the power of the state to punish those who rebel against it.[38]

It is understandable, then, that historians who have considered the ritual of public execution in Early National America generally have stressed its political significance. Following the pioneering work of Michel Foucault, these historians argue that the ritual of public execution in early New England functioned primarily to demonstrate the power of the state. Louis Masur is representative of these historians when he claims that "above all else, authorities designed public hangings as a demonstration of the power of government and a warning to those who violated the law." While remnants of religious significance may have survived as carryovers from an earlier time, the ritual of public execution after the American Revolution especially was dominated by messages of deference, obedience, and submission to state authority. Gabriel Gottlieb also concludes that public executions were significant primarily as demonstrations of "ultimate state power." In her study comparing the rituals in early New England, the Middle Atlantic, and the South in the early national period, she argues that the ritual taught lessons aimed ultimately at building "community cohesion and order by reinforcing principles of social discipline and morality."[39]

Even with this new emphasis on state power, the ritual of public execution in Early National New England continued to follow the basic pattern that had been set as early as 1700. The length of time that the accused remained in jail awaiting trial, however, shortened considerably after the American Revolution. In fact, the accused typically waited no more than three months to learn his or her fate. As it had been the practice for a century or more, local ministers and laypeople visited the accused in prison in order to prepare them spiritually for their probable execution. After the American Revolution, the courts typically granted longer reprieves to those who were condemned, permitting even more time than before for them to repent. Even though the time was distributed somewhat differently in the Early National context, the total time between the arrest and execution of a capital criminal was about the same as it had been throughout the eighteenth century.[40]

There were, however, variations that developed in the ritual of public execution in Early National New England. For one thing, a military presence became more common on hanging day in the years following the American Revolution. Detachments of a hundred armed militiamen—and sometimes many more than that—guarded the local gaol for weeks before execution day, surrounded the meetinghouse during the delivery of the execution sermon, escorted the condemned to the gallows, and generally maintained order during the hanging itself. The aforementioned highway robbers Bly and Rose, for example, had an escort of 250 militiamen for every activity of their hanging day in 1787. Vermont governor Jonas Galusha ordered a detachment of a hundred soldiers to preside over the 1818 execution of Samuel Godfrey, who had murdered the keeper of the Vermont State Prison. These soldiers added another new element to the ritual: a sonorous military drumbeat as the condemned walked or rode in a horse-drawn cart to the gallows.[41]

Civil authorities had good reason to be vigilant because the crowds at public executions in Early National New England often swelled to ten thousand or more. These crowds were sometimes intoxicated with the antiauthoritarianism that had developed during the American Revolution and continued to grow amidst the social unrest of the 1780s and 1790s. The behavior of these crowds was unpredictable, authorities suspected, and rather than demonstrate the power of the state, the ritual of public execution had the potential to become a spectacle of anarchy. New England authorities probably feared the kind of riot that broke out in Cooperstown, New York, in 1806. Child-murderer Stephen Arnold received a last-minute reprieve, and a disappointed crowd nearly started a riot. Some drunken men even rounded up a stray dog, named him "Arnold," and swung him from the gallows before a cheering crowd. There is no evidence that similar unrest ever broke out on a New England hanging day, but the potential certainly existed.[42]

At the very least, commercial interests threatened to subvert the official religious, political, and social message of hanging day in Early National New England. Chapmen hawked their execution broadsides containing the criminal's biography, a brief trial account, or execution poem, all of which by then catered to the prurient interests of the gallows crowd. Such broadsides sometimes attempted to foment disgust and arouse a spirit of vengeance against the condemned. The 1795 broadside sold at the execution of twenty-year-old "Negro Pomp," for example, describes in graphic detail how the slave hacked his master to death with an ax because Pomp believed that he was the beneficiary of the estate. Many people in the crowd probably reacted like Rev. William

Bentley, who wrote in his diary that such an account "has a tendency to make Dying Speeches ridiculous." At other times, execution broadsides attempted to foster sympathy for the condemned, and those distributed at the Fairbanks execution are probably representative. Either way, commercial interests—the profit from the selling of broadsides—often overturned the intended ritual significance of public executions in Early National New England.[43]

Following the American Revolution, most state legislatures revised their capital jurisdiction in ways that they thought consistent with the values of an enlightened republic. Between 1780 and 1812, Vermont and New Hampshire gradually restricted the number of crimes punishable by death in those states to three or fewer: murder, treason, and robbery. Massachusetts and Connecticut, however, resisted this reforming trend. In 1780, Massachusetts treated seven crimes worthy of death: murder, sodomy, burglary, bestiality, arson, rape, and treason. In 1805, the state legislature removed sodomy and robbery from the list of capital crimes but in 1819 reinstated the death penalty for robbers who used dangerous weapons in the course of committing their crimes. In 1784, Connecticut defined six crimes as capital: murder, rape, sodomy, burglary, robbery, and treason. The "land of steady habits" did not revise its death penalty laws again until the middle of the nineteenth century.[44]

In the Early National context, New Englanders occasionally challenged the propriety of public execution amidst these varying death penalty laws and the developing spirit of penal reform. A crime considered worthy of death in one state could be punished with far less severity in another state. In 1790, career criminal Joseph Mountain was convicted in Connecticut of raping a fourteen-year-old girl. Even though he frankly confessed that he "abused her in a most brutal and savage manner," he claimed that he deserved a pardon because he had been raised in Philadelphia and lived in London, where rape was not a capital crime. The New Haven judge and jury were not impressed, and Mountain was hanged five months later as ten thousand people looked on.[45]

More problematic was the case of Ephraim Wheeler. This discontented, illiterate farmer eventually was arrested for raping his thirteen-year-old daughter, Betsy, something that apparently had become a habit. Throughout the summer and fall of 1805 the case dragged on as politically driven, and partisan legal professionals debated not only the facts of his case, but the merits of counting rape among the crimes worthy of death in an enlightened republic. Eventually over a hundred townspeople—including Wheeler's wife and victimized daughter—petitioned the courts to spare his miserable life and sentence him instead to a life of hard labor. Throughout the whole ordeal, Wheeler himself adamantly maintained his innocence of the crime. The courts denied their petition, and Governor Caleb Strong refused to grant him a pardon. In spite of popular opposition, Wheeler was executed in Lenox, Massachusetts, on February 20, 1806.[46]

As a result of these developments, most execution preachers after 1800 found themselves in a difficult position. If the clergy delivered their sermons as a part of the ritual of public execution, then they most often did what they always had done: to attempt to drive the capital criminal to repentance and salvation, and thereby heal the breach in the community caused by serious crime. Most often, the condemned obliged by playing their expected role. But execution preachers could not ignore the fact that the ritual of public execution was under attack. Precisely because the ritual purpose of public execution was changing in Early National New England to demonstrate the power of the state, many execution preachers chose to deliver their sermons *after* hanging day. Like the two delivered in Dedham following the Fairbanks execution, these sermons highlighted the moral lessons to be learned, made a report of the spiritual progress of the condemned as he or she came to execution day, and urged the divided community to seek reconciliation.[47]

Although the New England clergy continued to preach execution sermons and to participate in the ritual of public execution throughout the Early National period, their published execution sermons slowly lost their popular appeal after the turn of the nineteenth century. In part this was due to a major change in the culture of early New England. In the Puritan and Provincial contexts, the clergy—especially those of the established Congregationalist Church—were virtually unrivalled as public intellectuals and spoke and wrote with authority on virtually all issues of public importance, including crime and its punishment. After the middle of the eighteenth century, however, the rise of the legal profession in New England meant that the clergy eventually would have to vie with a new professional class for the right to speak and write on these matters. Although the New England clergy continued to deliver and publish execution sermons until 1825, two other genres of crime literature began to eclipse them in popularity and importance.[48]

The trial report was probably the most significant of these genres. As noted earlier, the trial report emerged as an independent genre of crime literature in New England as early as the 1710s and 1720s but never really took hold. After 1800, when the operations of the new judiciary became a matter of intense public interest, trial reports reemerged in large numbers. Cohen notes that in the first decade of the nineteenth century, at least ten trial reports issued from the presses of New England; in the second decade, more than twice that number; and hundreds more by the middle of the century. These reports conformed quite closely to the trial proceedings themselves: indictment, opening arguments, witness testimony, verdict, and sentencing. In some cases, the reports were issued as brief pamphlets, but the reports of more celebrated or controversial trials might run more than a hundred folio pages. It is clear that the trial report was beginning to eclipse the execution sermon as the most important and widely consumed genre of crime literature in early New England. Indeed, between 1800 and 1825 (when the last execution sermon was published in New England), trial reports outnumbered published execution sermons nearly two to one.[49]

The sentimental criminal biography also emerged after 1800 in New England to challenge the authority of the execution sermon and—as it turns out—that of the trial report as well. During the era of the Great Awakening, the distinct focus of published criminal biographies had been their spiritual transformation. Gradually over the course of the eighteenth century, these criminal biographies had evolved into more elaborate factual accounts of the criminal's birth, parentage, education, and petty criminal activities. But after 1800, criminal biographies came under the influence of the sentimentalism that characterized the literature of

Victorian America. These narratives often manipulated the emotions of their readers, generating intense feelings of empathy for the misfortunes and even the misdeeds of the condemned. Often these romantic criminal biographies paid very little attention to factual evidence and instead narrated a quasi-fictional account that evoked from readers both pity and mercy. Cohen and Halttunen rightly suggest that criminal biographies of the early eighteenth century are precursors to the fully developed romantic fiction of later nineteenth-century American literature.[50]

Conclusion

The ritual of public execution in early New England followed patterns that had been established in England. The prison visits, the "condemned sermon" preached by the Ordinary of Newgate, and the last dying speech delivered by the condemned gave the ritual in early modern England some religious significance even if the overwhelming purpose in that context was to demonstrate the power of the state. In the New England Puritan context, the religious significance of the ritual apparently dominated, in part because the crimes for which a person might be executed were clearly defined by biblical precedent. Apparently, the Puritans looked primarily to their ministers to make sense of hanging day. They taught that public executions cleansed the land of egregious evil and thereby prevented the fearful judgment of God. In doing so, the ritual healed the breach in the moral community caused by serious crime. The conversion and ultimate salvation of the criminal—though not wholly ignored—appears to have been a secondary concern of the Puritan ritual of public execution.

After the turn of the eighteenth century, the conversion and ultimate salvation of the capital criminal became the most important element of the ritual of public execution in Provincial New England. Under the growing influence of evangelical revivalism, the ritual required a sinner-turned-saint if it were to heal the breach in the moral community caused by serious crime. Indeed, when the condemned failed to achieve repentance or actively refused to strive after it, the ritual virtually was robbed of its significance entirely. Even as the religious significance of the ritual continued, the laws prescribing death in Provincial New England actually became more "secular." Property crimes long considered punishable by death in England were increasingly punished with death in New England, too.

By the time of the American Revolution, the ritual of public execution in New England was undergoing a significant transformation. Although the clergy continued to play an important role in maintaining its religious significance, the ritual appears to have been increasingly focused on demonstrating the power of the state and the ability of civil government to rule effectively. Public execution was used against traitors, army deserters, and those who would rebel against properly constituted civil authority. But it was also used against murderers, rapists, and burglars to maintain the peace and security of society. Even as popular opposition to them mounted, public executions continued and the New England clergy by and large supported them.

The authority to interpret the ritual of public execution initially was vested with the clergy. Unlike the Ordinary of Newgate and his "condemned sermons," Puritan ministers in New England regularly published their execution sermons to reinforce the lessons of hanging day long after the ritual itself was concluded. The execution sermon initially was the unrivalled genre of crime literature in New England, but during the first three decades of the eighteenth century new genres developed that generally reinforced the message of published execution sermons: trial reports, criminal biographies, execution broadsides, last dying speeches, and other ephemeral literature. Certainly by the 1750s, these other genres of crime literature came into their own; criminal biographies especially began to challenge the execution sermon by offering an alternative interpretation of crime and its punishment. The commercial value of crime literature soon increased as an eager readership craved the sensational accounts of both the lives of these criminals and their actions on hanging day. During the early decades of the nineteenth century, formal reports that described every detail of criminal trials emerged as the most important genre of crime literature, both satisfying the curiosity of their readers and legitimating the operations of the new nation's judiciary. Increasingly influenced by the romantic fiction of

Victorian America, criminal biographies aimed more at entertaining than informing their audience; this certainly added to their popularity but devalued them as a factual source. Amidst the developing body of crime literature in early New England, the execution sermon quickly lost its currency after 1800. Although the clergy continued to publish them until 1825, execution sermons had been eclipsed by genres of literature that appealed more to an Early National readership.

Having situated the early New England execution sermon in its ritual, literary, and historical contexts, it is possible now to consider their theological content and its development over time.

CHAPTER TWO

Human Sinfulness

> Wherefore, as by one man sin entered into
> the world, and death by sin, and so death passed
> upon all men, for that all have sinned.
>
> —*Romans 5:12*

Few people in early New England would have questioned the correlation between criminal behavior and human sinfulness. In fact, the terms *crime* and *sin* were virtually interchangeable across the period because both connoted primarily a moral failing on the part of the offender. The origin of this identification is not difficult to discern: the earliest criminal codes of New England were modeled upon what the Puritans believed to be the law of God as expressed in the Ten Commandments and other moral teachings in scripture. As the criminal code of early New England expanded beyond the confines of Puritan biblicism, the identification of crime with sin expanded as well. Most people probably trusted that legislators would enact laws that were consistent with the will of God because their duty was "to translate the divine moral law into criminal statutes in the interest of morality."[1]

New England execution preachers naturally took the identification of criminal behavior with human sin very seriously. Indeed, prior to about 1750, few of them openly questioned the federal doctrine of original sin as it had developed in Reformed theology and had been codified in the creeds of Anglo-American Puritanism. This doctrine furnished Puritans and their immediate heirs with a ready-made explanation for the origin of criminal behavior: the depravity resulting from Adam's initial act of disobedience had been imputed to all of his descendants. Because this depravity was the corrupt fountain out of which actual sins flow, all crimes could be traced back to that source. Moreover, the federal doctrine of original sin provided Puritan execution preachers with the rhetorical means to fashion a moral identification between the condemned criminal and the audiences of hanging day. Because human depravity was understood to be universal, capital crime differed only in magnitude from the ordinary sins that otherwise law-abiding New Englanders committed on a daily basis.

After about 1750, however, some clergy of the Provincial period began to question this federal doctrine and to articulate a revised understanding of human sinfulness. From the Enlightenment they generally learned an improved assessment of human nature, one that made room for increased human autonomy, freedom, and responsibility. More specifically, some New England theologians of the eighteenth century began to question on logical grounds how some essential moral corruption of human nature was passed down from Adam and Eve to their posterity, and why God would hold anyone accountable for the actions of another. While a few execution preachers after 1750 continued to employ the federal doctrine of original sin in their sermons, most others relied on a revised understanding of human sinfulness that made room for the "moral peculiarity" of the capital criminal.

The present chapter begins with a brief description of the federal doctrine of original sin as it was articulated in Anglo-American Puritanism. The purpose of this description is to provide the context within which to make sense of New England Puritan execution preaching and its reliance on the doctrine of original sin as a way of making sense of capital crime. The chapter then describes briefly how understandings of human sinfulness developed in New England after the middle of the eighteenth century. Late colonial and early national execution sermons are used to illustrate how this revised understanding of human sinfulness impacted how some preachers made sense of capital crime. The central claim of this chapter is that human sinfulness—however it was conceived doctrinally—remained a compelling explanation for the origin of criminality in New England execution preaching. Moreover, developments in the understanding of human sinfulness brought about important shifts in the explication of capital crime in New England: as human sinfulness became less a consequence of innate depravity and more a consequence of individual choice, the moral peculiarity of capital criminals grew proportionately, making them logical targets of the moral reformers of the early national period.

The Federal Doctrine of Original Sin

For about a century New England Puritan ministers held a nearly unanimous belief in the federal doctrine of original sin. Although it had gained currency among some continental Reformed theologians before 1600, this understanding of human sinfulness reached the status of orthodoxy in New England by about 1650 and would remain dominant until about 1750. Although he cannot be credited with single-handedly formulating the doctrine, William Ames was an important authority to whom New England Puritans appealed for their understanding of human sinfulness.

Ames taught that humanity had been created in the image of God, consisting of both the inward perfection of the soul and the outward perfection of the body. This perfection included the freedom and the ability to live according to the commands of God, that is, in perfect obedience to the divine will. Further, Ames taught that as a dimension of God's "special government" of humanity, God covenanted with Adam, "not only as a private person . . . but as a public person of the head of the family of humanity." Accordingly, "his posterity were to derive all good and evil from him." Motivated by pride and marred by ingratitude and faithlessness, however, Adam failed to render the obedience that he owed to God. In so doing, he brought upon himself and all of his posterity two consequences for his transgressions: first, a depraved nature, which Ames described as a "corruption of the whole man" and an "ineptness and perversity of all bodily faculties"; and second, physical death as the final punishment for sin. This depraved nature, Ames continued, was the origin for all actual sins. The human will, in bondage to the depravity of original sin, motivated all persons to habitual deviation from the obedience owed to God. Indeed, Ames argued that all human actions reflect original sin as "a daughter [reflects] her mother," and "original sin is rightly called the tinder of all sins."[2]

The federal doctrine of original sin as formulated by Ames and others in the 1620s reached the status of orthodoxy when the Westminster Confession of Faith and related catechisms were ratified by the Puritan parliaments of England (1647) and Scotland (1649). Meanwhile in New England, delegates of the Congregationalist churches met in Cambridge in 1648 to adopt this Confession as their standard as well (except for the chapters dealing with church polity, which they replaced with the Cambridge Platform). The Reforming Synod (1679–1680) reaffirmed the commitment of Massachusetts Congregationalism to the federal doctrine of original sin, in part because Puritan leaders feared a further decline in religious piety. Connecticut Congregationalists, too, declared their belief in the doctrine by adopting it at the Saybrook Synod in 1708. As a result, the historian would be hard pressed to find a Puritan on either side of the Atlantic who did not at least formally declare his or her belief in the federal doctrine of original sin, because it was enshrined in the creeds and confessions of Anglo-American Puritanism.

Relying in part on Ames's formulation, the Westminster Confession of Faith asserted that Adam and Eve were tempted by Satan and sinned by eating the forbidden fruit. Thus, they "fell from their original righteousness and communion with God, and so became dead in sin, and wholly defiled in all the faculties and parts of their souls and bodies." Because Adam and Eve were "the root of all mankind," the guilt of their sin was imputed to their descendants and the "same death in sin and corrupted nature conveyed to all their posterity descending from them by ordinary generation." All of humanity, therefore, is "utterly indisposed, disabled, and made opposite to all good, and wholly inclined to all evil." This inherited corruption is the source of all actual transgressions, for which the sinner alone must bear sole responsibility. These transgressions against the "righteous law of God" bring down guilt upon sinners, and they are bound over to the wrath of God with all of its miseries: spiritual, temporal, and eternal.[3]

In spite of their unanimous acceptance of the creed, New England Puritan ministers developed their commitments to the federal doctrine of original sin in different ways. Indeed, their sermons and theological treatises reveal that they spoke and wrote about human sinfulness in multivocal and sometimes ambivalent ways. Even as early as the 1630s and 1640s, some Puritans like Revs. Thomas Shepard, Thomas Hooker, and Peter Buckeley depicted original sin as an active principle of internal evil that constantly threatened to overwhelm helpless individuals. They employed imaginative metaphors to stress the vileness and incapacity of fallen humanity in contrast to the holiness and sovereignty of God. Yet others like Revs. John Cotton, John Davenport, and John Wheelwright spoke of original sin as the passive absence of good in humanity, assuming that the image of God had been obliterated by the Fall. They understood human depravity primarily as the occasion for God to lavish forgiveness on fallen men and women, thereby enticing them to love God in return.[4] This tension was by no means restricted to the first generation of Puritan preachers; indeed, even after the turn of the eighteenth century New England preaching down to the Great Awakening exhibits similar tensions in its use of the federal doctrine of original sin.[5]

While assenting to the federal doctrine of original sin, Puritan execution preachers developed it in rhetorically different ways. Some relied on a rationalist understanding of original sin to explain the source of capital crime. Typical of this group was Rev. Samuel Danforth, who preached a sermon in 1674 at the execution of seventeen-year-old Benjamin Goad, sentenced to death for bestiality. According to the Roxbury minister, the young man's crime exemplified just how utterly depraved all persons were: original sin so vitiates human souls and pollutes human bodies that "the Temple of the Holy Ghost is become a Stew, and Brothel-house, yea, a Cage of unclean Birds, yea, a very Hog-sty!" Because the young man acted out of his depravity to bugger his father's horse in broad daylight, he was delivered into the hands of Satan to be "swept away as dung and filth from the earth." Only his death could remove the pollution of the land caused by his sinful act. Even if the prospects of Goad's repentance and salvation were slim, his execution represented a "tremendous dispensation" from God designed to awaken New Englanders out of their slumber. Danforth said that all needed to recognize their own depravity and to beware their own sinful natures. Indeed, the hanging day was an opportunity for God to "pluck poor sinners out of the snare of lasciviousness"—at least those who were willing to repent—lest they continue to indulge their natures and end up on the gallows themselves.[6]

Others developed the federal doctrine of original sin more like Rev. Increase Mather did in two sermons preached before the execution of infanticide Sarah Threedneedles in 1698. Already punished at seventeen for giving birth to an illegitimate child, she "repeted her Whoredoms" two years later and gave birth to a second. She claimed that this second child was stillborn, but magistrates surmised from the bruising on the newborn's neck that the young mother had strangled her baby. During her trial, her crime was compounded by her false claim of paternity against respected Boston shopkeeper Thomas Savage and by the fact that she was caught having sexual intercourse with a fellow prisoner just days before her execution.[7]

Both of Mather's sermons focused on the foolishness of making a "light matter" of human sinfulness. His reliance on the federal doctrine of original sin is obvious: he said that in eating the forbidden fruit Adam was acting as a "publick person, representing all mankind" and his original act of disobedience was imputed to his posterity so that all have sinned "after the similitude of Adam's transgression." This original sin and all of the actual sins that flow from it are the cause of manifold temporal judgments from God: illness, loss of reputation, even physical death. But the most "woful fruit of sin" is a spiritual judgment from God: the loss of the divine image in humanity. This loss means that "by nature no man has the least spark of grace or holiness in him." Of course, the final judgment of God on human sinfulness is everlasting punishment in hell. "All these things considered," Mather concluded, "surely sin is an Evil not to be mocked at, not to be made light of."[8]

But for Mather this emphasis on the fundamental sinfulness of humanity served as a foil against which to understand the possibility of forgiveness and salvation. As he specifically turned his attention to Threedneedles in his sermon, the president of Harvard held out the possibility of the sinner's salvation. "That Sentence of Death which is passed on you as to your Body, cannot be reversed," he began. "But the Sentence of Everlasting Death may. . . . There is merit enough in the Death of Christ to make atonement for as great a Sinner as you are." Mather then detailed a prescription for the young woman: she must develop a godly sorrow and repent, forsake her sinful behavior, and go to Jesus Christ, praying that he will "pour his Blood on thy Soul." "If that precious blood be sprinkled on you," he concluded, "then notwithstanding your sins have been as Scarlet and red like Crimson they shall be white as Snow."[9]

However they chose to develop the federal doctrine of original sin rhetorically, Puritan execution preachers always used the doctrine to fashion a moral identification between the condemned person and the audience. Because the doctrine taught that natural depravity is total, innate, and universal, preachers often argued that capital criminals do not differ qualitatively from ordinary New Englanders; they only differ quantitatively in terms of the number and severity of their actual sins. In other words, Puritan execution preachers did not preach that capital criminals are morally "deviant" due to the innately and equally depraved natures of all human beings. This emphasis on the universality of human depravity was not unique to Puritan execution preaching, but it surely had increased rhetorical value when the comparison was made between ordinary New Englanders and capital criminals about to be executed.[10]

At the Morgan execution in 1686, for example, Rev. Cotton Mather skillfully fashioned a moral identification between the convicted murderer and the execution audience. "We are not only undeserving creatures, but also Hell-deserving sinners," Mather reminded his audience. "When our First Father began a desperate Warr against the Omnipotent God, we were a part of the mad Regiment involved in his perfidious Treason." No less than the convicted murderer, Mather explained, "our Enmity against our Maker hath from our very Cradles been so enormous, that we should long ere now been Devils-in-the-flesh if the Checks of restraining Grace had been taken away." The fact that Morgan was qualitatively no more depraved than the average New Englander must have been a hard pill to swallow: in a drunken rage Morgan attacked Joseph Johnson with an iron spit and ran it through Johnson's belly so that he died a few days later.[11]

Puritan execution preachers sometimes fashioned a moral identification between the condemned person and the execution audience by drawing upon a principle from the teachings of Jesus in his Sermon on the Mount. Jesus equated murder and adultery—both clear violations of the Mosaic Law and punishable by death—with the more common sins of unrestrained anger and lust (Matthew 5:21–30). Rev. John Williams followed suit by claiming in 1698 that, in the assembled audience, only Sarah Threedneedles was guilty of murder "in the highest degree of it." But the Deerfield minister continued, "I fear that there are several that have Murdered in their hearts, and some who have been guilty of interpretive Murder." This latter category included sins like drunkenness, sexual misconduct, anger, and hatred. And in 1721, at the execution of formerly enslaved Joseph Hanno for murdering his wife, Cotton Mather asked, "Is that Black Thing that you have in Irons here before you the only One that may be charged with Murdering his Wife among us?" The answer he gave was *no:* all husbands who speak harshly to their wives, fail to provide them with sufficient food, or break their hearts by their "vile carriage" are guilty of murdering them.[12]

Even after the turn of the eighteenth century, most execution preachers continued to rely on the federal doctrine of original sin to explain the origin of capital crime and to fashion a moral identification between criminal and audience. Typical was the sermon preached by Rev. Benjamin Colman at the execution of murderer David Wallis in 1713. At one point in his sermon, the minister of Boston's liberal Brattle Street Church ticked off a list of biblical characters who were guilty of murder, linked them with Wallis himself, and asked a jarring question: "Are we any better than they?" "No," he declared, "For we are incident to [murder] thro' the horrid Corruption that is in our Nature; and the very best of us are by no means our own Keepers. There is no sin," he continued, "but what the vile and cursed nature of man is prone to, and capable of; and the same vile Nature is common to us all." Rev. Cotton Mather joined Coleman in his sentiment at this same execution when he declared, "We are every one of us Depraved with Original Sin; it contains in it a propensity to every Sin. We must every one of us confess, 'Behold, I was shapen in Iniquity.'" Even as late as 1733, Rev. Thomas Foxcroft appealed to the federal doctrine of original sin to fashion a moral identification between the execution audience and infanticide Rebekah Chamblit. "The sorrowful Spectacle before us should make us all reflect most seriously on our own vile Nature, which the Falls of others are but a Comment upon." He continued by suggesting that the only proper response would be "to humble ourselves under a sense of the Corruption of our Hearts, which are naturally as bad as the worst."[13]

Surely at times the moral identification between the capital criminal and the audience assembled on hanging day seemed to be strained. Perhaps this was the case when Jeremiah Meacham was hanged in 1715, having been found guilty of a gruesome double murder. Meacham was a weaver by trade, living in Newport, Rhode Island, with his wife Patience and her sister Constance Garvey. On March 22, Meacham inexplicably struck his wife over the head with an ax; when his sister-in-law attempted to intervene, he struck her as well. While both women lay unconscious on the floor of their home, Meacham slit the throats of both women with a knife. He then flung hot coals all over the house, hoping to burn it to the ground to cover his crime. The tumult attracted some neighbors to the Meacham home just in time to see him jump from a second-story window, brandishing his bloody ax, in an attempt to escape. Some neighbors subdued the crazed maniac while others recovered the bodies of the two women from the burning home. His crimes were so self-evident that he was convicted in an extraordinarily brief trial and was hanged on the Newport gallows less than three weeks after his crime. His corpse was not buried but was placed in irons on Wanamatoming Hill alongside the bodies of two Native Americans who had been executed two years before.[14]

Prior to Meacham's execution, Baptist minister Nathaniel Clap preached a series of three sermons in which he reflected on the extraordinary circumstances. In the first of these sermons, he warned the audience that the Lord's voice had been crying to his people through the doctrine of original sin. People should be more mindful that they, too, suffer from the same depravity that explained the actions of this maniac: the "dreadful venom of Original sin," the "vicious disposition" that filled the vacuum created by the deprivation of Adam's original righteousness means that all of his posterity are "born into the world with Hearts full of Sin, with Corrupt Natures empty of Grace." Like Meacham, all of humanity is "ready to Sin, ready only to Sin, always ready to Sin."[15]

Yet this moral identification between the condemned criminal and the audience of execution sermons usually was tempered with some recognition of the quantitative difference between capital crime and the garden-variety actual sins of which all New Englanders were guilty. Execution preachers before about 1750 often argued that "little sins make way for greater." In other words, seemingly innocuous sins were understood to clear a moral path toward more grievous ones. Most probably agreed with Rev. Joshua Moodey, who advised his auditors at the execution of the aforementioned James Morgan to "see whither lesser sins will lead you, even to greater, till at last you come to a great Transgression." This inexorable pattern of sinful behavior truly is a slippery slope: "Custom of sin," Moodey continues, "will take away conscience of sin; and when conscience of sin is gone, what sin is there that you are not ready for?" Sometimes Puritan execution preachers were quite creative in their warnings against "lesser sins." In 1704 Rev. Cotton Mather rhetorically imagined what advice the six condemned pirates might give to the audience, and he came up with this: "When I was first Enticed to Evil, I was Tender and Fearful of it . . . by degrees I was emboldened in Sin; at last it became as familiar as my daily Food." He concluded with the pirate's pathetic exhortation, equally imaginative: "Oh! As you love your Souls, Take heed of the Beginning of Sin. Oh! That I could prevail with Young Persons, to cast away Sin and Check it in the first Beginnings of it!"[16]

It seems, then, that execution preachers before 1750—both Puritan and Provincial—would be eager to describe in graphic detail the sinful history of the condemned in an effort to illustrate the natural progression of sin as clearly as possible. However, they were usually content to describe in general terms the connection between lesser sins and greater ones. In part this is due to the probability that those hearing and reading these sermons already were familiar with the details of the case and the reputation of the condemned. It also may be the case that execution preachers before 1750 specifically avoided the details of criminal biography in order not to cater to the morbid curiosity of their audiences. But a theological reason is equally probable: execution preachers sought to fashion a moral identification between the condemned and his audience not only with reference to original sin, but also to the universality of "lesser" actual sins. Indeed, all struggle equally with lesser sins—cursing, swearing, lying, drunkenness, sexual promiscuity, and Sabbath-breaking—while in the lives of capital criminals these lesser sins have somehow yielded to greater ones.[17]

Sometimes, however, execution preachers before 1750 did turn their attention specifically to the condemned and described in some detail their specific lesser sins. One example should suffice to make the point. Rev. John Williams told infanticide Sarah Smith in 1699 that she had progressed from "little Follies" to "solitary Filthiness" to "secret Fornications" and finally to "secret Murders." Rev. Samuel Willard berated her as well about specific lesser sins: "your pride, your disobedience to your Parents, your impatience of Family Government, your company keeping, your Whoredoms, and your despising of Christ" led her finally to her capital crime. Although such instances were not common, Puritan execution preachers illustrated even further the moral kinship between the condemned and the listening audience while simultaneously holding out the condemned as a warning.[18]

This emphasis on the universality of original sin and this differentiation between lesser and greater sins, however, begs the question of *why* some sinners progressed from garden-variety actual sins into more serious ones, especially capital crime. Puritan execution preachers regularly argued that fallen humanity was ordinarily held back from committing actual sins by the "restraining grace of God." Although the notion appears in John Calvin's theology, New England Puritans found biblical sanction for the idea of God's "restraining grace" in Genesis 20:6. In this passage God "withheld him [Abimelech, King of Gerar] from sinning against me [Abraham]."

This manifestation of God's grace was doctrinally connected to their understanding of original sin, and execution preachers before 1750 regularly relied on this connection. Rev. Samuel Willard explained this connection best of all as he inquired in a 1698 sermon why "so much horrid wickedness is committed in the world." He postulated that the fountain of original sin always sends forth its bitter streams, and anyone with the slightest capacity for self-reflection could see abundant evidence for this fact. But God provides restraints by which innate depravity is "held back from breaking forth into prodigious Enormities." This restraining grace of God is a "chain with which God ties men up, and sets bounds to their violence." Without these divine restraints, everyone is in dire straits. Willard asked, "What then will not the impetuous lusts [of men] dare to make them do?" A contemporary of Willard thought that he knew the answer: "a man would soon Murder his Father and Mother, Destroy his own Wife, and Debauch his Neighbors, Blaspheme God, and Fire the Town, & run a muck among the people."[19]

This understanding of God's restraining grace found its fullest expression in Rev. Cotton Mather's 1713 sermon occasioned by the David Wallis execution. Mather argued that God keeps most persons from sinning in at least five ways: by disallowing Satan's "army of evil spirits" from having access to the person's soul; by "finding something else for us to do"; by convincing persons that sin is not in their best interest; and by arousing the conscience against sin. The fifth and most important way is also the most mysterious: "by infusing into the Soul a Principle of Grace which is contrary to Sin, a principle under the power whereof, men cannot sin like other men." This unknowable restraining grace of God can only be described metaphorically: it is a dam that holds back the "rapid streams of sin," and "whole Torrents of iniquity." Rather than question divine providence in allowing some to sin while others are held back from it, Mather concluded that our duty is only to praise God for the restraining grace in our own lives, which is both merciful and wonderful.[20]

Execution preachers before 1750 often argued that the restraining grace of God had been withdrawn providentially and that God explicitly allowed the offender's innate depravity to pursue its natural course to excessive wickedness. Rev. Increase Mather, for example, alluded to the withdrawal of God's restraining grace in a 1674 sermon occasioned by the execution of two servants for murdering their master. He admonished his audience to obey their social superiors, for "God is so provoked with such children as that he does sometimes leave them against nature to destroy themselves as a just punishment for their unnatural disobedience." Similarly, Rev. John Williams encouraged his audience to be humbly thankful to God that they had been restrained from sins like those of infanticide Sarah Smith. His meditation on God's restraining grace is worth quoting at length. "Everyone by nature," he explained, "hath the seeds of all Sin and disobedience. Religious Education, our own Wisdom, and resolutions can't restrain even such wickedness." But there is hope: "It is God that makes us to differ from one another, that keeps us from such pollutions. . . . We are not to be unthankful for restraining grace; we are humbly to acknowledge God when he keeps us back from presumptuous sins."[21]

Further evidence could be cited, but the most important points are certainly clear. Execution preachers before 1750—both Puritan and Provincial—relied on the federal doctrine of original sin to fashion a moral identification between the condemned criminal and the hanging-day audience. Because the stream of actual sins issued from the corrupt fountain of original sin, capital criminals differed morally from ordinary New Englanders only in the magnitude of those actual sins. Like all people, capital criminals committed numerous "lesser sins." Only the restraining grace of God, providential and mysterious, prevented some persons from sliding down the slippery slope from lesser to greater sins. Those whom God's grace continued to restrain were called to rejoice in that fact, even as they pitied the capital criminal on execution day. It is important to keep in mind, however, that this emphasis on the federal doctrine of original sin was not merely a homiletic strategy for execution preachers; it was a fundamental theological conviction that helped them make sense of capital crime and justify punishing such crime with death.

The Revised Doctrine of Human Sinfulness

After the turn of the eighteenth century, some New England ministers began tinkering with new ideas about the nature of religious faith, ideas that permitted them to moderate the strict confessionalism of New England Puritanism. Following English latitudinarians, they began to prize religious toleration, to emphasize morality as the essence of faith, and to reconcile the historic Christian teachings with the discovery of modern science. Historians usually refer to these developments as the "anglicanization" of New England religion and culture.[22]

The revised Massachusetts Bay charter of 1692 certainly aided this drift toward moderation by mandating religious toleration, at least for New England Protestants. Equally important was the transformation of the curriculum at Harvard College at the turn of the eighteenth century, which made room for the works of Enlightenment philosophers, natural scientists, and Broad Churchmen. Pushing the boundaries of Puritan creedal orthodoxy, a few bold theological innovators challenged openly some of the most cherished theological convictions of the New England Way and began to flirt with the latest trends in philosophy. The point is this: working in a new climate of religious toleration and armed with a host of new intellectual resources for formulating Christian faith, some New England ministers after about 1700 began to think outside the bounds of creedal orthodoxy.

By about 1750, this "anglican drift" precipitated developments in how some New England ministers understood human sinfulness, and John Locke was a significant intellectual influence on those developments. For a variety of complicated political and philosophical reasons, he intentionally steered a middle course between the determinism of the Puritan federal doctrine of original sin and the free-will philosophy of the Cambridge Platonists. Locke taught that the Fall occurred because Adam's reason had been overrun by his naturally unruly passions. Adam had been created with a perfect constitution: his reason and his passions were in proper balance, with reason maintaining governance of his will. In his act of disobedience, Adam's passions usurped the governing power of reason, clouding his powers of discernment in such a way that he no longer was able to exercise his will according to the dictates of reason alone. In other words, Adam's nature had become depraved, marked by an unremitting struggle between his passions and his reason. Without relying on any hint of federalism, Locke maintained that Adam's progeny was born after his image, that is, suffering from this same imbalanced constitution. His own life experiences convinced Locke that all humanity shared in this depravity, and that the only antidote finally effective in remedying it was the redeeming work of Christ.[23]

Significantly, Locke developed his understanding of original sin in the context of his writings on epistemology and education. He believed firmly that human beings could learn the discipline of controlling their unruly passions and of forcing them to submit to the governing control of reason. Moral education, beginning at a very young age, is the principal means for a person to "get a Mastery of his Inclinations and submit his Appetite to Reason," even if there are no guarantees that persons will always act accordingly. Like many seventeenth-century moral philosophers, Locke painted a very grim picture of a child whose mind had not been made "pliant to Reason" and in whom virtue had not been "woven into the very Principles of his Nature." Such a child grew to be a slave to his or her own appetites and passions, bent on gratifying every desire of his or her depraved nature. "Our first actions," Locke insisted, "being guided more by Self-love, than Reason or Reflection, 'tis no wonder that . . . Children should be very apt to deviate from the just measures of Right and Wrong." Guided by the "improved Reason and serious Meditation" afforded by a sound moral education, however, children learn to overcome the desire for self-gratification and to keep in check their depraved passions and appetites. Moral education, Locke concluded, helped people approximate the nature with which God had fitted our first parents at creation.[24]

This revised understanding of human sinfulness also emerged amidst open theological controversy over the federal doctrine of original sin. In England, the controversy began as early as 1710 and grew increasingly vigorous by midcentury.[25] Certainly the most significant treatise opposing the federal doctrine of original sin in England was *The Scripture Doctrine of Original Sin Proposed to Free and Candid Examination,* published about 1740 by Hebrew scholar and Presbyterian minister John Taylor. His biblical and philosophical arguments set the terms of the debate over human sinfulness that dominated Protestantism in both England and New England until the middle of the nineteenth century. For this reason, it will be helpful to review his basic argument in this important treatise.

Taylor first moved systematically through the five biblical passages in which he saw the consequences of Adam's first sin clearly treated. He quickly dispensed with four of them, but Romans 5:12–19 proved to be the greatest challenge because it appeared to teach the essence of the federal doctrine: through one man judgment for sin fell upon all persons. After painstaking exegetical and linguistic analysis, however, Taylor concluded that this passage teaches nothing different from the other four, namely, that God's judgment on Adam and his posterity for Adam's sin was nothing more than physical death. In no sense was the fictional "innate depravity" to be understood as God's judgment on human sinfulness, whether Adam's or anyone else's.[26]

More important than his exegetical analyses were Taylor's philosophical arguments against the federal doctrine of original sin. Like Locke, Taylor argued that Adam had been created in a state of moral neutrality—not in a state of original righteousness—and that Adam possessed the ability to choose his moral path. If Adam had exercised his natural capacities appropriately, then he would have developed the righteousness that God required of him. But the story of the Garden of Eden teaches us that he had not; Adam's sin consisted solely in his willful decision to disobey the commands of God and his acting on that decision. This, Taylor insisted, was not a "fall" from original righteousness but a failure on Adam's part to live up to the moral potential with which God had created him.[27]

Taylor's more devastating philosophical attack on the federal doctrine of original sin was his vigorous rejection of the notion that natural depravity could be imputed from one moral agent to another. In fact he called such an idea "one of the greatest absurdities in all the systems of corrupt religion." Human beings are independent moral agents, he said, and thus guilt for whatever sins they commit is personal and nontransferable. More specifically, Taylor rejected all notions of inherited depravity; indeed, he was outraged by the claim that moral corruption is passed from parent to child through the process of reproduction. If this were the case, then no person could be held accountable for his or her sin. "If we come into the world infected and depraved with sinful disposition," he argued, "then sin must be natural to us; and if natural, then necessary; and if necessary, then no sin."[28]

Taylor's ideas concerning human sinfulness reached the shores of New England by the mid-1740s, and a few ministers cautiously appropriated some of his ideas without wholly repudiating the federal doctrine of original sin. But the real firestorm over Taylorism in New England began in 1757 with the publication of a treatise by Rev. Samuel Webster in which he claimed that the federal doctrine of original sin was "unscriptural, emotional, and dangerous." Largely repeating Taylor's arguments, the liberal minister of the Congregational church at Salisbury rejected the notion of a covenant before the Fall that made Adam the "federal head" of humanity; he spurned the notion of imputed sin much as Taylor had; and he warned that the federal doctrine of original sin might tempt some to question the goodness, justice, and compassion of God.[29]

Webster's treatise touched off a paper war over the doctrine that raged in New England for the remainder of the eighteenth century. Liberal Calvinists like Revs. Jonathan Mayhew and Charles Chauncy emerged as champions of Taylorism and eventually folded his enlightenment understanding of human sinfulness into the theological worldview of emerging Unitarianism. Other Calvinists—most notably Rev. Jonathan Edwards and his "New Divinity" disciples Joseph Bellamy and Samuel Hopkins—vigorously defended the federal doctrine of original sin, even if they modified it slightly in order to make it more rationally defensible.[30]

The doctrinal unanimity that characterized New England ministers concerning original sin prior to 1750 clearly was collapsing under the weight of Locke's philosophy and theological controversy. This transition was clearly reflected in execution preaching. Drawing largely on Lockean notions of human depravity and to a lesser extent on Taylorism, many execution preachers after 1750—both Provincial and Early National—explained that sin consists of willful transgressions against the law from which persons have the capacity to restrain themselves. Born morally neutral, capital criminals become "depraved" because of their environment, experience, and custom of sinning. Moreover, many execution preachers began to assume that human depravity referred principally to a constitutional imbalance between a person's reason and his or her passions. Moral education, especially for the young, corrects this imbalance and thus prevents the sinful progression that would lead to capital crime. This redefined doctrine of human sinfulness opened up a sizeable chasm between the condemned and the execution audience by suggesting that capital criminals were, in fact, qualitatively different from ordinary New Englanders, morally speaking.

Consider the 1768 case of repeat burglar Isaac Frasier, for example. Like so many of his predecessors, Congregationalist minister Noah Hobart explained in his execution sermon that sinners become "overmuch wicked" and that such persons justly meet an untimely death. The Fairfield pastor claimed that "sin is justly stiled a transgression of the law . . . it means going beyond the bound or limits prescribed." As a result, persons who fail to restrain themselves from sin become "wicked overmuch": their sinful course becomes progressively more wicked, they repeat the same sins, and they become numb to the plain and repeated warnings of their danger. Although Hobart admitted that "we all have the same corruptions of the soul," he asserted that Frasier's persistence in transgressions made him morally peculiar: every transgression that he committed weakened his natural resistance to sin, robbed him of the power of conscience, dulled his fear of shame and punishment, and stripped him of regard for his own reputation. Such "habitual practice of wickedness" often provoked God "to leave sinners to be as vile as unbridled corruption can make them." Notice especially that repeated sinful acts account for Frasier's depravity, not vice versa.[31]

Presbyterian minister Samson Occom argued similarly in a sermon occasioned by the execution of Native American murderer Moses Paul in 1772. Occom certainly sounded like his Puritan forebears when he claimed that "Sin had vitiated the whole man, both soul and body; all the powers are corrupted" so that sin had "stupefied mankind," "blinded their eyes," and rendered them as "deaf as adders." But Occom referred here to sin as a volitional act, a willful "transgression of the law." Like Hobart before him, Occom seemed to be arguing that the habit of actual sin corrupts the body and soul of humanity, not that a preexistent corruption leads humanity to commit actual sins.[32]

More commonly, preachers of execution sermons after 1750 directly reflected Locke's understanding of human sinfulness: the constitutional imbalance between a person's reason and passions. Because human reason generally held the passions in check, sinners and criminals alike were understood as those whose affections had overcome the governments of reason. Indeed, Rev. Nathan Strong warned the audience assembled at the execution of Moses Dunbar in 1777 to beware especially the depraved passions of human nature. "Our passions," he explained, "like the most combustible matter, may instantaneously kindle at the touch of a single spark . . . our appetites, which are hushed into moderation one hour, may the next be fierce and victorious over reason. . . ." Rev. Thomas Thacher repeatedly made the same point in his sermon occasioned by the Fairbanks execution. In his sermon, Thatcher argued that "profligate, licentious youth" are particularly susceptible to these "black impetuous passions." Such young people tend to ignore the "sources of moral improvement"—the inspired precepts of Scripture, the public institutions of Christianity, the advice of parents, and the wise laws of the country—and to continue their "mad career" of unrestrained passions. "Swallowed up by [this] passion," Thacher concluded, "their reason is totally dethroned."[33]

Interestingly, this redefinition of human sinfulness was most noticeable in the sermons and related crime literature occasioned by the execution of New England blacks. In these cases, racist assumptions about the fundamental nature of black people combined with the ordinary anxiety that white colonists had about their presence among them to intensify the rhetoric of all genres of New England crime literature, including execution sermons. The result is an exaggerated social, legal, and theological ideology that differentiated "black crime" and depicted it as a greater threat than crime committed by whites.[34] Because of the frequency with which they were punished with death in early New England, two crimes—rape and arson—were particularly associated with blacks, and the intensified rhetoric of the crime literature associated with these executions reinforced prevailing racist stereotypes.[35]

There can be little doubt that the stereotype of the young black man as a hypersexual beast was one of the oldest and most durable themes of Anglo-American racism. Historians generally agree that the origins of this stereotype can be located in the travel accounts of sixteenth-century European explorers who brought back extravagant tales of the sexual behavior of the inhabitants of Africa. As the North Atlantic slave trade intensified in the eighteenth century, anxiety among white English colonists concerning black sexuality expressed itself in legal codes prescribing gruesome punishments—especially castration—for black men who committed sexual offenses. Moreover, lurid accounts of black sexual crimes in early American popular literature reinforced the existing stereotype of the young black man as sexual predator and guaranteed that the punishment for black sexual crimes would be both swift and harsh.[36]

An example might help illustrate how the stereotype of black hypersexuality impacted the application of criminal law in eighteenth-century New England. On October 2, 1742, the sixteen-year-old enslaved African known only as "Negro Cuff" was working on the farm of his master in East Haven, Connecticut. The sight of a fifteen-year-old white neighbor named Diana Parrish walking on the road, Cuff later confessed, filled him with sexual urges that he could not control. Seeing that no one was nearby, Cuff grabbed the girl and dragged her into the woods where he forced her to have sex with him. Cuff was apprehended and confessed to the crime of rape. When his case finally came to trial in early 1749, two lawyers represented the unfortunate young man, but he was nonetheless found guilty and sentenced to death. His lawyers urged the court in a defense motion that abounded with Scripture references to commute the sentence of death in light of Cuff's age. The motion was defeated. Losing all hope, Cuff even offered to submit to gruesome punishments in exchange for clemency: he was willing to be branded, flogged, castrated, and sold out of the colony as a eunuch slave. The court received his desperate petition but voted it down. So, the adolescent was hanged at New Haven on May 15, 1749.[37]

The few sermons preached in connection with the executions of black men for sexual crimes both reflected and reinforced these prevailing prejudices with their redefined theology of human sinfulness. Sometimes, these prejudices can be discerned in the intensified rhetoric that the preacher used in describing the sinful lives of black criminals. This was certainly the case with the sermon occasioned by the execution of nineteen-year-old convicted rapist Thomas Powers, who was born into slavery in Wallingford, Connecticut, on September 15, 1776. According to his own account, at the age of 11, he engaged in sexual intercourse for the first time and "began [his] career in the gratification of that corrupt and lawless passion" that led to his execution. In addition to his frequent sexual promiscuity, throughout his teens Powers took to burglary and pilfering whenever he needed money. At seventeen, Powers laid plans to commit his first rape at Norwich, Connecticut, but his plans failed when his victim never showed up. But on December 7, 1795, Powers accosted Sally Messer and pulled her from her horse "determined to make an attempt on her virgin chastity." Messer reported the rape, and Powers was jailed until he could stand trial. Powers escaped from jail at least twice to resume his life of crime but was caught each time. When his case was finally heard in June 1796, Powers was sentenced to death and was hanged at Haverhill, New Hampshire, on July 28. Powers donated his body to a local anatomist, who took the corpse to a tanner and had a pair of boots made from Powers's skin.[38]

Without making the expected attempt to fashion a moral identification between Powers and his audience, Congregationalist minister Noah Worcester berated the nineteen-year-old black rapist in his execution sermon. "The great God," Worcester began, "gave you a rational soul, and placed you in a land blessed with gospel light." But the young man had "proved [him]self to be by nature a child of wrath, by being a child of disobedience." According to the Unitarian minister, the young man "by indulging [his] own vicious inclinations" paved the way to an infamous death.[39]

Similarly, Congregationalist minister Timothy Langdon preached a heady sermon before the execution of convicted rapist "Negro Anthony" in 1798. The human tendency of sin began when "the will chooses what reason sees to be wrong." Such a tendency reflected a conflict between the "noble faculties of the soul," until it grew "to an enormous maturity" and became a "worm which dieth not" and a "devouring flame . . . that goeth not out." This was precisely what happened in Anthony's case. "You are one of those that have lived contrary to the dictates of your conscience," the

Danbury pastor explained. As a free black, he should have known better. "You were educated, having lived in a Christian land . . . having lived where the means of information were within your own reach, you cannot now come forward and claim ignorance as an excuse." Only Anthony's willful choice to sin, Langdon explained, could account for his execution.[40]

It should come as no surprise, then, that some execution preachers even argued that the natural inclination of black men to follow their passions rather than their reason makes them more susceptible to the temptations of the demonic. Such was the case with "Negro Arthur" in 1768, according to Congregationalist minister Aaron Hutchinson. He explained that the enslaved African ran away from his master at the age of fourteen, and thereafter he was "soon debauched and hardened in sin." He was idle, drunken, sexually perverse, and contemptuous of the gospel. Led captive by the devil for over seven years, the young man "wearied himself to commit iniquity." Surely the Grafton minister's rhetoric was revealing: "If all his enormous villanies, and wrongs to men, could be enumerated . . . what a black catalogue would there be of his crimes!" Hutchinson said that the young man showed signs of repentance in his last days but doubted that his conversion was sincere.[41]

Satan also was the master of Joseph Mountain, claimed Congregationalist minister James Dana, as the black rapist roamed "to and fro in the earth, seeking whom [he] may devour." Furthermore, satanic influence over Mountain produced in him an "unprincipled and shameless character" that led him to commit multiple crimes, of which rape was the most serious.[42]

Black passions stemming from original sin ran especially high not only in sexual crimes but in other crimes as well: arson and murdering the master or a member of his family. Historians have noted that early American secular crime literature related to black arsonists and dominicides often depict them as "ungrateful servants," who do not appreciate the "benefits" of their servitude. Although this literary trope echoed in execution sermons, more often the preacher relied on a theology of human sinfulness to explain these unspeakable crimes.[43]

The narrative of convicted arsonist Fortune Price illustrates how the crime of arson was racially coded in colonial New England.

Negro Fortune, as he was called, confessed to setting a fire that eventually engulfed and destroyed the entire wharf at Newport, Rhode Island, in February 1762. He started the fire in a warehouse containing lamp oil, ammunition, and other flammable goods. As barrel after barrel exploded, the fire spread out of control. Those living along the wharf were forced to evacuate their homes, and the shipmen who had docked their vessels in the harbor frantically cut anchor. The citizenry of Newport worked long into the night, and by dawn the blaze was more or less under control. Price was identified as the arsonist, arrested, and held for trial, miraculously without mob action against him. He was hanged on the Newport Commons in May 1762. In the published account, Price's actions were openly compared to the Great Negro Plot and similar insurrectionist activity at midcentury, and Price himself was characterized as the quintessential ungrateful servant. Lest the reader miss the dramatic character of Price's actions, the cover of his confession included a finely detailed impression of the Newport wharf wholly engulfed in flames.[44]

Interestingly, black arsonists like Price never inspired an execution sermon or any other theological explication of their crimes. But black murderers like sixteen-year-old Negro Bristol certainly did. Bristol was enslaved in the house of a physician in Taunton, Massachusetts, where he showed no propensity for violence or even disobedience. Nonetheless, during a visit from his master's sister, the young man conceived and nurtured an inexplicable hatred for her. One morning in 1763, Bristol struck her in the face with a hot flatiron. He then threw her down the stairs to the basement, where he bludgeoned her repeatedly with an ax. Bristol then stole his master's horse and rode as far as Newport, Rhode Island, before he was caught. The teenager pled guilty to the charge of capital murder and was hanged in December 1763. Congregationalist minister Sylvanus Conant alluded in an execution sermon to the ungoverned passions that overcame Bristol, the same ungoverned passions that inspire all insurrectionist activity among enslaved Africans. Such sinful behavior calls for increased vigilance against this threat to the peace and security of New England religion and culture. Indeed, he admonished slaveholders and others "who have the care of Negroes" to be "very vigilant in removing the natural Prejudices of their Barbarous disposition" by increased physical restraint and compulsory religious instruction. More to the point, white people needed to prevent "their companying together, that grand Source of all the Evils that have arisen so frequently from that Nation, when in their Conspirings they cry out 'Let us wait for Blood, let us lurk privily for the Innocent without a cause.'"[45]

The point here is that the redefined notion of original sin in late eighteenth-century theology—in which the baser passions and appetites have usurped the governing power of reason—appears to have been applied with specific vigor to black capital criminals, because blacks already were assumed to be governed by these baser passions and appetites. Execution preaching and especially popular forms of crime literature in this context appear to have given theological sanction to the racism that led to disproportionate punishment of black capital criminals.

Regardless of the race of the condemned, undoubtedly this revised doctrine of human depravity accounted for the frequent reference execution preachers after 1750—both Provincial and Early National—made to the importance of religious education for youth. Like Locke, they argued that an appropriate moral education would provide children with a mastery of their depraved inclinations and would subjugate their appetites to reason. As early as 1739, for example, Anglican divine Arthur Browne argued that a want of religious education led the young Penelope Kenney to murder her newborn infant. Because, Browne admitted, the very souls of all human persons are "vitiated by Sin" and "naturally inclined to evil." The neglect of religious education "lays Children under a kind of Necessity of pursuing what they are by Nature inclined to." So early intervention is the key: "[Children] are supple and pliable in their first and early Years," he claimed. "But they grow fix'd and stiffen'd as they ripen into Age, then preserving the same Shape, Figure and Frame into which they had been first moulded."[46]

Of course parents bear the chief responsibility for providing such an education, that is, to "train them up in the exercise of Obedience, and Modesty, of Diligence and Sincerity, of Tenderness and Humanity" and most of all "to accustom them to the government of their Passions." Only then, Browne continued, could children learn the "Practice of Piety & Devotion toward God; of Sobriety and Chastity with regard to themselves; and Justice and Charity toward all Men." To be sure, parenting is a "Concern of great Weight and Moment," Browne argued, because families are, after all, "Nursuries for both Church and State." In no greater way can parents become "greater Benefactors of the World, than by training up their Children in the Principles of Vertue and Goodness." Uncultivated by religious education, Browne warned, children would probably turn out like the morally peculiar infanticide herself: "wild and savage, unfit for society."[47]

Few executions afforded as much opportunity to reflect on the importance of the religious education of children than the 1786 case involving Hannah Ocuish. The twelve-year-old Native American girl stood convicted of bludgeoning to death a six-year-old playmate with rocks because the younger girl allegedly stole some strawberries from her. Although Connecticut authorities debated for almost six months about the appropriateness of executing a child at such a young age, the courts refused to hear any appeals for outright clemency.[48]

Rev. Henry Channing, one of the most respected Unitarian ministers of his generation, was left no other explanation for the unthinkable crime committed by Ocuish than her unchecked depravity. Referring directly to the young girl near the end of his sermon, Channing lamented, "We here see the natural productions of a heart uncultivated and left to itself; that indeed, it is deceitful above all things and desperately wicked."[49] As the neglected daughter of an alcoholic mother, Ocuish grew up very quickly to be morally peculiar: from her very birth she was "ignorant of the first principles of Religion" and thus appeared to have "no higher principle than the pleasure of gratifying her ungoverned passions."[50]

This melancholy example afforded Channing an opportunity to urge parents and masters to be scrupulous about the religious education of their children and servants, even if it was no longer fashionable. What was really "shameful" and "unpardonable," he argued, was "neglect of family Instruction and Government." Daily family devotions, doctrinal instruction, regular attendance at worship, cultivation of social deference, and discipline of vicious behavior are all essential elements of instructing and governing a family properly, according to Channing. The execution of Ocuish was God's way of reminding God's people of these duties, and nothing less than the spiritual destiny of New England religion and culture hung in the balance: "when a people favored of the Lord will not hearken nor incline their ear to his instruction, their national blessings are accursed from Heaven, and their pleasures will be bitterness in the latter end." Although it was certainly too late to stave off God's judgment on the ignorant waif condemned to die on that day, returning with intentionality to the religious education of her children and servants alone would secure God's continued favor on New England.[51]

This increased emphasis on the importance of religious education for restraining the passions of youth and on the responsibility of parents to provide such an education led at least one execution preacher to conclude that the sinful criminality of one young man was actually the responsibility of his parents. Intoxicated and weary, twenty-six-year-old Horace Carter took refuge in an almshouse in Brookfield, Massachusetts, on a rainy February night in 1825. He became enraged when an elderly woman tenant of the house did not move quickly enough to restoke the fire in the commons room. He pounced on the woman, tore off her clothes, and raped her in the presence of the other helpless elderly residents of the house. Carter was apprehended, charged with capital rape, and sentenced to death. He swung from the gallows on December 7, 1825.[52]

In the last extant execution sermon published in New England, prominent Baptist minister Jonathan Going essentially excused Carter's behavior by calling attention to the deficiencies of his family life. Carter was the son of an absentee father and of a mother whom the preacher described as "cruel." Indeed, the apple did not fall far from the tree, it seemed, because Carter's mother also was a habitual criminal, passing on to the young man "all the strong lines of his future character." Neglecting his religious education, his mother "left the mind of her child a perfect blank, open to receive the crooked lines impressed upon it by the casual hand of circumstance." Worse than that, she actually encouraged his early criminal behavior by dispatching him to "pilfer the neighbours' fields, and orchards, and gardens" rather than to bother raising produce of her own.[53]

"Carter might have been a good citizen," Going argued, "with an education." But his mother's negligence condemned him to "enter a life ignorant of its dangers, without experience, without education, unsupported by a cultivated moral principle; and worse than all without the habit of self-control." Like his Puritan forebears, Going argued that want of restraint permitted the rapist to progress from lesser sins to greater ones. What is different here, as with other Early National execution preachers, is that religious education is able to restrain human depravity, but in Carter's case it was lacking, and his parents were to blame. Indeed, while certainly not minimizing Carter's own responsibility for his heinous crime, Going minced no words in identifying who held ultimate responsibility: "Every parent ought to be deemed a felon, and punished as such, who suffers his children to grow up in ignorance of their duty as members of a Christian society, and as creatures accountable to God."[54] Clearly, Going advocated visiting the sins of the children upon the parents.

References such as these to the importance of youthful religious education in restraining the natural depravity of humanity abound in Early National execution sermons. On one level, these sermons illustrate larger theological developments in the doctrine of human sinfulness, and that has been the point of the present chapter. Yet on another level they reflect a fear among many Early National leaders of a "revolution against patriarchal authority" following the American and French revolutions.[55] For this reason, execution preachers extolled the coercive norms of colonial New England religion and culture for both family and social relationships. The value of public execution for such a message was clear: without these coercive norms—instilled through proper religious education—the rising generation would be left to pursue their passions, eventually leading them to the gallows. Ultimately, such a conservative understanding of education would lead New England to a reformation in educational theory and to the development of common schools by the 1830s.[56] But for now, the weight of the evidence for the importance of a specifically religious education seems to have been on the side of execution preachers. It might even be said that the notion of God's restraining grace commonly used by early execution preachers was preserved by later execution preachers in domesticated form. In other words, the mysterious dam that providentially held back the torrents of human depravity became less mysterious because it was built by religious education and proper family government.

Conclusion

As the Puritan doctrine of original sin began to yield to an improving assessment of human moral agency among New England ministers, explications of capital crime in execution preaching underwent a significant transformation. Their doctrine of original sin allowed Puritan execution preachers to argue that capital crimes are qualitatively indistinguishable from the actual sins that everyone commits every day. Instead, capital crimes differ only in degree. Thus, execution preachers prior to 1700 were able to fashion a moral identification between the condemned and the audience and could hold out the condemned as a fearful warning: the lesser sins with which everyone struggles could lead to greater ones, as they have in the case of the capital criminal.

The turn of the eighteenth century brought with it a subtle shift in the way Provincial execution preachers made use of the federal doctrine of original sin. These preachers rediscovered the systematic connection between the federal doctrines of original sin and salvation, and thus could argue that, if all are identical in terms of original sin, then even capital criminals are eligible for repentance and ultimate salvation. In Provincial execution preaching, the theme of warning yields to the homiletic trope of the sinner-turned-saint as proof of the magnitude of God's saving grace. This theme will be explored in detail in the next chapter.

Under intellectual pressure from the British Enlightenment, after 1750 Provincial and Early National execution preachers abandoned the federal doctrine of original sin as an explanation for the source of criminality. While never fully abandoning a commitment to innate depravity, they redefined the essence of human sinfulness, arguing that sin consists in the transgression of the law. Although all are guilty of such transgressions, capital criminals are indeed morally peculiar because of the magnitude of their transgressions. Even in these later execution sermons, the theme of warning persists, but preachers no longer grounded their warning in the universality of human depravity. Rather, they warned their audiences to beware lest their corrupt passions and appetites overcome the moral governance of their uncorrupted reason, surely a Lockean conception of depravity. Religious education, Provincial and Early National execution preachers argued, is an effective means of restraining those corrupt passions. While not exempting offenders from punishment, want of such religious education often was held out as a mitigating factor in their behavior and as a warning to others to be diligent about providing such education. Because of prevailing racial stereotypes, capital criminals who were young, black, and male sometimes were singled out as especially instructive examples of this internal contest between their reason and their passions. Surely, too, the race of such capital criminals served only to reinforce the assumption of their moral peculiarity.

It is certain that the nature and extent of human moral agency and its relationship to human sinfulness were issues that engaged the ministers of early New England. It is also certain that many execution sermons illustrate this engagement with helpful clarity. But the question remains whether execution sermons—either in oral or written form—played any significant role in eighteenth-century debates over human moral agency. Probably not. It is more likely that execution sermons simply reflect the broader debate among the ministers of early New England about human sinfulness, a debate that was worked out more fully in systematic, specifically doctrinal treatises.

CHAPTER THREE

The Economy of Conversion

And Jesus said unto him, "Verily I say unto thee,

today thou shalt be with me in paradise."

—*Luke 23:43*

In early New England, few theological issues generated as much interest and controversy as the economy of conversion. How precisely are people saved? What roles do God and humanity play in the process of salvation? Are there discernible steps in that process, and, if so, how can people know what those steps are? What assurances, if any, can people have that they are saved? Theological treatises, sermons, devotional writing, diaries, and a host of other genres of literature from early New England illustrate a preoccupation with these questions that characterized the religious lives of most people in this context. Moreover, in all the major theological controversies of early New England—from the Antinomian Controversy to the Great Awakening to the Second Great Awakening—contending parties aligned themselves against one another largely based upon how they understood the economy of conversion.

Such questions were just as pressing when they were asked concerning capital criminals and the prospects of their eternal fate. Prior to the early eighteenth century, most Puritan execution preachers believed that capital criminals were not likely to have the chance of eternal salvation. Relying on the doctrine of double predestination, they assumed that capital criminals suffered under God's decree of reprobation and developed a number of homiletic tropes to illustrate this assumption vividly in their sermons. Yet because they also believed that no one could discern with certainty whether another person is saved or damned, Puritan execution preachers also held out some hope of salvation to capital criminals. Their sincere repentance and trust in the saving grace of God might—just might—be an occasion for God to save. Most of them, however, probably agreed with Increase Mather, who was fond of saying that "late repentance is seldom true."[1]

In the early eighteenth century new understandings of the economy of conversion emerged, reaching a high water mark during the First Great Awakening, roughly 1730 to 1760. Provincial execution preachers appropriated these new understandings and argued more forcefully than their Puritan predecessors that capital criminals might be converted and saved. By midcentury, execution preachers were downplaying the doctrine of predestination as the starting point for their theology of conversion, and they attempted vigorously to "raise the affections" of the condemned person. They used fiery images of damnation to inspire fear in the condemned but balanced them with rapturous descriptions of the unmerited grace of God. Generally speaking, it appears that Provincial execution preachers had more confidence in "late repentance" than the Puritans had.

In the period of the American Revolution and following, Early National execution preachers continued to emphasize the evangelical economy of conversion in much the same way as their predecessors. Yet they nuanced this economy of conversion in ways that reflected the concerns of the troubled times in which they lived. The concern of these preachers for the conversion of capital criminals seemed less to be their actual salvation and more their submission to the established religious and political authorities. Often they held out the penitent thief on the cross from Luke 23:33–43 as a model, stressing his submission to the state by his admitting that his condemnation was just. Moreover, execution preachers emphasized the link between heterodox religious opinions and criminal behavior; renunciation of errant religious views and submission to orthodox faith, then, were often understood as "proof" of a criminal's conversion.

The discussion in this chapter will trace these developments in detail. But it will also suggest that execution sermons substantively influenced larger developments in New England theology. As new ideas about the economy of conversion were employed in these execution sermons, they acquired an even greater persuasive power, because they were applied to those persons who were perceived in New England to be the least likely candidates for salvation. Ultimately, of course, the ruminations of execution preachers about the conversion of capital criminals concerned more than the criminals themselves. Theirs was a question about how far God's redeeming grace reached, thus involving every member of the New England religious and social order. If capital criminals were not beyond the pale of God's redemptive activities, neither were the masses of otherwise law-abiding colonial New Englanders. It seems, then, that the gallows, no less than the meetinghouse, was an essential theatre in which the economy of salvation was worked out theologically.

The Puritan Economy of Conversion

New England Puritans inherited a theory of conversion from Theodore Beza, who after Calvin's death in 1564 became the leading teaching pastor in Geneva and the principal instructor at the city's theological academy. Beza founded his theory of conversion upon a clearly articulated doctrine of predestination: some time before the creation of the world, God determined who would be saved to eternal life and who would be condemned to eternal damnation. This "double predestination" brings glory to God on both accounts because the elect are recipients of God's unmerited mercy, while the damned are deserving victims of God's righteous judgment against human sinfulness.

But Beza's theology of predestination raised an immediate question: "How do people *know* whether they are elect or reprobate?" In other words, "How can people have the assurance of faith?"

Beza argued that persons can discern from their spiritual experience whether they are among the elect. When Jesus Christ truly dwells in a person by faith, he works in them to destroy their natural corruption and its influence over their moral lives, to sustain them during times of trial and temptation, and to empower them to obey the will of God. By discerning such activity in their lives, the elect can be assured of their status as such and can expect that they will receive eternal life. Naturally, of course, if persons lack such spiritual experience, they should take it as evidence of their reprobation, or at least as evidence that God has not yet given them saving faith.[2]

Anglo-American Puritans appropriated the Genevan reformer's insight and expanded it into a comprehensive theory of conversion, sometimes called "preparation." Assuming double predestination as Beza did, English Puritan theologian William Perkins understood preparation as a four-step process. First, the elect develop knowledge of the Law and the Gospel, chiefly through preaching and devotional Bible reading. The Cambridge theologian believed that even the reprobate are capable of some such knowledge, but they lack the assistance of God, who leads the elect to greater biblical understanding. Second, the Holy Spirit inspires the elect to clearly see the heinousness of their sin and its consequences. Again, the reprobate are capable of admitting their sinfulness but are lacking the Spirit. They never come to a full appreciation of sin's consequences. Third, the elect are motivated to contrition, or a sorrow for their sins. The elect are "pricked in the heart" not so much by a fear of their eternal damnation in hell as by an apprehension of God's severe displeasure at human sinfulness. Finally, the elect reach a state of desperation, surrendering all hope of relying on their own merit to achieve salvation and realizing that only the grace of God through Christ is sufficient. After progressing through these stages of preparation, Perkins concluded, the elect receive as a gift from God the faith that secures their salvation.[3]

On the other side of the Atlantic, New England Puritans typically simplified Perkins's scheme into two stages, but these stages reflected a full reliance on the Cambridge theologian. For example, Thomas Hooker spoke only of contrition and humiliation as the preparatory stages to receiving saving faith. Through the apprehension of the Law, the Holy Spirit drives the elect to contrition and inspired sorrow for sin. Through the apprehension of the Gospel, the Holy Spirit teaches the elect not to rely on their own merits but on only the merits of God's grace for salvation. Similarly, John Cotton spoke of the "double work" of the Holy Spirit: the "spirit of bondage" convinces the elect of the danger of sin and inspires a fear of damnation, while the "spirit of burning" obliterates in the elect any trust in their own merit and inspires in them a dependence on God alone to save. Although they often differed in the finer points of their theory of conversion, New England Puritans agreed on the broader ones that had been traced out by the generation of Reformed thinkers before them.[4]

Naturally, this theory of conversion impacted the worship and devotional lives of New England Puritans. From their pulpits, Puritan preachers pounded away at the theme of human moral debility and urged the faithful to rely on God to blot out the stain of original sin. They drove their parishioners to contrition with evocative images of hellfire and raised them to the heights of joy with the rapturous expectation of heaven. And they called them to love God and neighbor and to be zealous in their labor, all of which was pleasing to God and was befitting of "visible saints." They understood conversion to be a lifelong, Spirit-led process, oscillating between periods of faith and doubt, strength and temptation, but culminating for the elect in the promised heavenly reward.[5]

Second, in Puritan New England those who sought admission to a church and participation in the sacrament of the Lord's Supper were usually required to present a personal confession to the congregation, a kind of spiritual autobiography. They were expected to recount their awakening to sin, describe their lifelong struggle against it, and declare their conviction that salvation comes only through the death of Jesus Christ. Although New England Puritans believed that no one could judge definitively the spiritual experience of another, applicants were admitted to church membership and the Lord's Supper only if their confessions convinced the minister and the congregation that they had undergone a genuine conversion. Indeed, this was the principal way in which the New England Puritans believed that the purity and integrity of the church was preserved. Even after the Halfway

Covenant (1662) significantly reduced some of these burdensome requirements of church membership and admission to the sacraments, most New England churches continued to practice the more strident requirements of preparationism.[6]

Affirming the doctrine of double predestination and a theory of conversion based on "preparation," Puritan execution preachers generally assumed that conversion and ultimate salvation were unlikely for the condemned. They could claim that those condemned for capital crimes probably suffered under God's decree of reprobation, because there were few or no signs that the Holy Spirit was preparing them for saving faith. The only real benefit that execution preachers might expect from their efforts, then, was to hold out the condemned as an example of divine justice from which other sinners might learn. God demonstrates the divine glory in the death of capital criminals by carrying out God's sovereign decree of predestination in a way that is visible to mortal eyes.

In order to reinforce their assumption that the condemned were irrecoverably lost, Puritan execution preachers developed a number of homiletic themes to refer figuratively to the reprobation of the capital criminal. First, most probably agreed with Rev. Joshua Moodey that the sentence of death passed on capital criminals was a portent of the impending judgment of God. "No sooner shall your guilty soul be forced out of your wretched body," Moodey told convicted murderer James Morgan in 1686, "but it shall appear before the God that gave it, there to receive another Sentence of Condemnation than what you have already heard from man . . . in that sentence there will be no mercy for your soul."[7] Similarly, Rev. Increase Mather warned infanticide Sarah Threedneedles about the consequences of dying with an impenitent heart. "Thou thinkest it is a mean thing that you are Sentenced to be hanged to death," he told her, "but Oh! What will it be when the Son of God shall doom thee to Eternal Fire!" As if this were not enough warning, Mather continued, "After thou hast been in that Fire as many millions of Ages as there are sands on the Sea shore, thou shalt be no nearer to an end of it, than thou wast the first hour it came upon thee."[8] Public execution of a capital criminal was—to continue our theatrical metaphor—only a dress rehearsal for the damnation reserved for all of the reprobate.

Moreover, Puritan execution preachers often spoke of the capital criminal's "judicial hardness of heart" that motivated his or her progress in sin despite fair warnings from God. Most often these preachers likened the heart condition of capital criminals to that of the Pharaoh of the biblical Exodus. Indeed, Increase Mather alluded to the plagues visited upon Israel's Egyptian bondsman when he warned his audience to avoid James Morgan's impenitency: "For the truth is, if men be not humbled and converted by such signal dispensations, many times they are judicially and everlastingly hardened. They never leave sinning until they have sinned themselves into Hell, past all hope of mercy or recovery."[9] Sometimes, however, opportunities for emphasizing the judicial hardness of the capital criminal's heart did not even require biblical precedent. Rev. Cotton Mather also developed this theme in reference to convicted murderer Hugh Stone in 1690. "Oh that you may not be hard-hearted any more!" Mather wailed pathetically. "Thou has the name of STONE; God forbid that thou should have the qualities and properties of a stone, in your obduration." Mather, however, offered no evidence that Stone's heart was softened by his vigorous admonitions.[10]

It is important to note that this hardness of heart was for these preachers "judicial" or "penal"—that is, it came as a judgment from God. Like Beza, Perkins, and key Reformed theologians of the seventeenth century, these Puritan execution preachers assumed that God's controversy with stubborn sinners had its limits and that God eventually abandoned reprobates to their sinful ways. Just like Sarah Smith was, "the abhorred of [God's] soul . . . are left of God to go the way of Hell." Indeed, their "many previous and foregoing sinful courses have provoked God to jealousie and hot displeasure . . ." so that God "will leave them to this sin, to prepare them for a day of Vengeance." Such sinners could escape neither this divine abandonment nor its consequences, eternal damnation.[11] Of course, Puritan execution preachers were careful to exempt God from all responsibility for human sin. They argued that the judicial character of this hardness of heart consists only in God's withholding mysterious "restraining grace" and permitting reprobates to follow their own sinful courses. Greater sins thus follow inexorably upon the heels of lesser ones when

God providentially removes this grace. Such instances are indeed dreadful cases of "sin punished with sin," as Rev. Cotton Mather explained, referring to the sinful life of impenitent infanticide Sarah Threedneedles.[12]

Evidence that capital criminals were most likely among the reprobate did not end there for Puritan execution preachers. They emphasized thirdly that the pollution of the land caused by the actions of the reprobate demanded his or her execution, lest the wrath of God fall upon everyone. Rev. Samuel Danforth developed this theme with particular vigor in a sermon occasioned by the Goad execution mentioned earlier. His "abominable uncleanness" dramatically represented that of New England society more generally, and Danforth felt a duty to warn his contemporaries about the wrath of God that would befall them unless they repented. "The Church cannot be cleansed," the aging minister declared, "until this wicked person be put away from among us. . . . The Land cannot be cleansed until it hath spued out this Unclean Beast. The execution of Justice upon such a notorious malefactor is the onely way to turn away the wrath of God from us, and to consecrate ourselves to the Lord, and obtain his blessing upon us."[13]

Sarah Smith brought similar pollution upon the land in 1698, as John Williams explained: "a whole land cannot be innocent but polluted that suffer innocent blood to cry against it in neglecting the Execution of Justice for such a transgression . . . a whole Land shall smart for sparing a convicted Murderer's life."[14] In case his audience had any doubts, Williams provided ample evidence from scripture for God's blessing Israel when they applied God's Law with severity and for God's cursing the chosen people when they neglected to do so. Not simply their biblical scrupulosity led Puritan execution preachers to defend the execution of capital criminals; their belief that doing so was the only way to turn away God's wrath against New England religion and culture as a whole was an equally compelling defense of the practice of public execution. The purity of the church, the purity of the land, and the larger witness of New England religion and culture had been jeopardized by the actions of the reprobate.[15]

Finally, Puritan execution preachers argued that the capital criminal's greediness in sin—what they often called being "wicked overmuch"—results in the untimely death of the reprobate. This theme served as the central focus of Rev. Increase Mather's 1674 sermon occasioned by the execution of two servants who murdered their master. Those who were "overmuch wicked" might be said to die before their time in respect to their expectation and preparation for death, and even in respect to the ordinary course of nature. But Mather argued that no death is to be understood as untimely with respect to God's decree. Indeed, God punishes with death those who have committed particularly heinous sins, those with multiple transgressions, those who have a mind only on the things of this world, and especially those reprobate who are "incorrigible in the wayes of sin." What made the crime of these murderers all the more wicked, Mather continued, was their rebellion against the divinely ordained social order. "Oh how you have risen up in rebellion against the glorious image of God, not only in that you have shed the bloud of a man who was made in the Image of God, but such a man as had particular dominion over you; in that respect you have offered fearful violence to the sacred image of the blessed God." Such reprobate persons, Mather concluded, were "too wicked to live long."[16]

Nonetheless, the theological worldview of Puritan execution preachers simply would not permit them to say with absolute certainty that capital criminals were beyond the pale of God's redemptive activity. To do so would compromise the sovereignty and mystery of God. As a result, they sometimes included in their sermons a direct appeal to the condemned, giving them specific instructions to demonstrate suitable repentance. They were quite clear that repentance would not spare them temporal death at the hand of the magistrate, but it just might commute their sentence of eternal death at the hand of almighty God. In order to have a chance for mercy, the condemned must consider truthfully the sinfulness of his or her life; repent, trusting only in Jesus Christ as the source of salvation; and offer a clear warning to others of the dangers of sin.

One instructive example of such an appeal should suffice to make the point—the one that Rev. Cotton Mather made to James Morgan in 1686. Addressing the convicted murderer directly, Mather thanked him for the "seemingly penitent confession of

[his] monstrous miscarriages" that the minister had received in writing earlier that morning. Yet this was insufficient for his repentance and salvation. As Morgan faced the moment of his execution, he must "look upon Jesus Christ, as not only able, but willing to be [his] savior." What Morgan needed to demonstrate more than anything else, Mather said, was a loathing of himself: "Abhor and condemn yourself as most worthy of all the crushes that you have in the winepress, of omnipotent fury, of all the howling Torments between the millstones in the pit below." With these harrowing images of damnation in his sight, Morgan was also to "give and get all the honor that [he] can unto Jesus Christ." This he could do by making a confession of his sin and guilt on the gallows: "When the numerous crowd of spectators are, three or four days hence, throng'd about the place where you shall then breathe your last before them all," the minister advised, "then do you with the heart-piercing groans of a deadly wounded man beseech of your fellow sinners that they would turn now every one from the evil of his ways." Only then, Mather concluded, would Morgan be permitted to trust in Jesus Christ for salvation. There appeared to be hope for Morgan's salvation, but not much.[17]

Such an appeal to the condemned was a common feature of execution preaching, of course. But, as the next section demonstrates, evangelical execution preachers seemed more confident that the salvation of capital criminals might actually happen.

The Provincial Economy of Conversion

Alongside the Puritan economy of conversion, in the early decades of the eighteenth century a new economy of conversion began to emerge among New England Puritans, and eventually it animated the First Great Awakening. American religious historians have been divided in their attempts to locate the exact origins of this evangelical economy of conversion. Some trace it to the influence of continental pietism in the region, interpreting these theological developments as a break with the traditions of New England Puritanism. Others see this new understanding of conversion as a seedling that grew out of the soil of Puritanism itself. Still others claim that it has multiple roots and no single source can be identified. Whatever its origins, this new economy of conversion greatly expanded the reach of God's saving work beyond the strictures defined by Puritan preparationism.[18]

What characterized this "evangelical" economy of conversion? To begin with, this new understanding of conversion downplayed the systematic connection between the doctrine of double predestination and salvation. Following the teaching of English Puritan William Ames and some of his admirers in seventeenth-century New England, evangelicals of the early eighteenth century believed that the glory of God was demonstrated most decisively in the salvation of sinners rather than in God's eternal decrees of election and reprobation. Thus, the evangelical economy of conversion not only admitted the possibility that the "chief of sinners" might be converted and saved but also suggested that God's glory was magnified to an even greater extent in such cases.[19]

The most obvious hallmark of the evangelical economy of conversion was its emphasis on religious affections as the constitutive element of true religion. In eighteenth-century parlance, religious affections began with the operation of the Holy Spirit upon a person's understanding and will and resulted in a radical reorientation of him or her away from the love of the world toward the love of God. Often these affections manifested themselves in bodily agitations and intense emotional fluctuations between anguish and joy. More important for understanding religious affections as a sign of true religion was the way in which this radical reorientation of the soul toward the love of God manifested itself in a life of piety. Indeed, this served as a generally reliable norm by which to judge the genuineness of a convert's religious experience. In this newly emerging economy of conversion, assurance of salvation came to be defined not in terms of doctrinal and experiential conformity to the expectations of the church (the heart of preparationism) but in terms of the moral life visibly flowing out of one's newfound love of God (the heart of evangelicalism).[20]

This emerging evangelical economy of conversion greatly impacted the theology of both preaching and the sacraments in the opening decades of eighteenth-century New England. Indeed, many preachers began to see their primary responsibility as "raising the affections" of their congregations so that God might work through those affections miraculously to save. Rev. Solomon Stoddard pioneered these developments in the Connecticut River Valley as early as the 1670s and presided over five seasons of "revival" before 1720.

Like his more orthodox predecessors, Stoddard believed that preaching was an instrumental cause of salvation, what he called an "antecedent to conversion." Potential converts come to understand the economy of conversion in part by listening to sermons. But unlike his predecessors, Stoddard set out deliberately to raise the affections of his listeners, principally by contrasting the fear of God with hope in Christ for salvation. This was by no means mere emotional manipulation; Stoddard believed and taught that through these raised affections, the Holy Spirit operates upon the souls of individuals miraculously to save.

Similarly, Stoddard rejected the traditional understanding of the sacraments as means of grace and refused to fence them in the way that his more orthodox contemporaries did. Instead, he taught that the sacraments were "converting ordinances" that also could raise the affections of communicants to drive them to immediate commitment to Christ. Stoddardism, as this innovative homiletic theory and sacramental theology was often called, contributed much to the development of the evangelical economy of conversion.[21]

By downplaying the doctrine of predestination and emphasizing the importance of religious affections, the evangelical economy of conversion allowed early eighteenth-century execution preachers to entertain with more certainty than their Puritan forebears that capital criminals might be converted and saved. Like other forms of evangelical preaching, execution preaching became an instrumental cause of conversion; preachers were expected to "raise the affections" of the condemned, through which the Holy Spirit might also work miraculously to save. The primary object of this unique form of conversion preaching remained, of course, the capital criminals themselves. But execution preachers hoped that members of the larger audience—made equally sensible of the penalties for sin, of the saving work of Christ, and the joyous rewards of salvation—might "improve" the solemn occasions as opportunities to take stock of their own spiritual conditions.

Such a miraculous transformation as that of the aforementioned Esther Rodgers in 1701 demanded an explanation. Rev. John Rogers preached and published three lengthy execution sermons in connection with the case. His text for all three sermons was Romans 6:23: "For the wages of sin is death; but the gift of God is eternal life through Jesus Christ our Lord." No less than the infanticide herself, Rogers asserted in the first sermon, all were guilty of sins that deserve death. Indeed, the sins of the condemned woman differed from those of everyone else only in degree: "God makes every breach of his Law to be Capital," he explained; "we have many Laws, but a few Capital; whereas God makes every law such." As a result, "He that breaks any one of his Commandments forfeits his life; God hath set Death as a stated penalty of every sin." At precisely this point of hopelessness and despair, Rogers explained in his second sermon, "God opens the rich Treasury of his Grace," making eternal life possible through Jesus Christ to all who embrace the Gospel. Interestingly, Rogers made the specific argument that, if eternal life cannot be the gift of God to *all* penitent sinners—including capital criminals—then it cannot be the gift of God to *any* penitent sinner. In his third sermon, Rogers affirmed that the very best way for young people in particular to avoid the punishment of death for their sins is the "heedful Observing of [y]our way . . . according to the Word of God." Unruly passions, unprecedented temptations in the world, and the devices of Satan all threaten to distract young people from their duty to cultivate holiness in their lives. Though Rogers concluded that the convicted infanticide had failed in this regard, the God of "infinite grace" had saved her nonetheless and made her an example, not of "holiness leading to blessedness" but of God's gracious sovereignty.[22]

Because a sinner's conversion and ultimate salvation depended in part upon his or her affective response to the Gospel, Provincial execution preachers employed rhetorical themes designed to bring about that response. The most commonly used theme was the fear of God, because "only the fear of God," Baptist Nathaniel Clap insisted in 1715, "will excite repentance from sin." Accordingly, he and his evangelical contemporaries utilized stock metaphors in their sermons to awaken the condemned to the reality of their guilt and to inspire in them a fear of God. While these images resonated with Puritan execution preaching from the previous generations, new emphases emerged after the turn of the eighteenth century.[23]

Predictably, images of hell and its torments found a central place in these sermons. For instance, Rev. Cotton Mather demonstrated some evangelical leanings when he dedicated an entire sermon in 1717 to describing the hell torments that awaited impenitent sinners like convicted murderer Jeremiah Fenwick. Not only will God deliver them into the hands of the earthly executioner, Mather explained, but God will "take him into his own Hands, and make him feel such scalding strokes of His Wrath, as will be more tortuous than flaming Sulphur, or than running Bell-Metal!" Similarly Rev. Samuel Checkley confronted a convicted murderer remembered only as "Julian" with a series of jolting questions at the end of his 1733 execution sermon: "Are you afraid of Hell, and Damnation? Can you dwell with devouring fires? Can you inhabit eternal Burnings? Are you willing to be damned and suffer the flames of Hell thro' endless Ages of Eternity?"[24]

According to the criminals themselves, whose conversion narratives were increasingly published with execution sermons after 1700, these images of hell often provoked feelings of intense despair and spiritual agony. "I thought that I had so dishonored God beyond all Example," admitted convicted murderer Patience Boston in 1738, "that he could not bear the sight of me among the Living on Earth . . . I saw that I deserved eternal Misery and Hell was the only fit Place for Me." If we are to believe Rev. Samuel Moodey's report, the constant ministrations of the pious—both clergy and laity alike—over the course of her yearlong imprisonment awakened the hardened woman to the reality of her guilt and inspired in her an evangelical fear of God.[25]

The fear of God, however, was a double-sided coin for these Provincial preachers: the terrors of hell were understood properly only in their stark contrast to the hope of salvation offered in Christ. "The fear of God in the Evangelical notion of it," Mather explained to Fenwick in the same sermon referenced above, raised "such a dread of Divine Displeasure whereto our Sin exposes us, as to Compel our Flight unto the only Savior from sin, that by him we might be saved from it." For, "without hope, there is no Genuine Fear of God." Evangelical execution preachers expressed this hope in final redemption for capital criminals with equally evocative images. In contrast to the agony of the impenitent when they fall into the hands of the living God, Rev. Benjamin Colman offered comfort to condemned pirates in 1726: "There are the merciful and saving Hands of the living God, the saving hands of an Everlasting Savior . . . and into these Hands shall every contrite, trembling, believing soul be taken at death." In contrast to the "dreadful sound" made by the ghost of his murdered wife crying for vengeance, a truly penitent Joseph Hanno might indeed hear the "joyful sound" of the glorious Lord saying, "Be of good cheer, thy sins are forgiven thee," according to Rev. Cotton Mather.[26]

But how might these condemned criminals demonstrate a sure sign of their repentance? Were the raised affections sufficient proof of a capital criminal's contrition? Put simply, how could they *prove* that their repentance—"dying" though it might have been—was genuine? In 1715, Rev. Nathaniel Clap suggested that a "last dying speech"—already a staple in the ritual of public execution—would in fact validate the repentance of the condemned, and this was a second theme new to evangelical execution preachers. Not surprisingly, he drew his insight from Luke 23:39–42, where a penitent thief makes a dying confession of faith to Jesus, even as they both hung on crosses next to one another. Clap divided the text according to the two parts of the thief's speech: one part to his "Impenitent Companion," and the other to his "Merciful Redeemer." He was especially interested in discerning from the text some "true signs, the certain tokens of his Repentance," and he found four: that he rebuked his companion for that criminal's impenitence, acknowledged the justice of his execution, recognized the divine sovereignty of God and threw himself on God's mercy, and humbly prayed for forgiveness. Provincial execution preachers and capital criminals alike embraced Clap's criteria, and for the rest of the eighteenth century gallows literature of all types was largely built around this evangelical economy of criminal conversion.

This evangelical emphasis on dying confessions as an element of the Provincial economy of conversion differs subtly from that of earlier Puritan execution sermons. Puritan execution preachers called upon the condemned to make a scaffold confession primarily to serve as a warning to the gathered crowd about the dangers of human sin. Provincial execution preachers, by contrast, emphasized the model of the penitent thief on the cross, whose salvation was guaranteed by Jesus' promise, "Verily I say unto thee, today thou shalt be with me in paradise." By making a scaffold confession in which they not only warned others, but also admitted the justice of their condemnation and humbly prayed for forgiveness, dying criminals were, in effect, securing their salvation.

The last dying speech of Hugh Henderson mentioned before represents those of most capital criminals executed in the eighteenth century and illustrates the foregoing point nicely. In 1737, the convicted "house-breaker" acknowledged that neglecting his catechism and discounting the warnings he received in his youth were the "great Reasons of my taking such Wicked Courses as have brought me to my unhappy, untimely end." This melancholy recognition was no excuse; however, he also acknowledged the justice of his conviction and sentence: "My Sins have been very many and hainous in the sight of God and Man . . . for which I must justly die, and [be] righteously exposed to the wrath of God forever." Henderson knew that, although his sentence could not be commuted, his eternal damnation just might because of God's grace offered in Jesus Christ. Indeed, because of the ministrations of the Worcester congregation and its pastor, he had come to a "Hope and Dependence upon the Lord Jesus Christ for the Pardon of many and great Sins, and for eternal Salvation."[27]

Henderson's task, however, was only half finished. He also rebuked his contemporaries—especially the young ones—who shared in his besetting sins and warned them to avoid such sins lest they lead to greater ones. In particular he spoke of excessive drinking, cursing, swearing, gaming, and whoring, all of which he associated with his life in the criminal underworld. As preventive measures against sliding down the slippery slope of sin and criminality, he beseeched parents to pray for their children, warned children to obey their parents, and even cautioned tavern keepers not to let their patrons drink too much. He even beseeched magistrates not to be like the Rhode Island magistrates (all of them Baptists), not to allow their citizens to persist in their unrighteousness by "breaking the Lord's Day." To end his pathetic confession and dying warning, Henderson gave himself over to prayer. "I commend myself to the infinite mercy of God, my dear Redeemer," he begged, "beseeching that through the Merits of his Blood I may this Day be with him in Paradise."[28]

This emphasis on the affective response and the public confession of the condemned, however, ran the risk of suggesting that the criminals themselves were responsible for their conversion and ultimately for their salvation. This danger led to the development of a third important theme in the execution preaching of this era: true contrition had to issue from a trust in the all-sufficient merits of Jesus Christ. Rev. Thomas Foxcroft perhaps said it best when he reminded infanticide Rebecca Chamblit in 1733: "See that you trust not in your Tears & Sorrows, Confessions and Resolutions; they can't atone for Sin nor cleanse the Soul. 'Tis only the Blood of Christ and the Spirit of Christ that can do this." Similarly, Rev. Mather Byles told infanticide "Negress Phillis" before her execution in 1751, "'Tis a Fatal Mistake to pray for a Pardon, and think we shall obtain it for the Sake of the Prayer." Indeed, he counseled further: "if we endeavor to repent of Sin & reform our Lives, it oversets the whole Work, if we depend upon this Repentance and Reformation, and not on God our Savior." Evangelical execution preachers wanted to make it plain that if capital criminals were to be saved, God would get the credit.[29]

For at least one Provincial execution preacher the all-sufficient merits of Jesus Christ inspired a confidence in salvation that bordered on arrogance. While it was common for execution preachers to remind the condemned that the magnitude of their sinfulness did not exceed that of the atoning power of Jesus' death, occasionally they attempted to "improve" the magnitude of the sinfulness of the condemned as an argument with God for a pardon. Rev. John Webb developed this point in his 1734 sermon occasioned by the execution of John Ormsby and Mathew Cushing for murder and burglary. As a proof-text, he cited Psalm 25:11: "For thy name's Sake, O Lord, pardon mine iniquity, for it is great," and made three observations. First, he claimed that God alone ought to be petitioned for the pardon of our iniquities because sin "opposes and tramples upon God's ruling authority," and God alone can forgive them. In requesting such a pardon, the sinner must approach God with visible signs of true repentance, especially a conviction of his or her unworthiness. The sinner must "freely acknowledge that Hell and the inconceivable Torments of it, are our just Desert; and that every thing, on this side of the everlasting Burnings, is of the free and sovereign Mercy of God to us." Moreover, the sinner must be convinced that only the "Merits and Mediation of Christ our Redeemer" effects his or her pardon.

But Webb pushed this basic evangelical message to its logical conclusion in making his final observations on this biblical text. He argued that whenever God pardons iniquity, God does so for God's name's sake "to magnify his free and sovereign grace and mercy in Jesus Christ." The very name of God implied mercy and pardon, Webb asserted, and this was demonstrated most clearly in the expiating death of Jesus Christ. God's justice was satisfied and all sins were forgiven by the death of God's Son. For this reason alone, Webb concluded with his third observation, namely, that the truly penitent sinner may thus "plead the greatness of his sin, as an argument with God, why he should pardon and forgive him." Webb explained his conclusion in two propositions: first, since the proper objects of God's mercy are miserable creatures, the more miserable they are in themselves, the fitter objects they are for God's mercy; and second, the greater our transgressions have been, the more the mercy of God will be magnified in pardoning them.

The real import of Webb's doctrinal argument came as he addressed the condemned criminals at the close of his sermon. "There is merit enough in the precious blood of Christ to cleanse you," he said, "I can assure you from the holy Scripture, that God now invites, intreats, and commands you to come unto him for eternal Life and Salvation." So far, Webb is advocating nothing particularly innovative. But then he said, "And you may go to him, under all your Sin and Guilt, and even make use of the greatness of your Sins as an Argument to move his eternal Compassions toward you." Mercy from God for the chief of sinners, Webb argued, magnifies the divine glory more than damning him or her to eternal torment.[30]

In developing their evangelical economy of criminal conversion from the example of the penitent thief on the cross, one would expect that execution preachers would rely principally upon

Luke 23:39–43 as the text from which their sermons were developed. Interestingly, this text would not become standard until after 1770. By and large, Provincial execution preachers continued to draw from the prophetic and wisdom literature of the Old Testament, but they nonetheless generally reached different exegetical conclusions about these passages than their seventeenth-century forebears.

For example, in a 1733 execution sermon, Rev. Samuel Checkley encouraged Native American murderer "Julian" to plead for the mercy of God based upon Isaiah 1:18: "Come now, and let us reason together, saith the Lord: Though your sins be as Scarlet, they shall be white as snow." In other words, execution preachers of Checkley's generation utilized the characteristics of Old Testament "fools" not as diagnostic criteria by which the reprobate clearly could be identified but as signals of impenitence out of which the condemned presumably had emerged. As truly penitent, these former fools could approach God, confidently yet humbly, expecting God to pardon their heinous sins and to welcome them into paradise.

Under the influence of the developing evangelical spirit in New England theology, execution preachers stressed the real possibility that capital criminals might be converted and saved, albeit with an economy of conversion very different from that of their forebears. Execution preaching, like evangelical preaching more generally, became for them an instrumental cause of conversion and salvation: they raised the affections of the condemned by juxtaposing a fear of hell with the hope of salvation; they insisted upon a "last dying speech" as an essential element of the condemned criminal's act of penance; they affirmed the objective ground of salvation in the all-sufficient merits of Christ's righteousness; they even suggested that the magnitude of criminal sinfulness might be "improved" as an argument with God for mercy. All of this was indisputable evidence that a capital criminal could be saved and that God's glory would be magnified more by saving these egregious sinners than by damning them."

The Early National Economy of Conversion

The fires of the evangelical revival began to die down in New England after 1745, but the theological controversies that it inspired were far from settled. Gradually three basic theological worldviews emerged in New England, each with a unique understanding of the economy of conversion. Liberals gradually stripped themselves of the doctrinal restrictions of orthodox Calvinism and championed a brand of Christian humanism that emphasized the benevolence of God, the freedom of the human will, and morality as the essence of Christian faith. For these Liberals, the economy of conversion could not be founded on the affections, as faith was understood to be essentially rational in character. "New Divinity" theologians, on the other hand, carried the torch of revivalism and emphasized the foundational doctrines of Puritanism—especially the innate depravity of humanity and the efficacy of the atonement—even if they modified these doctrines to meet the intellectual standards of their time. In their understanding of the economy of conversion, New Divinity theologians were thoroughly evangelical: accompanied by religious affections, the conversion experience consisted of a sinner's receiving a "new heart" from God. Finally, Moderates sought to uphold the doctrines of the Westminster Confession of Faith as the standard of theological orthodoxy but refused to be doctrinaire about these commitments. Although there are significant examples to the contrary, most Moderates generally appreciated the need of immediate, experiential conversion. Nonetheless, like the preparationists before them, they continued to insist that church membership, preaching, prayer, and Bible study were indispensable strategies by which the faithful cultivated a life of Christian piety.[31]

Generalizations about the economy of conversion in Early National execution preaching are difficult to make. This is the case in part because execution preachers of this era belonged to each of the three parties described above. Nonetheless, whether the preacher was a Liberal, New Divinity, or Moderate, he interpreted the economy of conversion through the lens of submission to both political and religious authority. While this theme was not absent from earlier execution preaching, it emerges in the sermons from this context with special clarity. It is probably the case that the unsettled political, economic, and social context—more so than the theological commitments of the individual preacher—accounts for this emphasis.

For most Early National execution preachers, the model of the penitent thief on the cross became the standard by which this submissive repentance at the gallows was to be judged. For this reason it is worth looking at the passage in some detail. According to all four authors of the canonical gospels, at the time of Jesus' execution, two convicted thieves were crucified alongside him, one on his right, and the other on his left. Only the author of Luke, however, records the exchange among the three dying men:

> And one of the malefactors which were hanged railed on him, saying, "If thou be Christ, save thyself and us." But the other answering rebuked him, saying, "Dost not thou fear God, seeing thou art in the same condemnation? And we indeed justly; for we receive the due reward of our deeds: but this man hath done nothing amiss." And he said unto Jesus, "Lord, remember me when thou comest into thy kingdom." And Jesus said unto him, "Verily I say unto thee, Today shalt thou be with me in paradise."[32]

From these verses, Early National execution preachers developed an economy of conversion specific to capital offenders like the thief, including at least five discernible steps: a realization that his or her offense deserves death, a demonstrable fear of God and a concern for the glory of God, a belief in the pardoning mercy of God available through Christ, a willingness to make a public confession of his or her sins and to rebuke others as a warning against further sinful behavior, and a confident prayer for mercy that inspires courage as the condemned faces death. So universal was the belief in this economy of criminal conversion that Fr. William Smith, Rector of Trinity Church in Newport, published a lengthy how-to manual on the subject. This popular work provided clergy who ministered to capital criminals with "suitable devotions" for the months before and at the time of execution. These devotions were designed to bring about precisely the kind of discernible conversion experience envisioned by Revolution-era execution preachers and modeled in the penitent thief of Luke 23.[33]

Generally speaking, the condemned fulfilled the expectations of the clergy in undergoing the perfunctory conversion experience, so that in many instances Early National execution preachers provided in their sermons little more than a status report to the audience and a final exhortation to the condemned. One poignant example will suffice to make this point. Unemployed transient Richard Doane wandered into Barrett Tavern in East Windor, Connecticut, on Independence Day, 1796. He and a local tobacco trader by the name of Daniel M'Iver spent much of the afternoon drinking and laughing together, until they apparently began trading drunken insults. Doane inexplicably threw M'Iver to the ground and began beating and stomping on him. Then, grabbing him by his collar, Doane repeatedly banged M'Iver's head on the stone fireplace in the bar, where the victim died of a fractured skull. While his attorney spent much of the next year defending his client's actions as manslaughter (a noncapital offense), Doane himself set out to repent of his horrid actions with the help of eminent Hartford minister Nathan Strong. Although Doane's appeal for clemency was unsuccessful, Strong was convinced that the drunken man had repented sufficiently. He preached an execution sermon based upon a text that the condemned man himself chose, Hosea 6:6: "For I desire mercy and not sacrifice, and the knowledge of God more than burnt offerings." After a rather clumsy exposition of the text—which Strong himself actually deemed "improper for the occasion"—the Presbyterian minister launched into a full-blown exposition of true repentance, emphasizing precisely the themes described above. His advice betrays the routinized economy of conversion that he expected from the condemned man: "Christ's promises in the gospel," he explained, "are many and glorious; but you have no right to place any dependence on these . . . unless your heart hath complied with the conditions on which they are made." In the Appendix to his sermon, Strong matched Doane's preexecution behavior with each of these discernible stages of criminal conversion: he acknowledged his sentence as a just one, grew fearful as the terrors of future misery hung upon him, very gradually realized that nothing but the infinite mercy of God through the blood of Christ could save him, made a public confession of his irreligious life and warned others of the dangers of excessive drinking, and prayed so earnestly that he could approach the scaffold "strangely strengthened both in body and mind." For this reason, Strong concluded that the condemned man was "one of those uncommon instances of true repentance and grace" granted by God "to magnify the sovereignty and greatness of his mercy, and to teach us to seek his favor to the last hour."[34]

Even if most condemned criminals ultimately conformed to this routinized economy of conversion, a number did not, and their examples were equally instructive according to Early National execution preachers. In other words, because these capital criminals refused to submit to the prescribed method of repentance, their salvation was placed in jeopardy. For one thing, a number of capital criminals from this era refused to acknowledge the justice of their execution by stubbornly maintaining their innocence in spite of their conviction. Salem pastor Rev. James Diman, for example, declared plainly to convicted rapist Bryan Sheehan before his 1772 execution that his continued denial of his crime was sure evidence of his impenitence and brought him perilously close to damnation. "I think you have not as yet discovered sufficient marks of real repentance," Diman charged. "You have not appeared to have that lively sense of your sin and danger, and of the great things of religion, and another world, which might reasonably be expected from one in your circumstances." The minister continued, "And what is most discouraging of all is your denying the main fact for which you are condemned, though it was proved to the full satisfaction both of the Judges and Jury, and almost all who heard your trial." Such a temper of mind at this important hour truly made Sheehen "fit only for the company of devils and the damned spirits of hell."[35]

Similarly, a prominent, middle-aged Massachusetts woman named Bathsheba Spooner conspired with three men—one of them her sixteen-year-old paramour—to kill her aged husband in the spring of 1778. Because only the men actually committed the murder, Spooner "went upon the mistaken principle that she was not an immediate actor" and thus was innocent of any capital charge. Though she maintained her "constitutional politeness" throughout her four-month ordeal and was even baptized on the day before her execution, she refused to admit that she had committed any crime. Rev. Thaddeus MacCarty thus remained unconvinced that her repentance, such as it was, had any merit at all. "It would have been very satisfactory," the Congregationalist minister would have told the woman if she had bothered to attend his sermon, "had you been free and ingenuous in acknowledging your guilt, and the justice of your sentence." He apparently had reason to doubt because she failed to follow the submissive example of the penitent thief. "It was a fixed principle with her," he explained in the Appendix to his sermon, "that confession of her faults was proper only to be made to her maker, not to men." In the Early National economy of criminal conversion, however, such insistence on private confession of sin was tantamount to impenitence and refusal to submit to the properly constituted civil and religious authorities.[36]

Convicted murderer Samuel Freeman also apparently went to the gallows at Windham, Connecticut, with the same kind of impenitent resolve in 1805. Although little else is known about this case, the young African American man stood convicted of beating to death his Native American wife and persisted in denying responsibility up to the very moment of his execution. Rev. Moses Cook Welch, the Congregationalist minister who oversaw Freeman's preexecution ministrations, pointedly reminded him in a sermon on execution day that he had the advantage of a fair trial: the accusation was certified by Grand Jury indictment, and he was represented by "able and learned counsel" at his trial before the Connecticut Superior Court. Even the jury verdict was deemed appropriate: "The evidence," Welch said, "was so clear against you as to induce twelve sober, judicious, disinterested jurors, on their oath, to pronounce you guilty." Nonetheless, the preacher seemed to imply that it made no difference whether Freeman actually committed the crime because his life of egregious sin was ample reason for his execution, a fact that seemed wholly to elude him. "I know not, certainly," Welch explained, "that you are guilty of the crime for which you are to die. The truth is known only to God and to your soul." But there were several things of which the minister was certain: "you have been a great sinner . . . if you murdered Hannah Simons, and persist in denying it, however you may confess your other sins, you will die with a lie in your right hand." Such impenitence, Welch implied in the Appendix to his published sermon, accounted for the "very great weight and burden on [Freeman's} mind" at the gallows. The "inward perturbation and horror" of seeing this young man die without truly repenting, Cook reported, was "truly affecting."[37]

In other instances, unorthodox, even heretical theologies sometimes prevented capital criminals from demonstrating the discernible marks of true repentance. William Beadle, for example, grew to distrust the doctrine of providence and embraced instead the "doctrine of mechanism," an atheistic belief that human persons exercised complete control over their destinies. As Rev. James Dana explained in his 1782 sermon, this error clouded his moral reasoning and led him to kill his wife and four children while they slept in their Wethersfield, Massachusetts, home and then to take his own life.[38]

More to the point, however, Rev. John Marsh explained in a second sermon occasioned by the tragedy that Beadle's "deism and fatalism" made him guilty of striving against God: he refused to submit to God as his lawgiver; he found fault with the dispensations of God's grace; and he was dissatisfied with the way in which God governed his temporal circumstances. His characterization of Beadle and his actions was truly unflattering. "Being too haughty to submit to the humbling dispensations of Providence, and not having fortitude and courage enough to encounter and sustain the inconveniencies arising from straightened circumstances," the minister said, "he entertained the cowardly thought of flying from them and taking sanctuary in the unknown world." Such actions were motivated by "Dreadful delusion! Strange inconsistencies! [and] Horrid blasphemy!" Indeed, the very purpose of Christian faith, according to Marsh, was to break the rebellious human spirit and to "reduce us to submission to [God's] government" so that our souls will be fit for the heavenly kingdom. Those, like Beadle, who refuse to submit, "are chargeable with the guilt of contemning his infinite Majesty, vilifying his Wisdom, disparaging his justice, abusing his goodness, and defying his power, as if they were stronger than He."[39]

Doctrinal error also contributed to the criminality and impenitence of Samuel Godfrey. While imprisoned for theft, Godfrey murdered the warden of the Vermont State Prison in 1814, an unprecedented case that was subject to three separate appeals over the next four years. Godfrey maintained that he was innocent of the murder and that "false accusers" were responsible for his conviction. These were not the principal factors, however, that would prevent Godfrey's conversion and ultimate redemption, according to the execution preacher; it was his universalism.

Woodstock minister Walter Chapin alluded to his doctrinal error in a sermon drawn from Romans 6:23: "For the wages of sin is death, but the gift of God is eternal life through Jesus Christ our Lord." Although earlier execution preachers generally utilized this text to inspire in the condemned a hope for their eternal future, Chapin utilized this verse to demonstrate to the universalist Godfrey that the wages of sin truly are *death*. Not just physical death, the orthodox minister explained: Godfrey was exposing himself to an eternal, miserable condition of estrangement from God and perpetual torment, something he apparently denied. Chapin warned him that his faulty theology would mean eternal disaster: "Do not imagine that I am your enemy because I have dwelt largely on the desert of sin, and the irrecoverable doom of the wicked in the world to come." The minister was not trying to torment the criminal but rather hoped that he may "calmly review the subject, and not hastily conclude that the wicked will universally be restored to the favor and enjoyment of God." Godfrey apparently persisted in his universalism when this sermon was preached five days prior to his execution, and Chapin was forced to conclude that the convicted murderer's "heart [was] not renewed" and that he would be judged with the "second death" if he remained unwilling to tow the line of doctrinal orthodoxy and submit to the established economy of conversion.[40]

On the day of his execution, Godfrey apparently remained impenitent. Baptist Elder Leland Howard warned him one last time of his fate: he emphasized the reality of the Last Judgment in an execution sermon drawn from 2 Corinthians 5:11, "Knowing, therefore, the terror of the Lord, we persuade men." The Day of Judgment was coming, Howard explained, when every person must be arraigned before the bar of Christ and the ungodly would be consigned to everlasting torment; this is the "terror of the Lord." The only way to escape this fate is to embrace God's "admirable system" of salvation: to embrace "an entire, unreserved trust in him for salvation, an unfeigned love to his character, and a willing and cheerful obedience to his commands." Godfrey's only hope was submitting to the economy of criminal conversion as the clergy had presented it to him, including a belief in future punishment, but Godfrey refused.[41] In fact, he was prevented from delivering his dying confession from the gallows, but it was published only after his execution, buried in a number of other materials related to the case. It is easy to see why his confession was censored, because he refused to recant his universalism. Because of the atoning death of Christ, he claimed, God will "eventually restore all things to himself . . . and all flesh, which he hath made in his image and likeness, will see his glory, and participate in the full fruition of his everlasting life." The economy of conversion held forth by the orthodox as the only means of salvation was immaterial to the condemned man, who expressed only confidence that he would "soon join the happy throng of the redeemed who surround the throne and sing the praises of him that liveth for ever and ever."[42]

The problem with these impenitent, unsubmissive capital criminals was their refusal to recognize and reinforce the staid, orderly, and deferent standards of respectable piety that Early National New England clergy intentionally tried to cultivate. These criminals rejected the process of developing true faith as it was understood at the time, preferring rather to strike out on their own, either by asserting and maintaining their innocence or by rejecting the theology that defined true repentance in the first place. In other words, they refused to submit either to the civil or religious status quo; as a result, the clergy assumed that their ultimate salvation was in serious jeopardy. It might even be said that the economy of criminal conversion—first defined according to a biblical pattern—had become routinized, so as to be drained almost entirely of its meaning beyond reasserting and strengthening the cultural and religious status quo. What is noticeable, of course, in each of these instances is the ease with which execution preachers equated submission to God and his authority to punish with submission to civil and religious leaders and their authority to punish. In short, the state assumes the prerogative of the divine in the minds of these execution preachers, at least when it comes to punishing crime.

Conclusion

By way of conclusion, it might be useful to speculate about some possible reasons that the prospects for the conversion and salvation of capital criminals improved so dramatically in Provincial New England execution preaching. As has already been demonstrated, the Great Awakening accounts at least in part for these developments, especially since a large proportion of execution preachers of the period were supporters of revivalism. But what about the period after the Awakening, when it seemed that the economy of conversion returned to at least a quasi-preparationist model? How can we account for the execution preacher's continued confidence in late repentance?

Ironically enough, growing opposition to public execution beginning in the late eighteenth century may help explain the phenomena. So long as execution preachers could meet that opposition with the idea that the criminal might be on his or her way to heaven following execution, it made the practice more acceptable. As Chapter Five will demonstrate, when anyone in the Early National period—sometimes even the execution preachers themselves—dared question the genuineness of criminal conversion experiences, execution preachers began to lose one of the most compelling arguments that they had in favor of capital punishment and public execution.

Moreover, changes in American attitudes toward death after the Great Awakening also help explain why criminal conversion might have continued to be a cornerstone of the drama of public execution. As a frightful reality for the individual, death proved to be a handy rhetorical device for evangelical preachers to arouse the impenitent during the early decades of the eighteenth century. Provincial execution preachers learned this lesson well, as they reaped a rich harvest of criminal conversions apparently by relying on the understandable fear of death among the condemned. After about 1760, dying well in New England came to mean that the one facing death exhibited a stoic suppression of his or her emotions, especially of fear. Execution preachers again reflected the trend of larger cultural attitudes toward death, arguing that submissive conversion was the most suitable way for the condemned to develop this confident resignation.[43]

Although this issue will be taken up in greater detail in the next chapter, concerns about the nature and scope of civil authority also help explain why Early National execution preachers continued to concern themselves with the conversion of capital criminals. Indeed, when a capital criminal was converted and saved, both civil and religious authority seemed both punitive and benevolent. These authorities were able to punish offenders consistent with both divine and civil law for the immediate benefit of the religious and social order. But they were able to demonstrate their concern also for the ultimate welfare of the condemned. Civil government thus maintained an appropriate balance between justice and benevolence. Because this balance was a hallmark of the Reformed understanding of God, it likely served to reinforce the power and authority of civil government.

The moral continuity between the condemned and the audience that execution preachers went to great lengths to fashion may also help explain why conversion was so important. If indeed even capital criminals were not beyond the pale of God's redemptive activities, then neither were the vast majority of otherwise law-abiding New Englanders. In the minds of the execution preachers themselves, it seems that the conversion and ultimate salvation of capital criminals ameliorated the ambiguity of New England religion and culture. By reabsorbing capital criminals back into the moral community and healing the breach in the social order caused by their crimes, New England religion and culture *appeared,* at least, to be fulfilling the demands of her charter as the Holy Commonwealth.

But it seems that the greatest concern of execution preachers —whether in the seventeenth or the nineteenth century—was bringing glory to God. Puritan execution preachers clearly understood fidelity to God's law in the severe punishment of wrongdoers to be the most appropriate way to bring glory to God. The moral identification between the condemned and the execution audience reminded everyone involved that salvation and damnation depended only upon God's sovereign choice. Provincial execution preachers clearly understood that God's glory was magnified most when God's grace reached the chief of sinners, in this case, the capital criminal. If convicted murderers and rapists were not beyond the pale of God's redemptive activity, then the otherwise law-abiding citizenry of New England could rest assured that God's grace could reach them, too. Early National execution preachers apparently believed that they could bring glory to God by maintaining a social order that demanded submission, conformity, and respect for godly civil authority.

CHAPTER FOUR

Civil Government

For he is a minister of God, a revenger

to execute wrath upon him that doeth evil.

—Romans 13:4

The people of early New England had good reasons to think constantly about the nature and function of civil government. The first royal charters created colonies that often were drawn into political contests in England, especially the struggles between Parliament and monarch. The Dominion of New England (1686–1689) consolidated all New England colonies into one large administrative unit and taught colonists the dangers of political absolutism, a lesson that they never forgot. The rapid numerical and economic expansion of Provincial New England required constant political accommodation at all levels of government. The American Revolution forged innovative ideas about representative government, and the Early National period witnessed the working out of those new ideas in actual practice. Amidst all of these developments, the people of early New England regularly revised their ideas about the nature and function of civil government.

One function of civil government that went unquestioned in early New England was its right—indeed, its responsibility—to execute those who commit capital crimes. In their sermons, the execution preachers of early New England almost always provided theological justifications for this right. Prior to about 1750, Puritan and Provincial execution preachers argued that civil government was a divine institution empowered by God to protect the true church, uphold the highest standards of morality, and punish those who disobey God's law. Drawing their political theory mainly from Romans 13:1–7, New England Puritans assumed that magistrates were "ministers of God" and occasionally referred to them as God's "vicegerents on earth." By executing capital criminals, these government representatives were fulfilling their divine responsibility to rid the land of egregious sinners, thus protecting the region from God's judgment.

At the same time that Puritans were asserting the divine origin of civil government in the early eighteenth century, however, new ideas about the nature and function of civil government began filtering into New England, especially those developed by John Locke. By the 1760s leaders of New England consistently taught that civil government came into being by a social contract and that its chief function was the protection of the inalienable rights of citizens: life, liberty, and the pursuit of property. Provincial execution preachers at midcentury adopted these new ideas, while not fully abandoning the Puritan ones, and argued that protecting these rights required the execution of capital criminals from time to time.

Amidst the social and political turmoil of the Early National period, many execution preachers—especially those who can be identified as "New Divinity men"—returned to traditional Puritan political ideas by reasserting the divine origin and dignity of civil government. By executing capital criminals, divinely appointed civil magistrates protected civic virtue and preserved social stability, ridding New England of those persons whose personal ambitions and passions threatened the good of the commonwealth as a whole. Yet other execution preachers of more liberal theological worldviews—Unitarians, for example—openly questioned these Puritan political ideas and asserted a more "enlightened" understanding of civil government. It may be that these liberal execution preachers did so to express their confidence in the new nation's civil authorities and to appeal to a wider, more secular audience. In rare instances, these liberal execution preachers even expressed their doubts about the right of civil government to execute at all and questioned the effectiveness of public execution in deterring crime. This latter issue especially will be taken up in the next chapter.

The present chapter offers a broad survey of developments in ideas concerning the nature and function of civil government in early New England. This survey is not intended to be exhaustive; rather, it provides sufficient background to illustrate how execution sermons reflected these political ideas. More than this, the chapter claims that execution sermons actually reinforced the prevailing political ideas by applying them to one of the most intractable problems faced by any civil government, namely, serious criminal behavior. Execution preachers almost universally supported the right and the responsibility of civil government to perform public executions, regardless of how they understood the nature and function of civil government theologically.

Civil Government in the Puritan Context

Puritan ideas in New England concerning the nature and function of civil government were extrapolations of a larger, more comprehensive worldview—one inherited from earlier generations of Reformed thinkers in England. Long ago, Edmund Morgan identified two notions that stood at the center of this Puritan worldview like the points of an ellipse: calling and covenant.[1]

Two centuries earlier, before the sixteenth-century reformations, the notion that a person was "called" by God generally was reserved for persons whose vocational lives were spent in service of the church: members of religious orders, priests, and other church functionaries. Following the lead of Protestant reformers, New England Puritans extended the understanding of calling to include all realms of honest human activity. Of course, for them the notion of calling referred primarily to God's bringing the elect out of their lives of sin to salvation, a distinctly theological conception. But God also called persons to specific vocations, and not simply religious ones; whether one functioned as a magistrate or a miller, a clergyman or a cobbler, God brought all persons to their vocations. Finally, God's calling established a distinctive ordering of society built upon a hierarchy of roles. The husband and father, for example, stood as the head of the family; his wife was to be his subordinate, and their children and servants were to be subordinates of both. Similar ordering characterized all spheres of New England Puritan life: the church, the town, and the colony.[2]

For the New England Puritans, the vocations to which God called all people also implied clearly defined duties and responsibilities, most of which were derived from Scripture and clarified in the context of Puritan systematic theology. Once they discerned their calling and acquainted themselves with the corresponding duties and responsibilities, Puritans could obey God only by doing what was generally accepted as appropriate to their vocation. New England goodwives, for example, were expected to perform a series of discrete duties defined not only by their biology as women and by their relationship to their husbands and children but also by their relationship to the larger community. Although goodwives held primary responsibility for the "internal economy of the family," they often functioned as "deputy husbands" with duties that were more public in nature. Whether private or public, the duties of the New England goodwife were well defined, and women who rejected or challenged goodwives often opened themselves up to scrutiny, criticism, and even outright violent hostility. In this way, then, the New England Puritan doctrine of calling was socially and politically conservative primarily because the duties and responsibilities associated with each vocation were believed to be divinely ordained and thus were immutable.[3]

Even if all callings theoretically were equal in the sight of God, New England Puritans nonetheless held two callings in special regard: those of the minister and magistrate. Most of them probably agreed with John Calvin in his assessment that these two callings were "the most sacred and by far the most honorable of all callings in the whole life of mortal men." Unlike the seemingly numberless "private" callings that God issued to human persons generally, the callings to ministry and magistracy were "public," in the sense that their responsibilities extended far beyond the relatively limited circles of family and trade. Ministers, for example, were called to the daunting task of serving as "faithful shepherds" whose calling and duty were sound preaching of the word and diligent pastoral care for the elect. God's calling to magistracy was public in a wider sense, because its task was to ensure the optimal functioning of society as a whole, including both the elect and the reprobate. Seventeenth-century New England Puritans believed that the success or failure of any political unit depended largely upon the magistrate administering it. In spite of the voluntarism of New England politics, which seemed to imply that those who elect magistrates hold a great deal of responsibility for this performance, most still believed that ultimate responsibility for the common good lay with the magistrate himself.[4]

Because the call to magistracy was public and involved such grave responsibilities, New England Puritans were very clear about the qualities that they expected in potential rulers. The "character of a good ruler" boiled down to five general characteristics: wealth, piety, moderation, wisdom, and justice. Wealth obviously signaled to Puritans that a potential ruler had both high social standing and political contacts. But on a theological level, a person's wealth also bore witness to a host of other personal characteristics that the Puritan prized, most notably industry and frugality. Naturally, magistrates were expected to be models of piety and moderation as well. They were required to be members in good standing of a Congregationalist church and to be trustworthy and vigorous in their devotional lives. To a greater degree than other Puritans, magistrates were expected to be moderate in their behavior, avoiding extremes of both opinion and action. Such moderation, Puritans believed, was the primary safeguard against political corruption. Most importantly, potential magistrates had to display discernible signs of wisdom and a firm commitment to impartial justice. In the Puritan mind, wisdom was the God-given ability to distinguish between truth and falsehood, good and evil in ordinary human affairs. While they believed that some degree of wisdom had been granted to the elect, potential magistrates displayed this characteristic with unusual clarity. Moreover, those magistrates who were truly wise always kept in mind that any success that they might have in ruling was not the result of their own cunning (another Puritan connotation of the word *wisdom*) but was a gift from God. If these were the marks of a good ruler, Puritan logic furthermore assumed that those who possessed such qualities were divinely called to exercise authority in civil affairs.[5]

Like the notion of calling, that of "covenant" had far-reaching implications for the organization of New England Puritan society. Generally speaking, a covenant was understood to be an agreement between parties in which each held binding obligations to the other, obligations that were treated as sacred duties. Of course, the covenantal ideal first appears in the Old Testament, but it formed the basis of a whole system of theological thinking, particularly in the Reformed tradition, on the European continent, in England, and in America. These Reformed theologians taught that the "covenant of works" struck between Adam and God promised eternal life for all of humanity in exchange for perfect obedience to the will of God. Adam, however, proved incapable of maintaining that obedience, and his sin became that of his posterity by imputation: we, too, are incapable of the perfect obedience to the law. Therefore, God struck a new covenant with Abraham, the "covenant of grace," in which God promised divine blessing to him and his offspring in exchange for their faith. God's unique election of the nation of Israel continued until the coming of Christ; because God's chosen people rejected Christ, God opened the covenant of grace to all those to whom God gives faith. Although the nation of Israel will be recovered just prior to Christ's promised return, the elect within the Christian church have become partners with God in a new covenant of grace through Jesus Christ.[6]

The covenant ideal also impacted New England Puritan political theory at every level, even if covenants struck between human persons were considered subsidiary to those struck between human persons and God. The Cambridge Platform (1648), for example, placed the covenant at the center of Puritan ecclesiastical polity, suggesting that it was the only appropriate means by which church members might have a "visible political union among themselves." By pledging themselves to the terms of a covenant, the company of faithful persons agreed to meet consistently for the public worship of God and to edify and encourage one another and to submit to whatever disciplinary actions that the church might take to keep them "in the way of God's commandments." Making such a commitment was a weighty matter, one that bound church members in sacred obligation to one another. Indeed, without such covenants and the sacred duties implied therein, Christ would be left without visible churches at all.[7]

New England towns came into being through covenants as well. Using Dedham, Massachusetts, as a representative model, Kenneth Lockridge has characterized the New England town as a "Christian, utopian, closed, corporate community" precisely because of the terms laid out in its 1636 covenant. That document emphasized Christian love as the guiding principle of town governance, thus setting an extremely high standard of conduct for all its inhabitants in their relationships with one another. Moreover, the terms of the covenant preserved the homogeneity of the town by specifically excluding those who might prove "contrary minded" and "receiv[ing] only such unto us as may be probably one heart with us." Finally, the town covenant laid out the mutual obligations of all inhabitants with regard to the arbitration of disputes, participation in electoral politics, and the bearing of financial costs of its government.[8]

Even the relationship between civil magistrates and the governed was understood in covenantal terms in Puritan New England. Puritans believed that God already had called certain men to govern and had equipped them with the character to be good rulers. In annual elections freemen merely confirmed God's choice for magistrates by electing them to office. Once in office, magistrates held two principal covenantal responsibilities. First, and most important, was their duty to defend religious orthodoxy against the encroachments of heresy. Positive laws that protected Puritanism as the official form of Christian faith in virtually all New England colonies helped magistrates considerably in performing this duty. Banishment and—in rare cases—even execution were the consequences for religious dissent. Second, magistrates had the covenantal duty to enforce the laws that regulated morality. Indeed, Puritans believed that God had placed magistrates in positions of authority to prevent the moral decay that would be a natural consequence of human sinfulness. Laws prohibiting such moral lapses as Sabbath-breaking, drunkenness, and swearing were regularly punished severely and publicly. In response to this understanding of the nature of civil government, the covenantal duties of the governed were simple enough: elect those persons whom God already had called to office and voluntarily submit to their rule.[9]

The ultimate sanction for this covenantal understanding of civil government was, of course, scriptural. New England Puritans consistently looked to Romans 13:1–7 in support of both the divine origin of civil government and the sacred duty of the faithful to submit to it. Because this text is so important, it is worth quoting at length:

> Let every soul be subject unto the higher powers. For there is no power but of God; and the powers that be, are ordained of God. Whosoever therefore resisteth the power, resisteth the ordinance of God; and they that resist, shall receive to themselves condemnation. For magistrates are not to be feared for good works, but for evil. Wilt thou then be without fear of the power? Do well, so shalt thou have praise of the same. For he is the minister of God for thy wealth, but if thou do evil, fear: for he beareth not the sword for nought: for he is the minister of God to take vengeance on him that doeth evil. Wherefore ye must be subject, not because of wrath only, but also for conscience' sake. For, for this cause ye pay also tribute, for they are God's ministers, applying themselves for the same thing. Give to all men therefore their duty: tribute, to whom *ye owe* tribute; custom, to whom custom; fear, to whom fear; honor, to whom *ye owe* honor.[10]

From this passage, New England Puritans deduced a number of political principles that appear repeatedly in treatises on civil government up to the turn of the eighteenth century. The authority of civil government was granted by God and therefore required submission from the governed. Indeed, rebellion against civil government was tantamount to rebellion against God. The function of civil government was the preservation of the common good, which for New England Puritans principally meant the purity and godliness of society. Only evildoers need to fear the authority of civil government because God also invested magistrates with the *jus gladii,* the "right of the sword." One of their principal functions was implementation of the severe punishment of lawlessness and impiety, and that right extended to include capital punishment. Submission to civil authority was not a function of compulsion but a voluntary act of obedience to God. Accordingly, subjects also held the responsibility to support the functioning of these "ministers of God" or "God's vicegerents on earth" by the payment of appropriate taxes.[11]

Puritan execution preachers apparently saw little need to include in their sermons any sustained explication of the nature and function of civil government. It is reasonable to believe that the political ideas described above remained so deeply sedimented in New England society that they were rarely questioned, at least with regard to the prosecution and punishment of capital criminals. In the rare instances in which Puritan execution preachers mentioned the nature and function of civil government, they almost always reflected these traditional political ideas.

When they did talk about civil government, Puritan execution preachers spoke about magistrates as "ministers of God" who have both the divine authority and responsibility to execute capital criminals. Rev. Increase Mather first used this image in a sermon occasioned by the execution of two servants in 1674. As noted earlier, he argued that their crime was especially aggravated because Robert Driver and Nicholas Feavor had murdered their master, a social superior. Not only that, their actions further showed contempt for the "severe & righteous laws" that the "Lords Vicegerents on earth" were specifically called to establish and enforce. In one act of violence, these servants had completely overturned the divinely ordained social order.[12]

In another sermon occasioned by the execution of James Morgan in 1686, Mather emphasized the public calling of the magistrate in expressly Puritan terms. "Private Revenge is evil," he began, "but publick Revenge on those that violate the Laws of God, is good. The Magistrate is 'God's Vice regent . . . God has put the Sword into his hand for that end, that so he might clear the Land of wicked Malefactors who were worthy of Death, and he was resolved to see Justice done.'" In fact, because the responsibility to such public revenge is divinely ordained, disaster would result if any civil magistrate were to shirk that responsibility. "One murder unpunished may bring guilt and a Curse upon the whole land, that all the Inhabitants of the Land shall suffer for it." Indeed, Mather concluded, "mercy to a Murderer is cruelty to a People." The only proper response that the public ought to have to God's vicegerent was thankfulness. "Therefore, none ought to blame those in Authority for causing the Murderer to be put to death," he began. Instead, "let us be thankful to God, that we are under such Magistrates as will do Justice, and Execute Judgment, and punish Sin according as the Word of God requireth that it should be done." As God's vicegerents on earth, magistrates stood at the top of the social hierarchy by virtue of their public calling and by virtue of the power invested in their office by God.[13]

In the early eighteenth century, Rev. Benjamin Colman occasionally appealed to the spirit of the traditional vicegerent imagery but preferred to use the phrase more closely reflecting the text from Romans 13, namely, "minister of God." Before the execution of convicted murderer David Wallis in 1713, Colman explained more fully than any of his predecessors how and why magistrates functioned as "ministers of God." After ticking off a long list of biblical passages that demonstrate "how severely the Law of God forbids Murder, & makes it Capital," he cautioned his audience. "Let no man think that this looks Cruel or Inhumane: The Justice of God has so fix'd it," he said. "Yea, his tender Mercies to Mankind do account for this His Righteous Law and Judgment. Let us not presume to arraign the infinite Wisdom and Mercies of God." Relying as Mather had done on the public nature of the magistrate's calling, Colman declared that murder for a "Private Person" is "the extreamest Injury to our Neighbor and one of the highest Offenses against Human Society." Nonetheless, as a "Minister of God" the magistrate had the duty of functioning publicly as "the Avenger to Execute wrath upon him that does Evil." Indeed, "God has put the Sword into his hands, to cut off Evil-doers from the Inheritance of the Lord."[14]

So far, Colman's understanding of the magistrate as a "minister of God" sounds no different from that of his Puritan forebears. But Colman linked this divine responsibility with a concern for the overall good of society, a distinct emphasis of Provincial execution sermons. Indeed, part of what made the crime of murder so heinous was the effect that it had on society as a whole: "The sin of Murder strikes at the very being, and all the comforts hereof," he said. If the ministers of God were not vigorous in the prosecution of murderers, then "there [would be] no more living in any quiet or safety [than] there might be among the wild and savage Beasts of the Woods, where the stronger and fiercer prey upon the weak and mild." Society itself would have to disband, and all the divine blessings that accompany social order would dissolve. The link between divine mandate and the welfare of society is clearest as Colman closes the first section of his sermon. Unless they executed murderers, magistrates would be able to answer neither to God nor the people: "It is their Obedience to the Divine Law, and their Fidelity and Tenderness to Humane Society that constrain them to the Condemnation and Execution of a Murderer."[15]

Colman again emphasized the magistrate's concern for the public good in a sermon preached before the execution of Margaret Gaulacher in 1717. Though the condemned infanticide apparently underwent a credible conversion experience, the ministers of God nonetheless had the responsibility to carry out her death sentence in the interest of the public good. "[Humane Governments and their Laws] ordain Death in many Cases as the Sanction necessary to the Ends of Government, or to the Restraint of Crime," he began. But he urged his audience not to infer from this fact that the ministers of God take pleasure in the execution of capital criminals. Instead, he maintained that "the provision of the Law, and the Execution of it is Wise, Necessary, Good, and a tender Care for the Publick." Like other Puritans, Colman argued that public execution deterred capital crime: "providence hangs up one Criminal in Chains for Warning and Terror to others," he claimed. But the net benefit of such severity was communal. Using a crude medical analogy, the ministers of God acted like a physician, who "cut off a gangrene member" in order to preserve the health of the patient's body. "The Public Justice may be Inexorable to a private Criminal," he concluded, "because the public Compassions to the whole Community prevails."[16]

Similarly, Rev. Samuel Checkley blended a need for adherence to the law of God with a concern for the public good in his 1733 sermon series occasioned by the execution of Rebecca Chamblitt for infanticide. It is important to realize that Checkley's three sermons are dominated by concern for Chamblitt's repentance and salvation; in this sense, his series reflects the central theme of execution preaching of his day. In the first sermon, Checkley set out to prove that murder is a "great and crying sin." Even though murder is an offense for which God might pardon the offender, he claimed, it nonetheless "cries aloud for Vengeance on those that are guilty of it." After establishing biblically that the Law of God commands that murderers be punished with death, Checkley concluded that "Humane Laws should be consonant to the Divine." In fact, the happiness of society depends upon the degree to which magistrates govern according to the rule of law. Without such laws, and the governments to enforce them, chaos would result: "what Confusion and Uproars would there soon be in it without them? Men would soon devour, and be devoured of one another, and much more Sin and Wickedness be committed." Although fidelity to the Law of God was important to Checkley, the real import of penal severity was the protection of society as a whole from those who seek only their own good. Concerning murderers and even their accomplices, Checkley concluded: "These are a set of Men not fit to live, and therefore must be cut off by the Hand of Justice." Although civil government might forgive lesser offenses, willful murder must be punished severely.[17]

The subtle differences in the perspectives of Mather, Colman, and Checkley indicate a shift consonant with larger developments in the New England clergy's ideas concerning the nature and function of civil government over the first half of the eighteenth century. Mather seemed content to defend the right of God's vicegerents to execute solely on the dignity of their office and on their strict obedience to divine law. Colman and Checkley, however, defended that right on these grounds *and* on the grounds that the ministers of God preserve the public good. This development reflects the larger context of New England political thought in the Provincial period. The biblical scrupulosity of the Holy Commonwealth, though it remained important, no longer was the only determining factor for the clergy's ideas concerning the nature and function of civil government.

Civil Government in the Provincial Context

This Puritan understanding of the nature and function of civil government based on calling and covenant did not survive the turn of the eighteenth century, however. Two factors—one experiential and the other theoretical—motivated the New England clergy to reevaluate their understandings of the nature and function of civil government. For one thing, the revocation of the charter of the Massachusetts Bay Colony in 1684 brought an end to colonial governance as the Puritans had known it for almost three generations. A new governmental structure—known as the Dominion of New England—consolidated the formerly independent colonies into a single political unit and vested all executive and legislative authority in a royal governor appointed by the monarch. More disconcerting to New England colonists were the abolition of all elective assemblies, the enforcement of religious toleration for all Protestants, and the revocation of all land grants that had no prior royal approval. When Sir Edmund Andros assumed the governorship of the Dominion in 1686, things went from bad to worse. Although New England colonists disliked Andros on a personal level for a variety of reasons, his apparent disregard for the colonists' right to property proved to be the most troublesome. Andros rigorously enforced the unpopular Navigation Acts, imposed unprecedented taxes to fill English coffers, and failed to protect the colonies adequately from periodic attacks by Native Americans. When the news of the Glorious Revolution reached New England in the spring of 1689, colonists were emboldened to overthrow Andros and effectively to dissolve the Dominion of New England. Provisional governments were established until 1691, when a new charter—in many ways resembling the old one—was put into effect.[18]

As might be expected, during the years between the imprisonment of Andros and the ratification of the new charter, commentators flooded the New England presses with thoughts on the nature and function of civil government. Surprisingly few, including ministers themselves, offered theological explications of the ordeals of the day. Rather, they emphasized a new theme: because protection of property is the principal function of civil government, subjects have a right to resist if it fails in this basic obligation. This new argument can be credited at least in part to the objective of these commentators to justify the rebellion against the Andros regime to the English crown. But Timothy

Breen rightly suggests that it signalled a significant shift in Puritan ideas concerning the nature and function of civil government. Indeed, throughout the eighteenth century, emphasis on the civil authority's responsibility to protect property grew in strength and frequency, while emphasis on its responsibility to preserve orthodoxy and—to a lesser extent, morality—diminished.[19]

Certainly, the theoretical factor that shifted ideas on the function of civil government was the appearance of John Locke's second treatise on civil government, first published in England in 1690 but widely available in New England by the 1710s. Excellent discussions and analyses of Locke's political theories can be found elsewhere; it is necessary here only to sketch in broad outline his influential understanding of social organization and civil government. Locke argued that the nature and function of civil government can be rightly understood only after due consideration has been given to how humanity existed in its state of nature. For Locke, this idyllic arrangement consisted of the inalienable liberty and equality of all human persons. Individuals were perfectly free to behave in whatever way that they chose, and God had not, after all, subordinated any person to any other by divine providence. Moreover, in this state the law of nature generally prevailed: the innate reasonableness of all persons motivated them to work toward maintaining the peace and prosperity of the state of nature, thus preventing them from doing harm to one another.[20]

For what reason, then, did social organization and civil government come into being? Locke argued in part that the Creator had implanted in humanity the natural inclination toward relationships and social organization, the most basic unit of which was the family. Beyond this inclination, however, social organization and civil government became necessary because some persons treated the state of nature as an opportunity to act with licentious self-interest. The unreasonable passions of such persons motivated them to usurp the rights of others, that is, to take away their life, health, liberty, and possessions. Such selfish behavior, even though only few engaged in it, threatened to undo the state of nature entirely. Ideally, every person in the state of nature had the right to restrain such individuals with private punishments aimed at preventing such transgressions of natural law. But such private punishments, he concluded, might also be subject to individual self-interest, which only compounded the problem.[21]

Precisely this deficiency in the state of nature—the inability of all persons to govern their actions according to reasonable natural law—drove individuals into social organization and necessitated civil government. Indeed, Locke argued that civil societies come into being when any number of individuals enter into a social contract in order to protect their property from the invasion of the self-interested. By entering into the social contract, every individual consents to surrender some measure of his or her natural liberty and equality in order to empower the majority with the right to rule. Because it is completely voluntary, all parties to the social contract are thereafter obliged to submit to the determination of the majority. For practical purposes, the social contract delegates to civil government the task of articulating and enforcing positive laws, consistent with the law of nature. The legislative body of any civil government was supreme for Locke, and in terms of its power and authority it was answerable only to the governed. Indeed, civil government can be dissolved only when some force—either from within the government itself or from outside it—prevents the legislature from fulfilling its duties under the social contract to protect the property of those whom it governs.[22]

These Lockean political ideas posed a direct challenge to the understanding of the nature and function of civil government cherished by New England Puritans. First, Locke's political ideas began with a significantly improved assessment of human moral capacity. Indeed, Locke's state of nature was one in which the majority actually proves able to govern themselves according to the law of nature accessible to their reason; only the minority proves incapable. Even if Locke equated the problem of ungoverned passions in the state of nature with the classic Puritan doctrine of human depravity, such depravity was clearly not universal or total in any sense for him. Second, Locke's treatise laid a different foundation than Puritan political thinking upon which to build an understanding of the nature of civil government. By explicitly denying the notion that God had ordained a hierarchical social order in which some are called to govern, Locke challenged one of the key assumptions of early modern political thinking, especially among New England Puritans. Instead, the nature of civil government was constitutional and was thus answerable almost exclusively to the governed themselves. Finally, Locke's treatise emphasized the protection of property as the principal function of civil government. In doing so, civil government relied upon positive laws derived from the law of nature and approved by the will of the majority. This understanding of the function of civil government challenged at least the New England Puritan belief that the principal end of civil government was maintenance of moral conformity based upon unchangeable laws revealed in God's Word. In other words, Locke's political ideas emphasized the function of government to protect individual, pecuniary interests rather than communal, religious ones.[23]

As early as the 1710s, a handful of New England clergy were embracing Lockean political ideas, but such voices were clearly in the minority. By the 1730s, however, more widespread support for Locke had emerged and many New England clergy synthesized Puritan political ideas and Locke's social contract theory. Influential ministers gradually learned that the divine origin of civil government and social contract theory were not, after all, mutually exclusive ways of understanding the nature of civil government. Lawrence Leder suggests that New England clergy by the 1760s began "viewing the divine role [in the origin of civil governments] more as a limiting factor than as one transferring all authority directly from God to the ruler." In other words, rather than teaching that God had ordained civil governments and empowered them with the authority to rule, they began teaching that God made known the divine will for civil government and empowered civil governments through constitutional and electoral processes. Important dissent from this developing synthesis continued on both sides of the debate; both defenders of Puritan orthodoxy and those who capitulated fully to Lockean political ideas could be found among the New England clergy into the nineteenth century. Nonetheless, it is reasonable to assume that, by the end of the 1760s, the majority of New England clergy embraced this synthesis.[24]

Concerning the function of civil government, some New England clergy had become thoroughly Lockean by the 1760s, owing primarily to their tumultuous political context. The demands that civil government fulfill this basic responsibility to preserve the liberties and property of its citizens grew with a steady crescendo during the colonial economic crises of the 1760s. Most New England clergy came to accept the argument that Rev. Jonathan Mayhew, pastor of Boston's influential West Church, propounded in a 1749 sermon that was issued in multiple editions throughout the second half of the eighteenth century. In his celebrated *Discourse Concerning Unlimited Submission,* Mayhew treated as axiomatic the responsibility of civil government to protect property, understood in the broad Lockean sense. He suggested that the submission to civil government required by Paul's injunction in Romans 13 applied only in cases where the civil government fulfilled its duty to foster the good of civil society. If civil government became negligent in this duty, or actively sought its own good at the expense of the people, then, Mayhew argued, rebellion against this tyranny became the people's only proper response. Taking inspiration from Mayhew, New England clergy learned to apply Lockean ideas concerning civil government in the ways that Locke himself intended: to limit its function to promoting the welfare of the governed.[25]

Beginning about 1750, execution preachers explicated the nature and function of civil government more frequently, and they more obviously blended together their Puritan ideas concerning the nature and function of civil government with Lockean ones. Generally speaking, Provincial execution preachers continued to rely on the assumption that civil authority ultimately issued from God and even continued to refer to magistrates as "ministers of God" as their Puritan forebears had done. Even in that capacity, however, magistrates had as their primary interest the protection of property, and vigilant prosecution of criminals was one way to safeguard that interest.

Perhaps the sermon occasioned by the execution of felon Hugh Gillespie in 1758 best reflects the earliest blending of Puritan and Lockean political ideas. Presbyterian minister Chauncy Graham likened Gillespie to Achan, the biblical figure who brought down divine judgment on Israel by his singular act of self-interest and greed and was stoned to death for his actions (see Joshua 7:1–26). Yet biblical precedent was apparently not the only justification that the execution preacher offered. Readers could not help but hear Locke's contract theory of society looming in the background as Graham described how criminals like Gillespie become "troublers of God's people." First, they "ruin the Interest of the Publick" by placing their own ambitions above the common good. "It is one of the first Maxims with this Sort of Vermin," he began, "that it is no Matter what Injury is done to any particular Person, or what Damage accrues to Communities, if it is but subservient to their own private Advantage." Indeed, such self-interested criminals do not care what becomes of the public good, even "though their own Advantage should finally terminate in its utter Destruction." Moreover, these troublers of God's people brought distress on the public by incurring the judgment of God on the land. Here Graham sounded more at home in the seventeenth than in the eighteenth century: God had a "controversy" with the land because sinners like Gillespie "make light of the blackest Crimes," and because the righteous are distressed to see how God is "publickly dishonoured by the bold Transgressions of his Law amongst them." Gillespie's guilt extended to the whole land, which mourns until divine justice is exacted.[26]

Accepting that capital criminals are troublers of God's people, Graham then drew a number of inferences as an improvement of the solemn occasion. First of all, those who "vigorously exert themselves to bring such Villains to punishment"—that is, the civil magistrates and the courts—must be esteemed by the citizenry as "cordial Friends to its truest interests." Graham praised their zeal and vigilance against "Disturbers of our Peace" and "Hinderers of our public Prosperity" and even called upon his audience to "transmit their Names with Honour to Posterity, and gain them highest Esteem from all honest Men, who have a true Regard to the public Interest and rejoice in its flourishing Prosperity." In other words, honor was due to civil authority not because of its divine origin but because of its effectiveness in promoting the peace and prosperity of the state.[27]

More than this, Graham implied that the execution of capital criminals like Gillespie was not only a divine responsibility but also a public service to the State. Graham compared wicked men like Gillespie to a "Wart or Wen of the Body" that needs to be lanced in order to prevent its spread and to a "gangreened Limb" that should be amputated lest the whole body perish. The minister admitted that the State owes to criminals "suitable Care and Pains" to effect their rehabilitation, but concerning those who are deemed to be "unsupportable to the State" and "unsufferable," the magistrate's responsibility was clear: execute them in the interests of the public good.[28]

A sermon occasioned by the 1768 execution of Isaac Fraiser reflected a similar blending of Puritan and Lockean political ideas. The career burglar and arsonist had become "overmuch wicked," Rev. Noah Hobart assessed, because of the degree to which he had violated the moral law. This wickedness needed to be considered not only in terms of how his actions affected those whose goods he had stolen and those whose houses he had burned but also in terms of its impact on civil society. "Every thing that disturbs the peace and safety of the public is evil," Hobart began. If the citizens' property cannot be secured, or if they are unable to rest safely in their own beds without the fear of having their houses burned down around them, then "such a state is little, if at all, better than the state of nature." A powerful and vigilant civil magistracy was the God-ordained antidote to such an unstable state of nature. "Civil magistracy is an ordinance of God," he began, and "the great end and design of it is the public good." The surest way to attain that end, Hobart continued, was for the magistrate to use his divinely ordained right of the sword, a right that "fully vindicate[s] the magistrate in putting to death the criminal against whose destructive practices the public cannot otherwise be secured and defended." As a minister of God, a "revenger to execute wrath on him that doeth evil," the civil magistrate thus became an ideal Lockean ruler, protecting the public good.[29]

Even as late as 1799, in a sermon occasioned by the execution of convicted burglar Samuel Smith, Rev. Ezra Ripley explicated Jesus' command to "love thy neighbour as thyself" in terms of Locke's social contract. The Congregationalist minister argued that a person who is truly benevolent, one who takes seriously Jesus' command to love, will feel "a disposition to do good and make [his] fellow creatures happy," regardless of the response of those to whom benevolence is shown. In this way, benevolent persons are most like God, who causes the rain to fall on both the ungrateful and the thankful. Though they ought to govern themselves according to this principle, magistrates nonetheless cannot let their "christian benevolence interfere with the proper exercise of justice." Civil government is obliged to "preserve the peace and order of society and the quiet possession of life, liberty, and property to individuals." This benevolence to society as a whole sometimes necessitates the punishment of those who do not govern themselves according to the principle of benevolence. Ripley concluded that members of society have this mutual obligation of benevolence toward one another because they enter into a social compact and institute civil government expressly "for the great purpose of preserving, in peace and safety, our property, our life, our civil and sacred rights and privileges." Every member of society is thus obligated "to aid and defend each other and the whole body against every one, who shall trespass on society or an individual." When civil magistrates punish grievous offenders, they do so both out of a disposition of benevolence to society as a whole and out of obligations laid out in the social contract.[30]

Certainly one reason that these execution sermons dealt substantively with the responsibility of civil government to protect property was that the condemned in both cases were found guilty of property crimes, understood in the narrow sense. Provincial legislators and courts were hesitant to expand New England capital statutes to include such property crimes, at least to the extent that the Bloody Code had done in England. Perhaps it is not surprising, then, to see execution preachers in this context specifically justify the execution of persons found guilty of such crimes. But an equally plausible explanation is the one suggested here, namely that Lockean ideas concerning the responsibility of civil government to protect the property of its subjects had begun to make their way into the intellectual arsenal of midcentury execution preachers.

Even if "property" is understood in the wider sense to include the right to life, execution preachers utilized similar Lockean political ideas to justify putting murderers to death as well. Although Rev. Timothy Pitkin declared in a 1768 execution sermon that the prohibition against murder is founded in divine law, he seemed equally impressed that it was also founded upon the "law of nature." Accordingly, Native American John Jacobs deserved to die for an act of willful murder. "Antecedent to all human compact, and forming into society," he argued, "every man has a nature right to his own life, and no one has any right to take it away; and therefore, whoever doth take away the life of another, forfeits his own." Despite this obvious and direct appeal to Locke, however, Pitkin proved his claim with an appeal to scripture, namely, Exodus 21:12.[31]

Of course, execution preachers frequently reminded their audiences that this natural right to life, even though protected by the social compact and civil government, ultimately originated in God, another key Lockean idea. Rev. Charles Chauncy argued as much in 1754: murder is an impiety to a great degree chiefly because "it is a downright Encroachment upon and Usurpation of that Right over Life, which the Sovereign Lord has reserved to be exercised by himself alone." The ordinarily astute theologian continued to make a rather tortured application of Lockean natural rights theory by arguing that the murderer actually dispossessed God of "his just Property." Indeed, the murderer "robb[ed] [God] of a Creature whom his Hands have formed; yea, of a Servant and Subject, from whom he might have received a Revenue of Honor and Service."[32] Noticeably absent from the execution preaching of the period are the earlier Puritan claims that a human person's creation in the image of God made murder a particularly grievous crime.[33]

The execution of Negro Arthur, a twenty-one-year-old black man convicted of rape in 1768, provides yet another instructive example of how midcentury execution preachers blended traditional Puritan political ideas with Lockean ones. In a sermon preached on the Sabbath day after Arthur's execution, Rev. Aaron Hutchinson provided an account of the occasion. Apparently convinced that the condemned man had undergone a credible repentance, the Grafton minister aimed to show his auditors that God purged iniquity with mercy and truth. After providing numerous biblical examples of how God governed the affairs of humanity by wisely preserving the delicate balance between mercy and justice, Hutchinson called on heads of families, leaders of the Church, and especially civil government to imitate God in this respect. Neither one extreme of "superabounding mercy" nor the other of "relentless severity" would do. Rather, civil government ought to steer a middle way between these extremes: "But let justice take place," the pastor argued, "so far as to suppress vice, maintain right and equity, and support the honor of government; but not at the expense of mercy, and even of humanity." He concluded, "Let the vilest criminals be pitied, as much as may be, consistent with truth and justice." It was this kind of balance alone, Hutchinson maintained, that could guarantee the stability of society while also fostering the holiness that God demanded of God's people. A civil government that exercised such "well tempered power" was the kind that the Apostle Paul had in mind when he enjoined his readers to be subject to ruling authorities.[34]

So far, Hutchinson developed themes that dominated Puritan political thinking from the beginning. Like many others of his era, however, he understood the nature of civil government as both divinely ordained and contractually limited. He could encourage his auditors to think about civil magistrates as a manifestation of God's "restraining grace" and could describe their function as "ministers of God." But he could also ascribe to them the function of protecting the public good. Blending biblical images of ideal political leadership with Lockean language, Hutchinson explained: "When he that ruleth over men is just, ruling in the fear of God; in that ingenuous pity that never fails to accompany the fear of the Almighty; the end of civil government is attainted, public judgments prevented, our lives and properties secured, and all our natural and charter rights maintained, and every man may live and rejoice under his own vine and fig tree, and thereby none to make him afraid."[35] Such blending, it should be clear by now, was characteristic of New England execution preaching throughout the middle of the eighteenth century.

Civil Government in the Early National Context

Following the American Revolution, the theological heirs of Jonathan Edwards known as the "New Divinity men" dominated the established Congregationalist church throughout Massachusetts and Connecticut, and their influence prompted among New England clergy a return to more traditional forms of political thought. Drawing both on the orthodox Calvinism of their forebears and on the Scottish Moral Sense school of ethics, preachers like Revs. Joseph Bellamy, Samuel Hopkins, and Jonathan Edwards, Jr. sought to defend the traditional doctrines of Puritanism against the encroachments of theological liberalism. This defensive posture, however, sometimes obscures in the minds of historians their more constructive theological contributions. These New Divinity men successfully formulated a far-reaching metaphysical system that structured their thinking on politics, ethics, and Christian faith. Perhaps surprisingly, these theologians abandoned the Puritan covenantal ideal in understanding God's relationship with mundane human affairs like civil government. Instead, they restricted the use of the covenantal language to describe the constitution of the church as a community of the elect. If not through a covenant with humanity, then how were God's commands to become known?[36]

New Divinity theologians taught that God governs the universe according to a natural moral law that is universally applicable to saints and sinners alike. For these thinkers, the key to understanding the moral law was their concept of true virtue. Jonathan Edwards himself established a starting point by defining true virtue as "benevolence to being in general," a disposition that is best exemplified in God's relationship to creation in the work of Christ. Although a full explication of the context and meaning of Edwards's definition cannot detain us here, it is important at least to note that Edwards defined true virtue principally in terms of the affections; he understood true virtue principally as an inward disposition that motivated a love for God and a benevolent response to fellow human beings.[37]

Caught up in different contexts and writing with more pragmatic concerns, the New Divinity theologians located the nature of true virtue in the loving, benevolent behavior itself, rather than in the affections motivating it. These theologians often described benevolence with the heady adjective *disinterested,* that is, devoid of even the slightest hint of selfishness or self-congratulation. In point of fact, they elevated "disinterested benevolence" to be the chief characteristic of God; thus it became incumbent upon all of those who profess a love for God to behave morally as God does.

In other words, faith demands that Christians act toward their fellow human beings with disinterested benevolence, because only then are they following the example of God in Christ. Moreover, they taught that the virtue of disinterested benevolence is not only a private standard of morality but a public one as well. Only when whole communities devote themselves to this virtue in their relationships with one another can social happiness be expected. Just as true virtue and happiness are inseparably linked on the individual level, so they are on the social level as well.[38]

Unlike Locke and the New England clergy who appropriated his ideas, however, New Divinity men taught that human reason alone is insufficient to provide access to this natural moral law. They remained more or less committed to the doctrine of human depravity and thus distrusted any moral conclusions that humanity might reach on its own accord, no matter how virtuous they might appear. Instead, they taught that God mediated this natural moral law through divinely ordained social institutions, such as the family, education, civil government, and, of course, the church. Concerning civil government in particular, these theologians flatly rejected both the divine right to rule and Locke's social compact, fearing immoral tyranny on the one hand and immoral anarchy on the other. Returning to more traditional Puritan political ideas, these theologians argued that civil government had its origins in the will of God, but, chastened by the Revolutionary experience, they argued that God wills only those governments that cultivate virtue and foster the happiness of those governed.

In terms of their understanding of the function of civil government, the New Divinity theologians also returned to traditional Puritan political ideas. Civil government has as its principal task cultivating civic virtue as defined by the religious establishment. Responding specifically to the domestic unrest attendant upon the American Revolution and to the extremist threat of the French Revolution, these ministers feared that anarchy and vice might soon overwhelm the new nation. Thus, they called on the faithful majority to renew their commitment to established religion and stable government. Much like the Puritan Jeremiahs of a century before, these clergy repeatedly explained that these institutions alone could foster the civic virtue that would please

God and thus secure the prosperity of the new nation; conversely, they also warned that rejecting these institutions would lead to rampant, unrestrained vice that would antagonize the Almighty and guarantee the nation's downfall. In the minds of these clergy, then, the church and the state were part of the same institutional strategy for developing a virtuous nation out of the potentially vicious ruins of the Revolutionary generation.[39]

How precisely were magistrates to fulfill their important calling to develop civic virtue? Many Early National clergy taught first of all that the civil government was called by God to defend the New England religious establishment, that is, Congregationalism. As the new nation drifted ever closer toward Thomas Jefferson's impenetrable "wall of separation" between church and state, these theologians argued that such an arrangement would render ineffectual the principal means by which God made God's natural moral law known. Without the church and Christian faith to define it, true virtue would have little meaning or relevance at all for larger society.

Second, magistrates were called to embody true virtue themselves and thus to be models of Christian piety for their subjects. Only those men who governed their private and public lives with discernible virtue were fit to rule, and subjects held a sacred trust to elect only those candidates whose moral lives pleased God and benefited society. It was not uncommon for New Divinity theologians to speak about the magistrate's relationship with his subjects in parental terms; civil government functioned for society as a stern yet benevolent father.

Finally, and most importantly for the concerns of this chapter, civil government cultivated civic virtue by punishing vice. The magistrate's strict application of the law of God as revealed in Scripture and of God's will as revealed in the law of the land reemerged in the political thinking of the New England clergy as one of his primary responsibilities. In fact, penal severity was the mark of a good ruler because this trait demonstrated the magistrate's fear of God and his tender concern for the well-being of society. Perhaps it is not too much to say, then, that the New Divinity theologians brought New England full circle with respect to political thinking, adapting traditional Puritan ideas concerning the nature and function of civil government to a new context.

Not surprisingly, the Early National era witnessed a dramatic increase in the frequency with which execution preachers discussed civil government in their sermons. The reasons for this increase are perhaps obvious: New England ministers discussed politics with increasing frequency immediately before and during the Revolutionary War, and execution preaching simply reflects that larger development.[40] Moreover, as Chapter Five will make clear, Early National execution preachers were forced to defend capital punishment and public execution in an era of increasing opposition to these practices. Because this opposition was based in part on liberal arguments in favor of limited government, execution preachers of that era developed counterarguments more fully. But for now, it is important to realize that Early National execution preachers retreated from discussion of Locke's contract theory and began to reassert the more traditional Puritan explications of the nature and function of civil government.

The execution of Moses Dunbar in 1777 afforded Presbyterian minister Nathan Strong a unique opportunity to reflect on the nature and function of civil government, thus providing us with an early example of this return to traditional Puritan political ideas in the Early National period. A Tory sympathizer when the Revolutionary War broke out, Dunbar apparently abandoned his home in Waterbury, Connecticut, and served as a recruiting agent for the British army. When he was apprehended in late 1776, he was charged with espionage and sedition under the assumption that he was British. During his trial, however, the courts discovered that Dunbar was in fact a Connecticut citizen, and the charges against him were upgraded to high treason against the state, a capital crime. It was perhaps fitting that Strong preached his execution sermon, because the Hartford pastor was also serving as a chaplain to the patriot troops stationed in Connecticut at the time. Dunbar was hanged on March 19, 1777.[41]

Strong drew his execution sermon from 1 Timothy 5:20: "Them that sin rebuke before all, that others also may fear." From this text he argued that civil government held the responsibility to punish sin severely and publicly for three principal reasons: the glory of God, the safety of mankind, and the deterrence of others from wickedness by example. He stated plainly what his Puritan forebears had assumed for at least two hundred years: "Government is a divine institution . . . rulers and judges of nations are called ministers of God for good unto men." Because of this divine directive, civil magistrates had an obligation to punish publicly those iniquities that God specifically had prohibited, in order to avoid tarnishing God's glory. In fact, promoting God's visible honor was a national obligation, he contended, because God promises "public blessings as a reward for . . . the honor of his name."[42]

Moreover, he argued that the degeneracy of human nature inclined each of us to "gratify himself at the expense of [the] rights, prerogatives, and existence" of others. Thus, civil government also has the responsibility to punish sin in order to preserve the safety of society. Without the protection of civil government, societies quickly degenerate into ruin. Whenever law and government do not have the energy to prosecute vice, he claimed, "a numerous swarm of unjust persons, murderers, assassins and tyrants have immediately appeared to indulge their lust and satiate their cruelty in the blood of innocence."[43]

Finally, the deterrent impact demanded that civil government diligently mete out severe and public punishments. Although he did not want to represent human nature as more wicked than it really is, Strong nonetheless argued that "if the restraint of fear were wholly taken off the world would exhibit a scene of confusion, or cruelty, of hellish wickedness unparalleled by all descriptions that have been given." Civil government, he concluded, is the first line of defense against such social chaos.[44]

For these reasons, Strong concluded that the execution of Dunbar ought to teach us "to love and revere our country, to obey its laws, to devote ourselves to its service, and to abhor every practice which hath any tendency to increase public calamities." There was good reason to do this: God apparently works through the democratic process in the constitution of American government, and whoever violates its laws also offends God. "Our country, its privileges and laws are sacred," he claimed, "being enacted in a public manner, with the free consent of the people, they become ordinances of God; and the transgressor offends against Heaven and earth." God had given the American people both their liberty and their constitution, he argued, and "is not that a cruel sinner who would defraud his brethren of Heaven's sacred and invaluable gift?" Dunbar apparently was such a sinner, a man who would "damn an empire to share a penny" and who would "knowingly injure the State by . . . plung[ing] [his] sword into its bowels." The execution scene itself ought to teach us "the venerableness of the state and of civil government . . . that the man who injures his country and will not be restrained by considerations of duty, justice and gratitude, must be cut off from the earth that others may be safe."[45]

Congregationalist minister James Dana also returned to these Puritan ideas concerning the nature and function of civil government in his timely defense of capital punishment occasioned by the execution of convicted highwayman and rapist Joseph Mountain in 1790. Like so many of his Puritan forebears, Dana draws his initial observations from Deuteronomy 19:19–20: "So shalt thou put evil away from among you. And those which remain shall hear and fear, and shall henceforth commit no more any such evil among you." Ultimately, Dana argued, this text implied a threefold intent of capital punishment: "to rid the state of a present nuisance . . . to prevent the extension of evil . . . [and] to reclaim or preserve those who have been or might be in danger of being seduced by example of profligate wickedness." Surely it is significant that he defended the first of these premises with a meditation on the nature and function of civil government. It is clear that the New Haven minister understood the biblical directive to "put away evil from among you" to be equally applicable in Early National New England as it was in ancient Israel. He directly linked this injunction with the passage from Romans 13. The vigorous prosecution of criminal behavior and the exacting of severe penalties on the most pernicious offenders was "a duty which the civil guardians of a community owe to God and their people" because in doing so, magistrates fulfill their obligations as "minister of God for good to the community and its virtuous citizens."[46]

Dana directly confronted one of the burning questions of the Early National period: how were civil magistrates to determine which offenses deserved the ultimate sanction? He explicitly rejected the expanding capital jurisdiction of his English contemporaries and embraced a very simple standard: "where the sovereign of life has declared his will, or the public safety clearly requires it." Murder and treason—which he called "murder increased"—are clear-cut instances because "the divine legislator has expressly interposed his authority" in making these crimes capital. Rape, however, was a different matter. Dana argued that because God vested civil magistrates with the authority to "provide for the personal safety and rights of every subject," rape should be included because of its especially pernicious character. "Ravishment," he began, "is such an outrage on humanity, an injury so great and irreparable, a crime so baneful and dangerous to society, that civilized nations have agreed to protect female honor from violence by making death the penalty for this crime."[47]

The duty of civil government to protect public safety, especially the safety of virtuous women, necessitated including rape among the capital statutes of New England. Rejecting life imprisonment as an alternative sanction for rapists, Dana argued that anyone whose "atrocious conduct" merited that sanction "doth not differ materially in his moral character" from one whose conduct was thought to merit death. Although biblical sanction did not mandate death as the penalty for rape, the example of civilized nations, the perniciousness of the crime, and above all the sacred duty of civil magistrates to protect public safety justified including this crime on the small list of those that merited death.[48]

Like their Puritan forebears, Early National execution preachers also frequently emphasized the responsibility of civil magistrates to embody a positive moral example to their subjects, and one example stands out in particular. Unitarian minister Noah Worcester made this a central theme of his execution sermon occasioned by the execution of young African American rapist Thomas Powers in 1795. His sermon, like so many others, concentrated on the example of dying-hour repentance that the penitent thief of Luke 23 provided to the condemned man. But in "improving" the occasion for his auditors, Worcester identified four classes of citizens "who have great influence in regulating, or corrupting the morals of society," and chief among these four were civil magistrates. He mourned the deficiencies of some magistrates, those who were "too negligent of their duties" and "too regardless of the morals of community" to punish adultery, drunkenness, "tavern-haunting," idleness, and profane swearing. He asked rhetorically, "If executive officers are negligent in their duty respecting such violations of law, does not this tend to encourage the vicious, and pave the way to capital crimes?" Worse still, Worcester noted, some magistrates of his day were "notoriously vicious in their characters, immoral in their lives, and profane in their language." By their very example, such magistrates encouraged vice, subverted government, corrupted the morals of the governed, and destroyed the happiness of the community. Such hypocrites, he argued, ought to "blush whenever they take the seat of judgment . . . to execute laws upon others."[49]

The evidence presented here from Early National execution preaching suggests that many of these ministers shared an ideal vision of the American republic. Their "godly federalism" assumed that the American people were essentially virtuous; that a divinely ordained and benevolent civil government maintained order and justice according to the Word of God; and that the church should be established, and ministers ought to function in society, with a moral influence that rivaled the political influence of elected officials. These three dimensions of "godly federalism" were interdependent in the minds of Early National New England clergy: the strength of one would lead to the strength of all, and if one were undermined, then the other two would surely fall as well.[50]

Most Early National execution preachers assumed that criminal activity undermined public virtue and morality because of its pernicious example. Only a swift and decisive response to it from both the church and the state could curb its deleterious effects. Divinely ordained civil magistrates held the responsibility to punish criminals according to the law and will of God; ministers held the responsibility to support the magistrates in performing their sacred duty and to "improve" the drama of public execution for the moral benefit of society. Thus, Early National execution preachers were able to defend the practice by incorporating it into a larger, organic vision of New England religion and culture.

Conclusion

The present chapter has argued that the political ideas shared by the Puritan founders of New England were grounded in the fundamental concepts of calling and covenant and were symbolized by the images of the magistrate as God's vicegerent and minister. The paternalistic care and scrupulous moral supervision that the Puritan magistrate was expected to exercise were essential to his vocation and to the sacred contract between God and New England. While early execution preachers infrequently invoked these Puritan political ideas explicitly in their sermons, they certainly implied them in their appeals to the imagery of the Apostle Paul in Romans 13. Civil magistrates reduced the region's offensiveness to God by cutting off those who threatened the moral integrity of New England religion and culture.

Even as Lockean ideas concerning the nature and function of civil government came to dominate the thinking of many New England clergy toward the middle of the eighteenth century, execution preachers seem to have been cautious in their appropriation of those ideas. This chapter has described a blending of Puritan political thinking with Locke's social contract theory and argued that execution preachers still understood the nature and function of civil government in fundamentally Puritans terms, even if its chief end was the protection of the public good.

Under the direct influence of the New Divinity theology, many Early National New England clergy rediscovered the value of Puritan political ideas and attempted to capitalize on American independence to fashion a godly republic. "Godly federalism" revived the older Puritan emphasis on the divine origin and dignity of civil government and charged magistrates with the duty of enforcing standards of public morality consonant with the law and will of God. Many Early National execution preachers once again referred to magistrates as ministers of God and looked to them to rule with paternal benevolence as God does. However, this revival of Puritan political ideas in the form of godly federalism, reflected in Early National execution preaching, would not survive beyond the first quarter of the nineteenth century.

CHAPTER FIVE

A New Moral Discourse

For the Son of Man is not come to destroy men's lives, but to save them.

—*Luke 9:56*

Prior to the American Revolution, opposition to public execution was virtually unheard of in England's North American colonies. The colonial consensus overwhelmingly favored the practice as essential to maintaining social order and preserving the moral integrity of the community. Beginning in the late 1780s, however, the winning of political independence inspired some leaders of the new nation to press vigorously for reform of the criminal justice system. Naturally the practice of public execution came under fire: some wanted to restrict the practice, while others wanted to abolish it altogether. By the 1820s, these reforming efforts had led to three fundamental transformations in criminal justice administration in most northern states: the development of the penitentiary as an alternative to corporal and capital punishments, the reduction of capital jurisdiction in state penal codes, and the privatization of executions.[1]

Generally speaking, New Englanders themselves did not take the lead in championing reform of the criminal justice system in the early decades following independence. The long shadow of Puritanism certainly covered New England criminal justice well into the nineteenth century. Penal severity was expected there because it had been a way of life since the first days of the settlement of the region and was buttressed by a theological tradition that assumed human depravity and prized conformity to divine law. Instead, the reformers emerged from the middle Atlantic colonies, and from Philadelphia specifically. Quakerism strongly influenced the religion and culture of this region, and the founders of these colonies had built into their charters and later their constitutions ideas concerning crime and punishment that they considered to be more "enlightened." Moreover, Quakers consistently emphasized the human capacity for moral improvement, making them more optimistic about the possibility of criminals being reformed.[2]

The present chapter describes a new moral discourse concerning crime and its punishment that emerged amidst the political and philosophical debates following the American Revolution. The chapter traces the origins of this new moral discourse to three principal sources: the Enlightenment, Quakerism, and the republicanism of early national America. The chapter then discusses two examples of influential leaders who relied on this new moral discourse to push for criminal justice reform: Philadelphia humanitarian and physician Benjamin Rush and Pennsylvania jurist Thomas Bradford. The chapter then examines the impact that this moral discourse had on the practice of capital punishment and the tradition of execution preaching in Early National New England. The central claim of this chapter is that in the early years of the nineteenth century this new moral discourse gradually eroded the intellectual support for public execution and interest in execution preaching in New England until both traditions quietly disappeared.

The Enlightenment and the New Moral Discourse

Not surprisingly, one taproot of the new moral discourse concerning crime and punishment in Early National America lay deep in the soil of the European Enlightenment. Perhaps the earliest figure to define some of its terms was Baron de Montesquieu, who published his *Spirit of the Laws* in 1748. In Book Six of his massive work, the Baron argued that severity in punishments belongs to despotic governments because they function solely on the principle of terror: the subjects of despots fear death more than they cherish life, and this is their only motivation for following the law. By contrast, monarchies and republics function on the principles of honor and virtue, principles that ought to be embodied in benevolent, moderate rulers. The shame attached to conviction and the accompanying punishment, he argued, are sufficient restraints against criminal behavior, and penal severity thus becomes unnecessary. It is important to note that Montesquieu never condemned capital punishment or public execution per se. But by linking penal severity with despotism and moderation with more enlightened forms of government, he set the stage for others, particularly Americans of the Revolutionary generation, to oppose these practices on similar grounds.[3]

Moreover, Montesqueiu was one of the first to advocate for a system of criminal laws that proportioned punishments more directly with crimes. Indeed, as he explained in Book Twelve, such proportion was in his mind constitutive of political liberty itself: "It is the triumph of liberty when criminal laws draw each penalty from the particular nature of the crime," he asserted. "All arbitrariness ends; the penalty does not ensue from the legislator's capriciousness but from the nature of the [crime]."[4]

As a starting point for developing such a system of proportions, Montesquieu divided crimes into four classes: those that run counter to religion, mores, tranquility, and the security of the citizens. As punishments for the first three classes, the Baron advised that offenders ought only to be deprived of the advantages provided by religion, mores, and tranquility: banishment, fines, or at most, imprisonment. Only for the fourth class did he cautiously admit that capital punishment might be an appropriate sanction. Obviously, in the case of murder, proportion dictates that the offender ought to surrender his own life. For property crimes—frequently punished with death in early industrial societies—Montesquieu favored less sanguinary punishments. Although he acknowledged that some property crimes may merit the death penalty, he argued that "it would perhaps be preferable . . . if the penalty for crimes committed against the security of goods were punished by the loss of goods."[5]

Montesquieu's Enlightenment emphasis on moderation and proportion in the construction of criminal law impressed a number of political thinkers of Early National America. For example, in 1776 Thomas Jefferson introduced a bill in the newly constituted Virginia legislature that proposed the "Proportioning Crimes and Punishments in Cases Heretofore Capital," drawing largely on Montesquieu's arguments. Jefferson's bill restricted the capital jurisdiction to two crimes—murder and treason—because he believed that only severe crimes such as these two conclusively demonstrated the incorrigibility of the offender. As an alternative punishment for most crimes, he advocated a graduated scale of public labor, based upon the severity of the offense. After being introduced three times, a modified form of Jefferson's bill finally passed the legislature in 1796, twenty years later. In place of Jefferson's graduated scale of public labor, the Virginia law provided for a similar scale of terms of imprisonment.[6]

Italian marquis Cesare Beccaria followed Montesquieu's lead and ended up writing one of the most influential treatises in the emerging penal reform movements worldwide. First appearing in Italian in 1764, his essay "On Crimes and Punishments" relied on an idiosyncratic combination of social contract theory and utilitarian philosophy. He believed, first of all, that rational people are forced by necessity to surrender some of their personal liberties in exchange for the safety, comfort, and benefits of an organized society. The laws of a given society reflect the boundaries of individual liberties, in some cases encouraging behavior and in others prohibiting it. The purpose of the law, then, is not to protect the liberties of individuals; rather, it is to promote the good of society as a whole: the greatest happiness for the greatest number. But because persons may not submit voluntarily to the terms of the social contract, it has to be defended against private usurpation. All societies, he admitted, will have individuals who violate the terms of the social contract out of self-interest, and laws provide the guidelines to civil rulers for dealing with them. It is essential to realize that Beccaria did not advocate a retributive theory of criminal justice in which laws provided a formula for punishing offenders. Rather, his understanding of criminal justice sought only to protect the social contract by providing a tangible incentive for individuals to maintain its terms.[7]

With regard to punishment, specifically, Beccaria taught that the purpose of the law is the deterrence of crime, both specifically (to prevent the criminal from doing further injury to society) and generally (to prevent others from also committing offense). The swiftness and certainty of punishment, not its severity, guarantee the effectiveness of a punishment in reaching its primary goal. Moreover, although he certainly believed in maintaining a rational proportion between crime and its punishment, he argued that proportion ought not be the guiding principle in choosing criminal sanctions. Rather, punishments should be chosen to "make the strongest and most lasting impressions on the minds of others." This same reliance on sensational psychology led some of Beccaria's English contemporaries—notably William Paley and Jeremy Bentham—to continue to defend the practice of capital punishment and public execution, even if they advocated trimming the list of capital crimes to a handful of offenses. Beccaria, however, vigorously opposed capital punishment, adding that all punishments should be chosen that provide "the least torment to the body of the criminal."[8]

Beccaria believed that capital punishment is an inappropriate sanction for any crime for three principal reasons: first, he argued that the authority of laws ought to derive their power from the will of the people living under them. Because it is unimaginable that anyone voluntarily would surrender to a fellow citizen the right to take his or her own life, the state—which is nothing more than the sum total of the individuals comprising it—should not claim that right, either. Second, drawing once again on sensational psychology, Beccaria argued that the duration of criminal sanctions produces a greater deterrent effect than their intensity. For this reason, he proposed replacing capital punishment with lifelong slavery so that every criminal remained a lasting example of justice. "The death of a criminal is a terrible but momentary spectacle," he wrote, "and [is] therefore a less efficacious method of deterring others than the continued example of a man deprived of his liberty, condemned, as a beast of burden, to repair, by his labour, the injury he has done to society." Third, and most convincingly to some of his contemporaries, he argued that capital punishment contradicts the spirit and purpose of the law itself. Law is designed to be a civilizing force, and if it sanctions a barbarous practice such as capital punishment, then it fails to meet its own standard. He best summarized his point by asking a rhetorical question: "Is it not absurd, that the laws, which detest and punish homicide, should, in order to prevent murder, publicly commit murder themselves?"[9]

Becarria's influence on the emerging discourse of penal reform was probably more direct than that of Montesquieu. The first English edition of his essay appeared in London in 1767, and by 1770 future president John Adams quoted from Beccaria in his defense of those implicated in the Boston Massacre. By 1780, his treatise was available for sale in most reputable bookshops in the emerging United States. It was surely significant that his ideals on penal reform had infiltrated the heart of the Calvinist establishment by 1786 when *The New Haven Gazette and Connecticut Magazine* serialized his treatise for popular consumption. The excitement generated by that edition encouraged the faculty at Yale, in 1788, to include in their commencement day exercises a disputation on the lawfulness of capital punishment. Harvard and Princeton Colleges held similar disputations in the early 1790s. It is probably not too much to say that Beccaria's essay was the principal resource to which Enlightenment thinkers, liberal theologians, and republican ideologues turned when they discussed penal reforms, especially those reforms that limited or abolished capital punishment and public execution.[10]

American Quakerism and the New Moral Discourse

In many ways this new moral discourse concerning crime and punishment was not especially "new" in America; Quaker settlers of the middle Atlantic colonies built their opposition to severity into legal codes as early as the 1670s and 1680s. Indeed, both the *Concessions and Agreements* (1676) of West Jersey and the so-called Great Law (1682) of Pennsylvania prescribed strict guidelines for the administration of criminal justice in these colonies. These legal codes limited the discretion of capricious magistrates and judges by guaranteeing the right to a speedy trial only by one's peers, insisting that punishments for crimes be administered fairly and without partiality, guaranteeing that the severity of punishment would never exceed the severity of the offense, and restricting the penalty of death to willful murder and treason only. In place of physical punishments that were all too public, the legal codes of the middle colonies prescribed private penalties designed to awaken the offender to repentance and reformation. Indeed, in the Quaker colonies, flogging, branding, and cropping of the ears were intolerable; instead, fines, restitution, and imprisonment replaced these gruesome punishments to aid in criminal reformation. This "holy experiment" in criminal justice lasted only about thirty years, until the death of William Penn in 1718, whereupon English authorities forced upon New Jersey and Pennsylvania British standards of criminal justice despite strident opposition from Provincial Quaker leadership. For most of the eighteenth century, then, criminal justice administration in the middle Atlantic differed little from that of the other English colonies.[11]

This early Quaker opposition to penal severity was not forgotten, however, and it reemerged following the American Revolution as a driving force in the development of penitentiaries and the reform of criminal law. American Quakers organized their first prison reform society in 1776. The goals of the Philadelphia Society for Assisting Distressed Persons were to investigate the conditions of prisons and jails and to publish firsthand reports of these conditions in order to build political support for prison reform. Although the Society's activities were greatly curtailed during the Revolution, afterward the group reemerged as the Philadelphia Society for Alleviating the Miseries of Public Prisons. The Society quickly succeeded in creating the first American penitentiary in 1790, namely, Philadelphia's Walnut Street Jail.[12] The revamped institution operated according to a revolutionary philosophy of punishment: the chief goal of penal sanction became rehabilitating offenders by means of a stern regimen of hard labor, solitary reflection, and moral education. Only four years after the opening of the jail, Quaker merchant and prison inspector Caleb Lownes published an account of the early success of the institution in which he described in glowing terms its systemic impact on criminal justice in Philadelphia. He credited the institution with lowering overall crime rates, decreasing recidivism, and emboldening juries to return convictions in cases in which they formerly would have been reluctant to do so.[13] Because of such early reports of success, the idea of prison reform and the penitentiary caught on. By 1817, eleven states had at least one penitentiary following the model of Walnut Street and most had prison reform societies to oversee their operation.[14] In almost all of these states Quakers remained the most important leaders of this reform movement, a fact that remained true for most of the nineteenth century.[15]

The development of the penitentiary was the penultimate goal of these Quaker reformers; the ultimate goal was an overhaul of state penal codes, beginning with Pennsylvania. Reflecting both Enlightenment and Quaker influence, the Pennsylvania state constitution of 1776 called for a criminal code that better proportioned punishment to crime. Ten years would pass before any tangible results of this commitment would be realized, but the result was worth the wait. The revised criminal code of 1786 provided for a graduated system of punishments utilizing monetary fines and imprisonment as the principal sanctions and completely eliminating bodily punishments. Most important for the present study is the fact that by 1794, the Pennsylvania legislature had limited the number of capital crimes to one, namely, willful murder. The preamble of the new criminal code succinctly explained two basic reasons for these innovative reforms: the punishments afforded under the old code were ineffectual because they "do not answer the principal ends of the society inflicting them, to wit, to correct and reform the offenders"; and even regarding criminals, "it is the wish of every good government to reclaim rather than destroy." Similar principles inspired most northern state legislatures to disallow bodily punishment and to trim their capital jurisdiction before the turn of the nineteenth century. By 1796, the New York legislature had completed a major revision of its criminal law, abolishing bodily punishments altogether and restricting the capital jurisdiction to only willful murder and high treason. A year later, the Vermont legislature made a similar move, but its capital jurisdiction included three crimes: murder, high treason, and robbery.

By 1815, all northern states except Massachusetts and Connecticut had undertaken similar revisions of their criminal law.[16]

It is important to note that the acts of the Pennsylvania legislature reflected an opposition to penal severity that had been growing in the region since the time of the Revolution. The response of Philadelphia Quakers to the wartime execution of Abraham Carlisle and John Roberts in 1778 clearly illustrated this developing spirit of penal reform and their opposition to extensive application of the death penalty. The details of the case are difficult to determine—even by examining court records—because of the sensationalism that surrounded it. Carlisle and Roberts, both Quakers themselves, were accused of everything from aiding General William Howe in his invasion of Philadelphia to poisoning the city's supply of flour. During their trial and imprisonment, the city's Quakers flooded the Supreme Executive Council with petitions for clemency. One petition from Philadelphia clergy hoped that the nation's liberty might be secured without shedding the blood of these "fellow-citizens." "Humanity, mercy, charity, and forgiveness," declared another of these petitions, are "characteristick of True Americans." Still another argued that a well-timed pardon often accomplishes more in the interest of public justice than an execution. Nonetheless, the Council determined that both men were guilty of high treason against the state, and they were hanged on November 4, 1778. One observer blamed the whole incident on the excitement of the "ultra Whigs," noting that such ardent patriots always had equated Quaker pacifism with loyalism. Public execution, even for high treason in the midst of the Revolutionary War, was unacceptable to many Pennsylvania citizens because it apparently smacked of the political self-interest and religious fanaticism of former ages.[17]

It should come as no surprise that Anglo-American Quakers led the way in penal reform and the development of the penitentiary. Most historians assume that Quaker opposition to penal severity originated in their experience of persecution under Charles II and James II between 1660 and 1689. Nearly a thousand were repeatedly arrested and imprisoned, and many died because of their severe treatment in English prisons. This experience compelled many of these Quakers to be very critical of English prisons specifically, and of the English system of criminal justice generally. Initially their reforming efforts met fierce opposition from the crown, but the more religiously tolerant policies of later English monarchs—especially William and Mary and Anne Stuart—permitted Quakers to work for the amelioration of the Bloody Code and for the improvement of the English prison system.[18]

Theological principles, however, provided an equally important motivation for Quaker reformism regarding crime and punishment. As early as the 1660s English Quakers had declared their opposition to all interpersonal violence—including war, slavery, and dueling—and by the turn of the eighteenth century the targets of this opposition included the death penalty as well. Early modern Quaker pacifism ultimately was grounded in an understanding of God: rejecting the puritanical emphasis on God's punitive nature, Quakers emphasized instead God's benevolence and forgiveness. These attributes of God were most clearly manifested in the life and ministry of Jesus, and his moral example served as a pattern for all who called themselves Christians. Moreover, early modern Quakers rejected the Calvinist emphasis on the depravity of humanity, preferring instead to speak of the "inner light" of Christ that dwells in all human persons. Accordingly, they believed that with God's help, individuals could effect a reformation in their own moral lives. This reformation could never be accomplished by coercive discipline but only by a cultivation of the individual's innate moral goodness. Opposition between these "liberal" theological principles and those of traditional Calvinism was certainly pronounced. As Quaker penal reforms gained ground throughout the North in the Early National period, bitter exchanges between those who supported and those who opposed public execution became commonplace.[19]

Republicanism and the New Moral Discourse

A third major taproot of this new moral discourse concerning crime and punishment was nascent American republicanism. Although social and intellectual historians have not come to a consensus on precisely what "republicanism" as a social ideology meant in the context of Early National America, some dominant themes can be identified. First, republicanism assumed that the American Revolution represented more than political freedom from England; it was an opportunity to reorder Provincial society completely. Accordingly, republicanism was characterized by "extraordinarily idealistic hopes for the social and political transformation of America." Like most movements of political and social reform, republicanism looked to classical antiquity for guidance. In ancient Greece and Rome the architects of the new nation could find models of the individual and social virtues according to which they wished to structure the new American republic. They prized the writings of classical authors who described frugality, industry, and patriotism as the ideals that guaranteed the strength and prosperity of nations. But even more than this, republicans considered the history of the tragic failure of ancient republics because of the wanton excess, laziness, and self-interest of their citizens and read in that history a clear warning: the new nation needed by all means scrupulously to guard itself against these besetting vices, lest it, too, suffer the same decay and failure. For republicans, only a virtuous nation can be a truly free nation.[20]

The promotion and defense of liberty became the clarion call of republicanism in Early National America, and this might be identified as a second dominant theme. It is important to realize, however, that the "liberty" of republican ideology is not that of liberalism: while liberals tended to define liberty in terms of individual, inalienable rights, republicans understood liberty in terms of the public good. Indeed, republican ideologues were fond of imagining that all members of American society were linked organically and were willing to sacrifice individual self-interest for the greater good of the whole. Moreover, they believed that this political organism was, so to speak, greater than the sum of its parts. The public good was distinct from and even transcended the collected private interests of the constitutive elements of the state. This was the spirit that inspired the Revolution itself and guaranteed its success; only a firm and widespread commitment to the public good would sustain the fledgling republic and guarantee its prosperity. Republicanism did not naively assume that the public good would never become a source of conflict between members of society, but it insisted that wise and benevolent rulers who embody the collective moral wisdom of those who elected them would maintain a steady course toward the public good, despite the conflict. "Liberty," then, consisted precisely in the vigorous dynamic that first determines, and then fosters, the public good.[21]

A third major theme of Early National republican social ideology was a commitment to the principle of equality. Contrary to popular contemporary misunderstanding, republican equality did not connote a radical social leveling that did away with all distinctions and hierarchies. Instead, republican equality relocated the origin of those distinctions and hierarchies away from divine will and monarchical preferment to individual merit and capability. Theoretically speaking, a pure republic would provide its citizens equality of opportunity for education, economic advancement, and other privileges; thus, the distinctions between otherwise equal citizens would be based only on how each made use of those opportunities. The fact remained that early American society remained highly stratified socially, economically, and politically, but the republican commitment to its principle of equality held out the hope that this arrangement could change eventually.[22]

Extraordinary optimism, public-spirited virtue, and commitment to egalitarianism thus emerged in the minds of Early National republicans as the unique and defining traits of the American character. Two dimensions of republicanism especially have impressed contemporary historians. First was its pervasiveness. Not confined to political arrangements only, republicanism represented a revolutionary social ideology that transformed virtually every facet of American culture, including the economy, family life, education, and—as we will see—religion and criminal justice administration. The second impressive dimension of republicanism was the swiftness with which this social ideology came to dominate America. In the two and a half decades between the Declaration of Independence and the turn of the nineteenth century, American society had been completely transformed politically, and the agenda had been set for social and religious reforms that would take at least three full generations to realize. Benjamin Rush captured the swiftness and the far-reaching implications of republicanism when he observed that "the American war is over: but this is far from being the case with the American revolution."

He explained further, "It remains yet to establish and perfect our new forms of government, and to prepare the principles, morals, and manners of our citizens for these forms of government after they are established and brought to perfection."[23] Even if contemporary historians can look back with amazement at Rush's optimism, none can doubt the power that this social ideology exercised over Early National America.

Drawing nourishment from these three taproots, the new moral discourse concerning crime and punishment that arose in Early National America emphasized five major themes: penal severity is a symptom of political despotism, and thus it has no place in an enlightened republic; punishments ought to be proportioned to the nature of the crime, rather than to the character of the offender; the principal aim of criminal laws and their enforcement is the reformation of the offender; deterrence from crime can be guaranteed only by the certainty and consistency of punishment, not its severity; and the optimism, egalitarianism, and freedom afforded by republicanism provide an ideal opportunity for the new nation to be innovative in its approach to criminal justice administration. As we will see in the following sections, public intellectuals in Early National Quaker Pennsylvania repeatedly marshaled these themes to mount an impressive counteroffensive against the ideology of colonial Puritan New England. This challenge would eventually lead to the abolition of two mainstays of New England criminal justice administration: public execution and execution preaching.

The Embodiment of the New Moral Discourse

As the eighteenth century drew to a close, two figures more than any others embodied the new moral discourse concerning crime and punishment. The first was Benjamin Rush. Under the religious influence of prominent revivalists Gilbert Tennet and Samuel Davies, Rush renounced his heritage in the Episcopal Church in favor of evangelical Presbyterianism at a very young age. He graduated from the College of New Jersey in 1760 and began his apprenticeship with Philadelphia's leading physician that same year. Beginning in 1766, he spent two years studying medicine under the most progressive physicians of the era at the University of Edinburgh, Scotland. Thereafter, Rush completed internships at hospitals in both London and Paris, where he met a number of Quaker physicians with whom he maintained a lifelong friendship and correspondence. Upon his return to Philadelphia in 1769, he quickly established himself as the leading voice in the emerging medical profession there. In addition to maintaining a private practice, he taught courses on the philosophy and practice of medicine at the University of Pennsylvania and circulated widely in the high society of late eighteenth-century Philadelphia. He was a signer of the Declaration of Independence, a contributor to Thomas Paine's *Common Sense,* and a regular participant in the program of Benjamin Franklin's Society for Promoting Political Enquiries. He published on a variety of subjects, notably medicine, law, education, morals, and politics.[24]

Deeply influenced by Scottish physicians and philosophers like Thomas Reid, Rush understood the relationship between the human mind and human actions according to the terms of eighteenth-century psychology. Building on Locke's notion of human understanding and rejecting Hume's skepticism, faculty psychologists argued that the human mind is composed of various faculties such as reason, the passions, and even a moral faculty. Each of these was as much an "organ" as was a person's heart or lungs; when exercised appropriately these faculties grew in strength and remained healthy. However, like the body's other organs, psychological faculties atrophied through neglect or even became diseased if subjected to pathogens from without. Indeed, defects in reasoning, poor impulse control, and immoral behaviors were understood to be symptoms of failing moral faculties.[25] Because of this intellectual influence, Rush rejected any notion of innate depravity, preferring instead to ascribe a person's misconduct entirely to environmental factors that somehow had corrupted his or her moral faculty. Because they were physiologically based, diseases of the moral faculty were treated appropriately by the physician rather than the pastor. To be sure, for Rush preaching was as likely to cure the "sinner" of immorality as it was to cure him or her of smallpox.[26]

Rush directly challenged the understanding of human sinfulness that prevailed among many New England clergy of his day in a 1786 oration delivered before the American Philosophical Society. First, Rush defined the moral faculty as the "power in the human mind of distinguishing and chusing good and evil; or, in other words, virtue and vice." He contended that virtue and vice consisted solely in human action, arguing that the moral faculty guided the human body, issuing in action. Consequently, the state of a person's moral faculty was to be judged only by what is visible, not by any assumption about his or her essential nature. Rush then reviewed some of the scientific observations of his contemporaries that suggested that physical causes influence mental processes; delirium and fever, for example, directly affected human perceptions and memory. In like manner, Rush argued, physical causes affected the moral faculty and the behaviors that issued therefrom. In fact, physical causes might only weaken the moral faculty (a condition that Rush called "micronomia") or they might obliterate the faculty altogether (a condition that he called "anomia"). In either case, he saw a direct causal connection between physical or environmental factors on human moral reasoning and the behaviors that issued from it. Rush clearly rejected all nonempirical explanations of human action, especially those that relied upon theological categories. Interestingly, among those environmental factors that have a positive influence on the human moral faculty, Rush listed solitude and silence. In doing so, he repeatedly cited as his authorities leaders of the English prison reform movement like John Fothergill and John Howard. Along with these reformers, Rush reasoned that the stimulus of "profane society and conversation" upon the moral faculty became an "exciting cause" of vicious behavior. Solitude and silence aided in reforming such behavior by "removing men out of the reach of these exciting causes" and producing a "sufficient chasm in their habits of vice." This solitude and silence paved the way for moral reeducation and the curing of the diseased moral faculty. Although we have already noted that some execution preachers shared his environmentalism in explicating the origin of vicious behavior, Rush was clearly working out a theory of criminal rehabilitation that even the most theologically progressive execution preacher likely would have rejected.[27]

This theory of the moral faculty provides the foundation of Rush's critique of public punishments that he published a year later. He began by recognizing that established opinions and universal practice argued that the design of punishment was threefold: to reform the offender, to prevent the perpetration of future crime, and to rid society of those who are deemed unfit to live in it because of their vicious behavior. Nonetheless, Rush ambitiously set out to demonstrate that public punishments accomplish none of these goals; in fact, he said, they "tend to make bad men worse and to increase crimes by their influence upon society." Public punishments can never effect reformation, Rush argued, because such sanctions destroy the sense of shame in the offender, and they fail to produce a lasting impression upon his or her behavior owing to their short duration. In fact, public punishments increased crime because the offender took from the whipping post or the stocks little more than a "spirit of revenge" against the whole community. To borrow Rush's vocabulary from his earlier treatise, it might be said that public punishments functioned as a physical cause on the moral faculty that excited, rather than suppressed, vicious behavior.[28]

When Rush turned his attention to the second and third purposes of public punishment, the theoretical underpinnings of his critique became clearer. Conventional wisdom held and execution preachers long heralded that in response to severe public punishments, the people would "hear and fear, and do no more any such wickedness." By contrast, Rush argued that such terrible displays excite admiration on the part of spectators when the offender faces punishment with fortitude, incite pity when the offender responds with insensibility, and garner sympathy for the offender's distress. He admitted that the effects upon the moral faculties of the spectators may be salutary, but he believed they are just as likely to be detrimental. Public punishments may excite the indignation of spectators toward the offender and "extinguish a large portion of [the] universal love" that persons owe to one another. They may excite contempt for the state because they appear to be "arbitrary acts of cruelty." Or, worst of all, public punishments may introduce the innocent to crimes of which they otherwise would have remained ignorant.[29]

Rush was quite concerned with the impression that public punishments make on the offender, and he considered that impression to be wholly and universally negative. Building upon this assumption, Rush advocated the construction of a "house of repentance," advised placing limitations on all punishments, and demanded that the practice of public punishment, especially public execution, be abolished. Civil government had an obligation, as its chief responsibility regarding crime, to reform the criminal, not to destroy him or her. Indeed, Quaker physicians and moral philosophers had championed this idea for some time, and others ought to follow their lead: "The great art of surgery has been said to consist in saving, not in destroying . . . diseased parts of the body. Let governments learn to imitate in this respect the skill and humanity of the healing art."[30]

Rush's early treatises, along with initial penal reforms undertaken by the Pennsylvania Assembly, sparked a blazing fire of controversy. In July of 1788, Rush squared off in a printed debate over the theological appropriateness of capital punishment with Philadelphia Presbyterian clergyman Robert Annan. The debate centered on the interpretation of Genesis 9:6, long held to be a central text in defense of the gallows: "Whoso sheddeth man's blood, by man shall his blood be shed." From one corner, Rush declared that the biblical precept was a prediction, not a divine mandate. Violence usually begets violence, the physician and moral philosopher asserted, unless persons exercise the restraints of reason. Furthermore, Rush declared that legislators who elevate their administration of criminal justice to the status of divine judgment flagrantly usurp the prerogative of God over human life. Rather than rely on a solitary scriptural text to justify an entire system of criminal law, Rush argued that legislators ought to be guided by the whole spirit of the gospel, namely that Jesus came to save the lives of humanity, not to destroy them. Any person, indeed, any nation worthy of the label "Christian" ought to have the same commitment; "a religion which commands us to forgive and even do good to our enemies," he concluded, "can never authorize the punishment of murder by death."[31]

From the other corner, Annan defended what he understood to be the plain sense of the scripture. The verse may indeed be a prediction, he responded, but this did not preclude it from being a divine mandate as well. He accused Rush of trying to undercut the authority of civil magistracy by taking from it the divinely given right of capital punishment. Far from being a sign of social barbarism, capital punishment is an expression of civility because it bears witness to the right of magistrates to rule according to the law of God. Moreover, Annan lamented that Rush embodied a larger trend among public intellectuals of his day to "undervalue the Old Testament" in their thinking about moral issues. However, not even the "spirit of the gospel" could be manipulated to oppose capital punishment, according to Annan. To think so is to confound the "spiritual kingdom of Christ with the kingdoms of this world." Jesus did not appear on earth as an earthly prince and made no attempt to reform the civil laws; he did not even oppose the execution of the two thieves hanging beside him on the cross. Rather, the Savior was interested only in their spiritual destiny, and with that destiny alone were American Christians also to be concerned.[32]

Eventually, the debate became intensely personal. Labeling his opponent's arguments as "flimsy," Rush judged them to flow naturally out of Annan's "severe Calvinistical principles." Moreover, Rush asserted that his ideas would have made Annan more at home "in the fifteenth, rather than the eighteenth century." Annan himself was no more kind to his opponent: he labeled Rush a "Socinian" and a "Deist" and charged him with denying the providence of God in governing the world. But these rhetorical barbs were more than *ad hominem* attacks. Indeed, they illustrate in miniature the emerging contest between two competing moral discourses concerning crime and punishment in Early National America.[33]

The debate in which Rush and Annan held exemplary positions was carried out mainly on the pages of Philadelphia's high society newspaper *The American Museum,* to which Rush made frequent contributions. Throughout the 1790s, too, his contributions to the debate were republished in a variety of forums, and eventually he would advocate the total abolition of the death penalty, a view with which few of his contemporaries had much sympathy. Nonetheless, Rush's contributions proved to be enormously influential in the anti–death penalty movement that emerged among northern social reformers in the 1830s and 1840s.[34]

The second exemplar of the new moral discourse concerning crime and punishment in Early National America was William

Bradford, a war veteran and leading jurist in Pennsylvania. Born in Philadelphia, Bradford completed his B.A. (1772) and M.A. (1775) degrees at Princeton College. Following a three-year appointment as a colonel in the Continental Army, he was apprenticed to eminent Quaker jurist Edward Shippen. Under his mentor's influence, Bradford himself joined the Society of Friends. After being admitted to the Pennsylvania bar for less than a year, Bradford was appointed in 1779 to be the state attorney general, a post that he held for eleven years. He was appointed to the Pennsylvania Supreme Court in 1790 and served in that capacity for three years until President George Washington chose Bradford to be the attorney general for the United States. Though his sudden death in 1795 prevented him from finishing his term of office, he was instrumental in negotiating terms of peace with the leaders of the Whiskey Rebellion.[35]

At the request of Pennsylvania governor Thomas Mifflin, in 1793 Bradford published a lengthy apologia for the sweeping penal reforms that were overtaking the state. But the chief aim of the Supreme Court Justice's treatise was to question whether capital punishment itself was consistent with the values of the newly established republic. He began by crediting both Montesquieu and Beccaria for supplying the state's government with three sublime principles of criminal jurisprudence: that the prevention of crime is the sole purpose of the law, that all punishments that are not absolutely necessary in achieving this purpose are cruel and tyrannical, and that every punishment ought to be proportioned to the offense. These were the only principles, he concluded, that could protect the hard-won republican values of the American and French Revolutions. Extensive use of severe penal sanctions—such as those contrived by European monarchs and indiscriminately employed according to their fancy—had no place in a nation where the will of the people dictated the policies and procedures of civil authority. "Sanguinary punishments," he suggested, had been "contrived in despotic and barbarous ages" and "have continued when the progress of freedom, science, and morals renders them unnecessary and mischevious." He concluded that "[Capital] laws, the offspring of a corrupted monarch, are fostered in the bosom of a youthful republic." The American Revolution remained unfinished, Bradford seemed to be arguing, as long as unnecessary penal severity continued in the United States. Regarding capital punishment specifically, he highlighted its inconsistency with the spirit of the law as a civilizing force, took note of the differing capital jurisdictions of the new states, and mentioned that other states like Virginia were undertaking similar penal reforms based upon Enlightenment principles.[36]

Bradford knew, however, that Pennsylvania provided an important test case in penal reform because of its Quaker heritage. He argued that the history of civil government in Pennsylvania bolstered his argument against continued penal severity. He noted that the colony's venerated founder advocated all of the appropriate virtues of an enlightened civil government, especially religious toleration and mildness in the application of criminal laws. In fact, he spoke of William Penn in hagiographic terms: "But the Founder of the province was a philosopher, whose elevated mind rose above the errors and prejudices of his age, like a mountain, whose summit is enlightened by the first beams of the sun, while the plains are still covered in darkness." Nevertheless, he noted that, contrary to the founders' intentions, the Pennsylvania Charter demanded in 1718 that the criminal laws of the province conform to English standards, and subsequent governors enforced these laws with brutal severity. Indeed, even the moral objections of the Quakers were largely ignored. Because of these factors, Bradford concluded that the severity of the new state's criminal law was "an exotic plant and not the native growth of Pennsylvania," and thus it needed to be uprooted.[37]

Bradford then moved on to enquire whether Montesquieu's inverse relationship between freedom and penal severity could be validated by empirical evidence. He noted that in the seven years since the Pennsylvania Assembly had replaced capital punishment with hard labor as the sanction in cases of crimes against nature, robbery, and burglary, instances of those crimes actually had decreased significantly. Moreover, because the penalty for these crimes had been ameliorated, the administration of justice had become more consistent: juries were more likely than before to convict the guilty in hopes of their reformation instead of their death without redemption. Given these encouraging results of penal reform, Bradford argued that "the principle of the new system . . . coincides with the public safety as much as with the dictates of humanity," and concluded, "there is little to apprehend from extending it to other crimes." Indeed, Bradford went on to argue that only premeditated murder and high treason should be punishable by death; even in these cases, however, he was willing to entertain the thought that death is not absolutely necessary and that a milder punishment might be sufficient.[38]

One significant feature of Bradford's argument is his critique of the authorities to which his contemporaries appealed in defense of penal severity, sources that he felt were no longer appropriate for the governance of an enlightened republic. When explaining why the Pennsylvania Assembly had abolished capital punishment for "crimes against nature," for example, he rhetorically quipped, "How dangerous it is rashly to adopt the Mosaical institutions." Indeed, he argued that context makes all the difference: "Laws might have been proper for a tribe of ardent barbarians wandering through the sands of Arabia which are wholly unfit for an enlightened people of civilized and gentle manners."[39] In other cases, such as counterfeiting and treason, he observed that Pennsylvania law still rested inappropriately on the decrees of the Tudor and Stuart monarchs, who had become the embodiment of despotism in the minds of Early National republicans. The shaky foundation of such laws was reason enough for Bradford to suggest trimming Pennsylvania's capital jurisdiction even further.

Bradford concluded that penal reform, penitentiaries, and the abolition of capital punishment still would prove insufficient in solving the problem of crime in the new republic. Because all criminal behavior issues from "the ignorance, wretchedness, and corrupted manners of a people," moral education was essential for the prevention of crime. Again, Bradford relied on both Beccaria and Penn when he argued that "no government has a right to punish its subjects unless it has previously taken care to instruct them in the knowledge of the laws and the duties of public and private life." He was surprisingly complimentary of the New England Puritan tradition of moral education that he saw extending even to his own day in the development of public schools in the region. He urged his readers to support also the efforts of the Pennsylvania Assembly to establish a similar system of moral education in their own state. Pennsylvania was on the right track toward genuine reformation, Bradford clearly believed, and could look forward to a day when "in the progress of civilization, the punishment of death shall cease to be necessary." When that day arrived, his state would have put "the key-stone to the arch" and would "triumph in the completion of their benevolent work."[40]

Expressing a more radical application of republican discourse to the issue of penal reform than either Rush or Bradford could have conceived was a discourse published in 1809 by an author who identified himself only as M.E. The author set out to demonstrate that capital punishment, far from being a legitimate right of the state, was in reality a "bloody power wantonly usurped by Society in defiance of Reason and Common Sense." More than this, the treatise looked forward to a "consoling epoch . . . when the American Nation, inspired by her virtuous liberty, will wisely retrace her steps from wild customs." One of those wild customs was public execution. After consulting the "unalterable laws of nature," the new nation should "blot forever out of the Code this infamous relic of ancient corruption and tyranny." In the body of the treatise, the author relied less on inflammatory rhetoric and more on well-reasoned Enlightenment arguments about the nature of civil order and the purpose of punishment. What is especially remarkable, and well worth noting given the emerging contest between penal reformers and the religious status quo, is the author's candid claim that religious belief was not an appropriate foundation upon which to build a philosophy of crime and punishment. In the most scrupulous manner, the author chose to "wave all kind of dependence on religious dogmas and interpretations" even if he claimed to have respect for "sincerity in religion" and considered genuine faith "a virtue in the highest order." Instead, the author embarked on a course charted only by "Reason and Common Sense." The author then relied on an idiosyncratic social contract theory to argue that although human persons are the "legitimate proprietors" of their own lives, they cannot surrender that right to another, and thus no such proprietary right over human life is vested in society, and the punishment of death can never repair the harm done by criminal behavior to individuals or to society. In place of capital punishment, the author advocated perpetual, lifelong "slavery to the state" as an appropriate punishment for crimes hitherto capital. This "political death," he argued, was less severe and ignominious than physical death. It is clear from the author's anonymity, however, that even he recognized the unpopular extremism of his own position.[41]

New England and the New Moral Discourse

What effect did this new moral discourse have on the practice of capital punishment and the tradition of execution preaching in Early National New England? The present chapter argues that in the early years of the nineteenth century, this new moral discourse gradually helped erode the intellectual support for public execution and execution preaching in New England until both traditions had quietly disappeared. Public executions, which had been a staple of New England criminal justice administration and had been justified by what supporters understood to be sound theology, effectively ceased when the Massachusetts legislature privatized executions in 1835. Within ten years, all other New England legislatures had done the same. Without *public* executions, there could be no salutary moral lesson for spectators; and without a moral lesson, there was no need for execution sermons to reinforce it.

Because Early National penal reformers either had failed to achieve or opposed the *total* abolition of capital punishment in the North, reformers of the early nineteenth century agitated for the next best thing: privatizing executions. Although the origins of private executions are properly located in legislative reforms beginning in the 1820s, evidence suggests that the idea was developing much earlier. Oddly, perhaps, some of the evidence comes from New England execution preaching itself. In Rev. Thomas Thacher's sermon following the execution of Jason Fairbanks, for example, he asserted near the close of his discourse that public executions were "pernicious in their influence on the minds and manners of the community." He admitted that magistrates and ministers had laudable motives in continuing public executions: the curbing of vice by providing examples of extreme punishment for those who indulge in it. But he argued that the practice had precisely the opposite effect. Perhaps reflecting the influence of faculty psychology generally, and of Rush specifically, the Dedham minister argued that persons already "habituated to wickedness" were unlikely to be reformed by witnessing a public execution and that "such exhibitions naturally harden the heart" of the virtuous "and render it callous to those mild and delicate sensations which are the out guards of virtue."[42]

Although Thacher agreed with his forebears that "fear and terror are necessary engines in controuling the conduct of mankind," he argued that thoroughly privatized executions would be more effective than public ones in exciting that response. His description of privatized executions is morbid, to say the least: "The guilty . . . suffer in dark and gloomy apartments, where none [are] permitted to approach but the legal ministers of vengeance, where they could discern no objects but through the glimmering taper which rendered visible . . . the surrounding instruments of death." Assuming that they were attended with this kind of propaganda, Thacher concluded, privatized executions actually "would impress more fear and terror on the multitude" than even daily displays of "wretches expiring under the protracted torments of a despot." Lest any in his audience miss his opposition to public execution, Thacher raised the specter of the "late revolution in France" as a warning; indeed, he argued that the Revolution was made possible only because French hearts were corrupted and their senses polluted by frequent "tragical and sanguinary exhibitions" of public execution.[43]

Rev. Jonathan Going made a similar point in the last extant New England execution sermon, occasioned by the hanging of convicted rapist Horace Carter in 1825. The Baptist pastor apparently was reluctant to preach and publish a sermon related to the execution, but "gross misrepresentation of Carter's case, and mistaken opinions of the propriety of his execution" had become widespread, and he felt constrained to address these issues. Interestingly, Going chose the text of Matthew 6:6 as the basis for his reflections: "What went ye out into the wilderness to see? A reed shaken with the wind?" This choice suggests that, like those who had come to see John the Baptist, mere curiosity inspired most of those in attendance at Carter's execution. Going's sermon really amounted to little more than a defense of Carter's conviction and a description of the execution day. But he also provided a clear rationale for the privatization of executions. Although the conduct of the gallows crowd was "creditable," he still believed that "the moral tendency of public punishments is pernicious." Indeed, he continued, "The object of public justice would be better secured, if executions took place in the Jail Yard, in the presence of only the necessary officers, and a competent military force." Going ended this brief argument in favor of privatization by asking a tantalizing question that must have been on the minds of many of his contemporaries: "Does not this subject demand the attention of the Legislature?"[44]

This evidence suggests that one of the factors that eventually led to the privatization of executions were already developing—even among New England execution preachers—by the turn of the nineteenth century. Specifically, that factor was a fear of the demoralizing effects of the spectacle on the gallows audience. This fear, coupled with the threat of the growing gallows crowds described in Chapter One, inspired many leaders to push for the privatization of executions, as England had done in 1783. Perhaps a developing preference for privacy among the middle class and elite of Early National American society also helps account for their subsequent retreat from the ritual of public execution. Perhaps even opposition to public execution had become a "class imperative" by the late 1820s, because middle-class and elite citizens associated the spectacle with the lower classes.[45]

Whatever the motivating factors, privatization required the action of state legislatures, and again Quaker Pennsylvania led the way. As early as 1824, the legislature had entertained its first resolution designed to "explore the propriety of executions in the prison yard," on the assumption that public executions were "highly demoralizing, and a great and unnecessary waste of public time and labor." The legislature was apparently flooded with reports and observations from many sectors of Pennsylvania society staking their claims in the protracted debate, and the debate was mirrored in the popular press as well. By and large, however, the most persuasive arguments favored privatization, offering a rationale grounded in the new moral discourse concerning crime and punishment and extending that argument to include more practical considerations. The 1823 report of Pennsylvania congressman Jacob Cassat is perhaps representative of those tendered for consideration. Public executions demoralized spectators, he argued, because they diminished their "sensibility of moral feeling" and excited in them "the most debasing passions and appetites."

Only the dregs of society attended such events, because they had not been conditioned by more refined values. Finally, he argued, the uncontrolled reveling of the gallows crowd disrupted both the peace and productivity of the more well-disposed citizens. After repeatedly suspending the debate and tabling proposed legislation that would have privatized executions, the Pennsylvania legislature finally voted in 1834 to move executions away from the public gaze.[46]

The Pennsylvania debate over privatization was replayed in virtually all other northern states during the early 1830s, and by 1835 New York, New Jersey, and Massachusetts also had abolished the practice of public execution. Within ten years every New England state had moved their executions within prison walls. Not surprisingly, in New England the clergy made more of a contribution to the debate than they did in other regions of the North, but by this time most had joined the ranks of those who favored privatization. Unitarian ministers were especially vocal, weighing in with contributions to popular publications that condemned the savagery of public executions as theologically indefensible, morally bankrupt, and politically unwise. Take Rev. Francis Parkman, the Unitarian minister of New North Church in Boston, as an example. In 1832, he reviewed four recent defenses of capital punishment and public execution for the *Christian Examiner* and found them all wanting, especially theologically. Hanging days were, in his judgment, "loathsome exhibition[s] of religious frenzy" that made a mockery of genuine Christian faith. In particular, he objected to the way that the spectacles excited in the condemned the delusion that he or she becomes a "regenerate child of God" simply because of a half-hearted, eleventh-hour conversion. Such disingenuous repentance communicates precisely the wrong message to spectators as well because it portrays "malefactors . . . as if they were martyrs, dying joyfully in Jesus, and ascending from the gallows to glory." For these reasons, hangings and any religious services associated with them should be entirely private. For the New England clergy who favored privatization, then, public executions were demoralizing to both the condemned and spectators.[47]

A full recitation of the debates concerning the privatization of executions in the Early National north is clearly beyond the scope of this study on execution sermons. The evidence presented here is sufficient to establish the claim that the traditions of public execution and execution preaching met their demise amidst these debates. The Early National commitment to privacy among the middle class and elites, along with their fear of the gallows crowd eventually drove the events of hanging day behind prison walls, where their demoralizing tendencies could be minimized. Without *public* executions, there could be no salutary moral lesson for spectators, and without a moral lesson, there was no need for execution sermons to reinforce it.[48]

Conclusion

By 1835, the new moral discourse concerning crime and punishment—including the development of the penitential ideal—and the privatization of executions throughout New England effectively eroded the intellectual support for public execution and execution preaching. Among the execution sermons that were preached and published during the first three decades of the nineteenth century, most issued from the pens of preachers who remain virtually unknown to the region's history, were occasioned by executions on the New England frontier, or expressed sentiments decidedly opposed to public executions. Very little is known, for example, about execution preachers like William Andrews, David Sutherland, Samuel Shepard, Joshua Spalding, and Holloway Hunt. In terms of geography, few hangings in New England urban centers occasioned execution sermons—a fact that is not especially surprising, given the developing fear of mob action at public gatherings. Instead, frontier outposts like Haverhill, New Hampshire; Woodstock, Vermont; and Scipio, New York, were the sites of most of the executions that occasioned published sermons after 1810. Finally, relatively well-known and influential ministers who *did* preach and publish sermons in connection with public executions expressed in them decided opinions *against* the practice. In other words, after about 1800, the new moral discourse and efforts toward privatization increasingly pushed the ritual of public execution to the intellectual and geographic margins of New England religion and culture. By 1835, with the stroke of a legislative pen, Massachusetts became the last state in New England to privatize executions, forever putting an end to the ritual of public execution and the sermons that went with it.

Conclusion

The wages of sin is death; But the gift of God
is eternal life through Jesus Christ our Lord.

—Romans 6:23

The typical way to tell the history of capital punishment in America treats the colonial and Early National periods with self-righteous incredulity. The story goes something like this: the people of that time—particularly the New England Puritans and those who lived in their long shadow—were slow in throwing off an oppressive political and religious worldview that demanded moral conformity and punished severely those who refused to comply. Their frequent use of capital punishment represented the lengths to which magistrates and ministers would go to exercise social control. Only the political revolution and the slow maturation of enlightened democracy would dismantle these oppressive structures. Indeed, the practice of capital punishment in America today represents nothing more than a regrettable legacy from a barbaric past.

There is, of course, a grain of truth to this version of history. As we have seen, theological explications of crime and punishment dominated early New England, and the ritual of public execution demonstrated the cooperative power of church and state. The experience of the American Revolution and of nation-building inspired some to think differently about crime and punishment and to challenge traditional ways. Overall, however, this version of history fails to take seriously one important fact: the people of early New England really did ponder carefully what they were doing when they executed capital criminals, and the corpus of execution sermons clearly illustrates this fact. Their assumptions, arguments, and conclusions differ radically from those of later generations and, perhaps, from our own, but the people of early New England cannot be accused of imposing the death penalty thoughtlessly.

This conclusion offers a longitudinal summary of the way in which the execution preachers of early New England made theological sense of capital crime and justified punishing such crimes with death. This summary returns to the original questions that this book set out to answer: how did the clergy of this context make theological sense out of capital crime and justify punishing such crimes with death, and how did their theological explications for capital crime and its punishment relate to broader trends in New England theology? Using the typology first introduced in Chapter One, this summary explores the broad theological arguments that dominated the execution preaching in the Puritan, Provincial, and Early National contexts.

This conclusion also offers some brief thoughts on the significance that reflecting on the ritual of public execution in early New England and execution preaching has for contemporary persons. Once a central plank in the platform of criminal justice, these activities seem quite distant from our time and place. What we find, however, is that the questions about crime and punishment with which the people of early New England struggled remain with us. Like them, we are still horrified by heinous crimes and long for answers to our questions when such crimes are committed. Even if we have very different assumptions and reach different conclusions than they did, perhaps considering the answers that the people of early New England found compelling will help us in our own search for answers to these vexing questions.

A Longitudinal Summary

Until about 1700, New England execution preachers generally relied on the doctrinal standards of Puritanism to make sense out of capital crime and to justify punishing it with death. The Bible was their starting point: only those crimes for which scripture specifically prescribed the penalty of death were considered worthy of death. In some ways this is not surprising because the ministers and magistrates of Puritan New England understood that they were God's new Israel and that they cooperated together to build a Bible Commonwealth. By executing capital criminals, Puritan execution preachers taught that the land was being purged of sin and that others thereby would be warned away from committing similar sins, just as the Bible said.

Yet, Puritan execution preachers also consistently relied on the federal doctrine of original sin to explain the origin of capital crime. Because they taught that all persons shared equally in this innate depravity, execution preachers were able to develop a moral identification between the condemned and the audiences of their sermons. The mysterious restraining grace of God ordinarily prevented persons from committing egregious sins, but in the case of capital criminals this restraining grace had been providentially withdrawn. Without this restraint, the torrents of innate depravity eventually overwhelmed capital criminals, and the current carried them along to destruction. Although Puritan execution preachers were reluctant to claim that capital criminals were beyond the pale of God's redemption, they often distrusted late repentance as disingenuous. More likely, capital criminals suffered under God's decree of reprobation, just as the Puritan doctrine of predestination taught.

Finally, Puritan execution preachers borrowed their politics directly from earlier Reformed thinkers and claimed that magistrates were God's vicegerents on earth. As such, they held the unpleasant but necessary responsibility of exacting divine judgment on those persons who violated God's law. The ritual of public execution afforded them an opportunity to reinforce that authority and to warn others of the potential consequences of similar transgressions. In so doing, they believed that they were preserving the moral integrity of the Bible Commonwealth.

Beginning in the early decades of the eighteenth century, most execution preachers were greatly influenced by the theology of nascent evangelicalism. Like all evangelical preaching in this Provincial context, their sermons broke from strict doctrinal orthodoxy and emphasized personal religious experience. Although most shared with their Puritan forebears a belief in the universality of original sin, Provincial execution preachers began subtly to imply that the condemned were morally peculiar after all. In other words, the condemned differed morally from otherwise law-abiding citizens because of the magnitude of their crimes but not in terms of their essential sinfulness. Ironically, this emphasis served a rhetorical end: the heinous nature of capital crime, they argued, could be presented to God as an argument in favor of the ultimate salvation of the condemned. God's glory would be all the more magnified by saving the worst of sinners.

Moreover, Provincial execution preachers generally downplayed the doctrine of predestination in their sermons, arguing that even the condemned are not irrecoverably lost. Like all revival preachers, they took on the responsibility of raising the affections of the condemned and driving them to a credible repentance. Execution preaching itself became in their minds an instrumental cause of the ultimate salvation of capital criminals. In cases where the condemned experienced a conversion, Provincial execution preachers sometimes held them up as a model of repentance to be emulated and as confirmation of the extravagance of divine grace. Indeed, the conversion of an egregious sinner was an inspiring story and undoubtedly inspired a great deal of confidence in the law-abiding citizenry of early New England that their own salvation was secure.

By and large, Provincial execution preachers shared their understanding of the nature and function of civil government with their Puritan forebears. They believed that magistrates were "ministers of God" who were responsible for maintaining justice in the community according to God's law. By the middle of the eighteenth century, however, they increasingly adopted Lockean contract theory to suggest that government existed to protect the God-given rights of citizens. The Puritan covenant theology that required New England to live scrupulously as God's New Israel began to relax, and Provincial society increasingly looked more like eighteenth-century England. Execution preachers in this context thus believed that magistrates came to power not by immediate appointment by God, but through constitutional and electoral processes: in addition to being accountable to God, magistrates were responsible to the people who elected them. Concerning capital punishment specifically, Provincial execution preachers argued that the protection of the rights of citizens from time to time required the execution of those who refused to abide by the terms of the social contract.

Early National execution sermons were more theologically diverse than those of the Puritan and Provincial periods, so generalizations about them are somewhat difficult to make. Nevertheless, it is fair to say that their preaching reflects a Lockean understanding of human sinfulness: sin originates from a constitutional imbalance between the reason and the passions of a person. To the extent that they would speak of human depravity, these execution preachers would claim that capital criminals have been shaped by their environment, their experience, and their habit of sinning. Capital criminals end up on the gallows, they argued, either because they have not learned to restrain their passions or because they choose to indulge them irrationally. Often this understanding of human sinfulness led Early National execution preachers to imply that certain segments of the population were more likely to commit capital crimes: insufficiently educated young people, women, and persons of color, including Native Americans. Early National execution preachers often argued, as did Locke, that a sound moral education was the best defense against the sinfulness that led to the gallows.

Concerning the economy of conversion, Early National execution preachers reflected the developing diversity of New England theology generally, ranging from a Liberal distrust of immediate conversions to an Evangelical embracing of them. A common theme unites the execution sermons of this context, however: submission to political and religious authority. The penitent thief on the cross, whose behavior is described in Luke 23:39–43, provided the model for last-minute submission to authority. In fact, from the thief's words, Early National execution preachers discerned a blueprint for true repentance. Particularly troublesome to these execution preachers were those capital criminals who stubbornly resisted submitting to political and religious authority by either refusing to admit the justice of their sentence or clinging to erroneous religious beliefs that marked them as unorthodox. Because so many execution sermons in this context were preached *after* the public execution occurred, they merely reported whether the capital criminal finally repented and was saved.

Amidst the political ferment of the period, Early National execution preachers naturally varied considerably in their theology of civil government. The New Divinity men, for example, essentially reasserted traditional Puritan understandings of civil government, arguing that its dignity and authority comes directly from God. This fact was reason enough, they claimed, for the magistrate to execute capital criminals. By contrast, those preachers who imbibed Enlightenment thought and developing republican ideas understood the power and authority of civil government to be more limited. Magistrates, they believed, ultimately were responsible to the people who elected them. Because they saw mounting opposition to public execution in some circles, and themselves believed that such displays debased the people who witnessed them, some preachers actually used execution sermons as a forum in which to argue that civil government ought to abolish the practice.

The corpus of execution sermons, taken as a whole, represents a detailed and careful theological explication of capital crime and its punishment that helped many in early New England make sense of these difficult issues. Naturally, the theological arguments developed considerably over the Puritan, Provincial, and Early National periods. But as the leading public intellectuals in each of these contexts, New England ministers exercised a great deal of influence over how civil magistrates and even average persons thought about these issues. Contemporary Americans may disagree with both their frequent use of capital punishment and their justification of it, but the people of early New England cannot be accused of imposing the death penalty thoughtlessly. As we will see below, there may even be important insights to be gained from their theological reflections, and these insights may help us clarify our own thinking about capital crime and its punishment.

Relevance for Contemporary Persons

Since the days of the public execution ritual and the preaching of execution sermons, pragmatic concerns and constitutional issues have dominated the public debate about capital punishment in America. The relative costs of lifelong incarceration versus execution; the frequency with which errors are made in capital cases; the political ramifications of both sides of the death penalty debate; and the inherent bias against the poor and people of color in the American judicial system all are issues that take center stage in the contemporary debate. Then, of course, there are debates about whether capital punishment violates the Eighth Amendment protection against cruel and unusual punishment or the Fourteenth Amendment guarantee of due process. If these are the burning issues of the debate about capital punishment in contemporary America, then why take the time to consider the theological arguments that these preachers made? What value is there in considering their theological reflections on capital crime and its punishment?

One of the best reasons to pay some attention to the corpus of execution sermons is that theological considerations continue to play a significant role in the thinking of many contemporary Americans concerning capital punishment, even if they often do not take center stage in the public debate. Almost all major Christian denominations have adopted some formal statement concerning capital punishment, either in favor of its use or opposed to it. While the connection between these formal statements and the actual beliefs of the people in the pews may be debated, it remains significant that American Christians continue to think theologically about the death penalty and attempt to influence the public debate with their insights.

Mainline Christian denominations in America began issuing statements *opposed to* capital punishment in the late 1950s. The Episcopal Church led the way in 1958, when the bishops argued that the life of an individual has infinite worth in the sight of God, and that taking such a life is the prerogative of God alone. A year later, the United Presbyterian Church—the largest of the bodies that in 1983 would unite to become the Presbyterian Church (USA)—issued a statement, based upon the revelation of God's love in Jesus Christ, claiming that capital punishment could not be condoned and that the death penalty tends to brutalize any society in which it is practiced.

Beginning in the 1970s, many other mainline Christian denominations in America began issuing statements against the death penalty. The nation was becoming increasingly aware of the inequities in the administration of capital punishment, and partly on these grounds the Supreme Court mandated a moratorium on executions in several highly contested decisions between 1972 and 1976. This growing awareness and the apparent indecision of the high court led some mainline denominations to issue statements against the death penalty for the first time. What is remarkable about these statements, in fact, is their reluctance to use obviously theological arguments.

For example, the statement adopted by the American Baptist Churches in 1977 argues that capital punishment has been abolished in Canada and most of Europe; that the death penalty continues disproportionately to affect the poor, racial minorities, and the educationally deprived; and that popular opposition to the death penalty continues to be strong in America. The statement speaks only in vague terms of how capital punishment is "morally unacceptable" and "inconsistent with religious and/or ethical traditions." Similar statements—almost always highlighting the racial and economic inequities in the administration of capital punishment—have been adopted and reaffirmed by almost all mainline denominations in the last four decades.

Yet, there is important theological content to statements like the one adopted by the American Baptist Churches. According to the gospels, the ministry of Jesus Christ centered on advocating for and defending the marginalized and the oppressed. In short, his ministry focused on justice consistently applied. So, when these statements draw attention to the fact that capital punishment disproportionately affects these segments of American society and ague that "this alone is reason enough for opposing it as immoral and unjust," they are making an inherently theological argument.

Far more obvious in their use of theological arguments are the statements adopted by American evangelical Christian denominations *in defense of* capital punishment. Almost always, these statements highlight the power of civil government's being divinely ordained as the primary argument in support of the death penalty.

For example, the resolution that the Southern Baptist Convention adopted in 2000 explicitly affirms the sacredness of every human life, and claims that all people, including capital criminals, have been created in the image of God. Nevertheless, with a reference to Romans 13, the statement claims that "God . . . has established capital punishment as a just and appropriate means by which the civil magistrate may punish those guilty of capital crimes." Because the Convention recognized the injustices in the administration of capital punishment, it called for its "fair and equitable use." But, for the Southern Baptist Convention, the divine origin and power of civil government meant that the use of capital punishment is theologically justified.

Judging at least from the formal statements that many Christian denominations in America have adopted, it appears that the most explicitly theological arguments concerning the death penalty have been in its favor. Such statements never equate the capital criminal's actions with his or her inherent sinfulness, and rarely do they argue for religious conversion as the primary expression of rehabilitation. But statements like that of the Southern Baptist Convention clearly favor the cooperative power of church and state when it comes to capital punishment, on almost identical theological grounds that most execution preachers did. So, one wonders whether this fact constitutes a faint echo of the ritual of public execution and the preaching of execution sermons that can be heard in our own time and place.

Even those statements adopted by mainline Christians in America opposing the death penalty can trace their theological arguments in part to early New England. They often assume that capital punishment is a regrettable legacy of America's barbaric past, that more subtle biblical interpretation is required when dealing with this issue, and that concerns for justice and mercy trump concerns of law and order. In such cases, these mainline denominations have relied on theological arguments that first were made as elements of the new moral discourse concerning crime and punishment that emerged in Early National America as part of an alternative worldview to the one propounded in generations of execution preaching.

It should be clear by now that the pressing existential questions with which execution preachers struggled remain with us in our consideration of capital crime and its punishment. This is a second reason that taking time to consider their sermons is useful. Like them, we struggle to determine what motivates persons to commit heinous crimes in the first place, we wonder whether rehabilitation is possible and whether the development of religious faith might be a part of that process, and we ponder whether civil government—however it is understood theoretically—has the power to put one of its citizens to death. The execution preachers of early New England developed theological answers to these questions that were appropriate to their contexts, and these answers likely do not have much currency in contemporary America. But the questions will never disappear as long as capital punishment remains a subject of debate.

One final reason that it is useful to consider the theological arguments of early New England execution preachers has to do with concerns about privacy. The belief remains very strong in contemporary America that the public should be shielded from observing capital punishment in practice. Today, only a small number of people are authorized to witness an execution; executions always occur within the confines of the penitentiary; and executioners utilize more "humane" methods, like lethal injection. All of these accommodations have been made in the interests of privacy.

One possible explanation for this aggressive concern for privacy in contemporary executions may, in fact, be that the executions in early New England were so intentionally public. And, as we have seen, execution preachers almost always provided a compelling theological rationale. Public executions warned otherwise law-abiding citizens of the wages of sin, reconciled the condemned to God and to the community, and clearly demonstrated the cooperative power of church and state. Public executions, the preachers consistently argued, had a salutary effect on society. Even in the Early National period, when the fear of large crowds often dominated hanging day, execution preachers continued to make this argument. Most contemporary persons do not agree, but understanding the concern in early New England for the public nature of executions may help us understand why we are so committed to keeping them private.

Notes

Introduction

1. This account of the Fairbanks execution generally follows the one published in the September 15, 1801, edition of the *Columbian Minerva,* Dedham's only newspaper. This account was reprinted in newspapers throughout the region in the week following the event. Two contemporary historians have reconstructed the events surrounding the Fairbanks execution, namely, Daniel Cohen, *Pillars of Salt, Monuments of Grace: New England Crime Literature and the Origins of American Popular Culture, 1674–1860* (New York: Oxford University Press, 1993), and Dale Freeman, "'Melancholy Catastrophe!' The Story of Jason Fairbanks and Elizabeth Fales," *Historical Journal of Massachusetts* 26:1 (Winter 1998): 1–19.

2. Louis Cook, *History of Norfolk County, Massachusetts, 1622–1918,* 2 vols. (New York: S. J. Clarke Publishing Company, 1918), 1:118; DeCoursey Fales, *The Fales Family of Bristol, Rhode Island* (New York: privately printed, 1919), 9–158; Lorenzo Fairbanks, *Genealogy of the Fairbanks Family, 1633–1897* (Washington, D.C., 1897); Kenneth Lockridge, *A New England Town: The First Hundred Years, Dedham, Massachusetts, 1636–1736* (New York: W.W. Norton and Company, 1970).

3. Erastus Worthington, *The History of Dedham from its Settlement . . . to 1827* (Boston: Dutton and Wentworth, 1827).

4. Ebenezer Fairbanks, *The Solemn Declaration of the Late Unfortunate Jason Fairbanks* (Dedham, Mass.: H. Mann, 1801), 19; Mary Caroline Crawford, *The Romance of Old New England Rooftrees* (Boston: L.C. Page and Company, 1902), 251–63.

5. Fairbanks, *Solemn Declaration,* 14; *Report of the Trial of Jason Fairbanks on an Indictment for the Murder of Elizabeth Fales* (Boston: Russell and Cutler, 1801).

6. Fairbanks, *Solemn Declaration,* 3–4.

7. Fairbanks, *Solemn Declaration,* 4–6.

8. *Columbian Minerva,* May 19, 1801; *Report of the Trial of Jason Fairbanks,* 12–14.

9. *Report of the Trial of Jason Fairbanks,* 28. The tombstone marking the grave of Elizabeth Fales can be found in Range XII of the First Parish Church in Dedham.

10. Dr. Nathaniel Ames noted in his diary how on Thursday, May 21, Fairbanks was transported to the Dedham gaol. Robert Brand Hanson, ed., *Diary of Nathaniel Ames, 1758–1822,* 2 vols. (Camden, Maine: Picton Press, 1998). The *Columbian Minerva* reported the determination of the coroner's inquest jury in its May 26, 1801, edition. Several papers erroneously reported that Fairbanks had died in prison, most notably New York's *Commercial Advertiser,* June 29, 1801. In his *Solemn Declaration,* 18, 29, Ebenezer Fairbanks attempted to answer the rumors that his brother was a deist and lacked remorse for his crime.

11. *Report of the Trial,* 5–7; *Columbian Minerva,* August 11, 1801; Thomas Amory, *Life of James Sullivan with Selections from his Writings* (Boston: Phillips, Sampson, and Company, 1859); Samuel Eliot Morrison, *Harrison Gray Otis, 1765–1848: The Urbane Federalist* (Boston: Houghton Mifflin, 1969). The members of the Supreme Judicial Court were: Francis Dana (Chief Justice), Robert Treat Paine, Simeon Strong, and Thomas Davis.

12. The trial transcript reveals that on the day of her death, Betsey had spent the morning reading Frances Brooke, *The History of Lady Julia Mandeville* (n.p., 1763).

13. *Report of the Trial,* 11–81.

14. *Report of the Trial,* 82–83.

15. *Columbian Sentinel,* August 19, 1801. This announcement of Fairbanks's escape was reprinted in newspapers throughout Massachusetts during the week he remained at large. The text of Fisher Ames's petition is included in the *Report of the Trial,* 83. The route of the two fugitives is recorded, among other places, in the *Columbian Sentinel,* August 29, 1801.

16. *The Boston Gazette,* August 20, 1801.

17. *Columbian Sentinel,* August 19, 1801; August 22, 1801; and August 30, 1801. See also the *Independent Chronicle,* August 20, 1801; August 24, 1801; and September 14, 1801. Dedham's own paper, the *Columbian Minerva,* ran a lengthy article in its August 25, 1801, edition to exonerate the community of any wrongdoing in Fairbanks's escape. On the Dedham "liberty pole affair" of 1798, see James Morton Smith, "The Federalist Saints vs. the Devils of Sedition," *New England Quarterly* 28:2 (June 1955): 198–215.

18. *Connecticut Courant,* September 7, 1801.

19. Thomas Thacher, *The Danger of Despising the Divine Counsel* (Dedham: H. Mann, 1802), 22.

20. *Columbian Minerva* of September 15, 1801, reports that a Roxbury woman counted 711 carriages full of spectators making their way to Dedham on the afternoon of Fairbanks's execution. Most contemporary accounts simply remark about the immensity of the crowd. More specific descriptions of similar executions of the day claim that crowds could number five to ten thousand people; given the public interest in the Fairbanks case, it is likely that that the crowd numbered toward the high end. Few in the crowd that day would have remembered the execution of "Negro London," who confessed to the rape of a 16-year-old white girl named Sarah Clark and was executed in Dedham in 1734. See Supreme Judicial Court case nos. 37890 and 38267 held at the Massachusetts State Archives and the *Boston Newsletter* for November 14, 1734. The broadsides that survive from the Fairbanks execution are: *A Poem on Jason Fairbanks who is to be Executed this Day* (Dedham, 1801), Early American Imprints, 2d Ser. no. 1161; and *A Mournful Tragedy*

(Dedham, 1801), Early American Imprints, 2d Ser. no. 964. On Fairbanks's walk to the gallows, see the *Columbian Minerva,* September 15, 1801; Thomas Thacher, *The Danger of Despising the Divine Counsel* (Dedham: H. Mann, 1802), 22; "Biographical Sketches of the Thacher Family, from their First Settlement in New England," *New England Magazine* 7:1 (July 1834): 4–6. Ministers who counseled condemned persons in the late eighteenth and early nineteenth centuries often appealed to the crucified thief of Luke 23:39–43 as a model of dying repentance to be followed.

21. *Columbian Minerva,* September 15, 1801.

22. *Report of the Trial,* 85. *Columbian Minerva,* September 15, 1801.

23. Thacher, *Danger,* 4–5.

24. Thacher, *Danger,* 19–24.

25. Thaddeus Mason Harris, *A Sermon Preached in the First Parish in Dedham* (Dedham: Herman Mann, 1801), 21, 25.

26. Fairbanks's tombstone can be found in Range III of the cemetery of the First Parish Church in Dedham.

27. Statistics about the frequency of New England executions have been drawn from Daniel Hearn, *Legal Executions in New England: A Comprehensive Reference, 1623–1960* (Jefferson, N.C.: McFarland and Co., 1999). I have chosen the dates 1623 and 1835 to limit this study because the first public execution occurred in New England in 1623, and 1835 marks the last *public* execution in New England. After 1835, executions continued but were performed in private.

Chapter One

1. This description of a hanging day in early modern England is drawn from Bernard Mandeville, *An Enquiry into the Causes of the Frequent Executions at Tyburn* (London, 1725), and Samuel Richardson, *Familiar Letters on Important Occasions,* ed. Brian Downs (New York: Dodd, Mead, and Co., 1928), 217–20. English painter, political cartoonist, and satirist William Hogarth captures the riotous scene of public executions in his *Idle 'Prentice Executed at Tyburn* (n.p., 1747). Also helpful is the work of modern historians, namely, David Cooper, *The Lesson of the Scaffold: The Public Execution Controversy in Victorian England* (Athens, Ohio: The Ohio University Press, 1974); J. S. Cockburn, *Crime in England, 1550–1800* (Princeton, New Jersey: Princeton University Press, 1977); Harry Potter, *Hanging in Judgment: Religion and the Death Penalty in England* (New York: Continuum, 1993); and V. A. C. Gattrell, *The Hanging Tree: Execution and the English People. 1770–1868* (New York: Oxford University Press, 1994).

2. Peter Lake and Michael Questier, *The Antichrist's Lewd Hat: Protestants, Papists, and Players in Post-Reformation England* (New Haven: Yale University Press, 2002), 1–183.

3. Lake and Questier, 281–314.

4. On Dorothy Talbye, see John Winthrop, *The Journal of John Winthrop, 1630–1649,* ed. Richard S. Dunn, et al. (Cambridge: Harvard University Press, 1996) 271–72, and the Records of the Quarterly Courts of Essex County, Massachusetts, vol. 1, held at the Massachusetts Historical Society. On Mary Martin, see Winthrop's *Journal,* 680–82. On Mr. Poster, see the New Haven

Colony Records (Hartford: Case, Tiffany, and Company, 1857), 440–43. Cotton Mather briefly describes each of these cases in his *Pillars of Salt: An History of Some Criminals Executed in this Land for Capital Crimes* (Botson: B. Green and J. Allen, 1699), 60–67. All of the quotations come from Mather's anthology.

5. Perry Miller, *The New England Mind: From Colony to Province* (Cambridge: Harvard University Press, 1953), 19–149; Robert Pope, "The Myth of Declension," *Religion in American History: Interpretive Essays* (New York: Prentice Hall, 1978).

6. David D. Hall, *Worlds of Wonder, Days of Judgment: Popular Religious Belief in Early New England* (Cambridge: Harvard University Press, 1989), 166–212, quotations from 167. See also Ronald Bosco, *Sermons for Days of Fast, Prayer, and Humiliation and Execution Sermons,* The Puritan Sermon in America, vol. 1 (Delmar, N.Y.: Scholars' Facsimiles and Reprints, 1978), lxxiii–lxxxiv; Ronald Bosco, "Lectures at the Pillory: The Early American Execution Sermon," *American Quarterly* 30 (1978): 156–76; Richard Gildrie, "The Ceremonial Puritan Days of Humiliation and Thanksgiving," *New England Historical and Genealogical Record* 136 (1982): 3–16.

7. Karen Halttunen, *Murder Most Foul: The Killer and the American Gothic Imagination* (Cambridge: Harvard University Press, 1998), 25–28.

8. Brief case summaries of all public executions in New England can be found in Daniel Hearn, *Legal Executions in New England: A Comprehensive Reference, 1623–1960* (Jefferson, N.C., 1999). These summaries almost always include dates of the crime, the trial, and the execution for each case, making it possible to calculate with a great deal of accuracy the length of time between each event.

9. Potter, 3–4. The benefit of clergy was not widely used in England's North American colonies, except for those of the South. George Dalzell, *Benefit of Clergy in America* (Winston-Salem, N.C.: J. F. Blair, 1955). "The General Lawes and Liberties of the Massachusetts Colony" in *Colonial Laws of Massachusetts,* ed. William Whitmore (Boston: City Council of Boston, 1890); George Haskins, *Law and Liberty in Early Massachusetts: A Study in Tradition and Design* (New York: Macmillan, 1960), 145–52; Edwin Powers, *Crime and Punishment in Early Massachusetts, 1620–1692* (Boston: Beacon Press, 1966), 264–73; David Grayson Allen, *In English Ways: The Movements of Societies and the Transferal of English Local Law and Customs to Massachusetts Bay in the Seventeenth Century* (Chapel Hill: University of North Carolina Press, 1981); Elizabeth Dale, "Conflicts of Law: Reconsidering the Influence of Religion on Law in Massachusetts Bay," *Numen* 43 (1996): 139–56; Eli Faber, "Puritan Criminals: The Economic, Social, and Intellectual Background to Crime in Seventeenth-Century Massachusetts," *Perspectives in American History* 11 (1977–1978): 83–144; John Murrin, "Magistrates, Sinners, and a Precarious Liberty: Trial by Jury in Seventeenth-Century New England," in *Saints and Revolutionaries: Essays in Early American History,* ed. David Hall (New York: Norton, 1984); and Edgar McManus, *Law and Liberty in Early New England: Criminal Justice and Due Process, 1620–1692* (Amherst: University of Massachusetts Press, 1993).

10. Harry Knerr, "The Election Sermon: Primer for Revolutionaries," *Speech Monographs* 29 (1962): 15–16.

11. Cotton Mather, *The Diary of Cotton Mather* 2 vols. (New York: Frederick Ungar, 1957), 1:122; Samuel Sewall, *The Diary of Samuel Sewall* 2 vols., ed. M.

Halsey Thomas (New York: Farrar, Straus, and Giroux, 1973), 1:99–100; "John Dutton to George Larkin, March 25, 1686," in *The Puritans: A Sourcebook of their Writings,* 2 vols., ed. Perry Miller and Thomas Johnson (New York: Harper and Row, 1963), 2:414; Lawrence Kennedy, *Planning the City Upon a Hill: Boston Since 1630* (Amherst: University of Massachusetts Press, 1992).

12. Cotton Mather, *Speedy Repentance Urged* (Boston: Samuel Green, 1690). Mather records the transcript in an appendix to his execution sermon. Mather had recorded a similar dialogue with the aforementioned James Morgan in 1686 in *Pillars of Salt,* 73–83.

13. The last dying speeches of James Morgan and Hugh Stone were published as appendices to their execution sermons. See Increase Mather, *A Sermon Occasioned by the Execution of a Man Found Guilty of Murder* (Boston: Joseph Browning, 1686), 42–44; and Cotton Mather, *Speedy Repentance,* 81–82. For comparative purposes, see J. A. Sharpe, "'Last Dying Speeches': Religion, Ideology, and Public Execution in Seventeenth-Century England," *Past and Present* 107 (May 1985): 144–67.

14. Samuel Danforth, *The Cry of Sodom Enquired Into* (Boston: Marmaduke Johnson, 1674). Cotton Mather's quote about the staying power of printed sermons can be found in the preface to his *Pillars of Salt,* n. p. Ronald Bosco, "Early American Gallows Literature: An Annotated Checklist," *Resources for American Literary Studies* 8 (1978): 81–107.

15. Perry Miller, *The New England Mind: The Seventeenth Century* (Cambridge: Harvard University Press, 1939), 332–33; Harry Stout, *The New England Soul: Preaching and Religious Culture in Colonial New England* (New Haven: Yale, 1986); Teresa Toulouse, *The Art of Prophesying: New England Sermons and the Shaping of Belief* (Athens: University of Georgia Press, 1987); Wayne Minnick, "The New England Execution Sermon, 1674–1800," *Speech Monographs* 35 (1968): 77–89.

16. Daniel Cohen, *Pillars of Salt, Monuments of Grace: New England Crime Literature and the Origins of American Popular Culture, 1674–1860* (New York: Oxford, 1993), 4–5; Kenneth Lockridge, *Literacy in Colonial New England: An Enquiry into the Social Context of Literacy in the Early Modern West* (New York: Norton, 1974).

17. Perry Miller, *The New England Mind: From Colony to Province,* 395–480. Dozens of scholars have followed this line of interpretation, including John Murrin, Bernard Bailyn, Timothy Breen, Richard Johnson, Richard S. Dunn, and David Lovejoy. More recent scholars have cautioned against overstating the impact of "anglicanization" on Provincial New England. See, for example, Jon Butler, *Becoming America: The Revolution Before 1776* (Cambridge: Harvard University Press, 2000).

18. Daniel Williams, "'Behold a Tragic Scene Strangely Changed into a Theater of Mercy': The Structure and Significance of Criminal Conversion Narratives in Early New England," *American Quarterly* 38 (1986): 827–47.

19. John Rogers, *Death the Certain Wages of Sin for the Impenitent, Life the Sure Reward of Grace to the Penitent, together with the Only Way for Youth to Avoid the Former and Attain the Latter* (Boston, 1701), 118, 124.

20. Theodore Ferdinand, "Criminal Justice: From Colonial Intimacy to Bureaucratic Formality," in *The Handbook of Contemporary Urban Life,* ed. David Street, et al. (San Francisco: Jossey-Bass, 1978), 261–87. Again, the duration of

the imprisonment of capital criminals before their execution was calculated using the data in Hearn, *Legal Executions in New England,* 107–39.

21. The case of pirate William Fly was reported in both the *Boston News-Letter* and the *Boston Gazette* over a three-week period in June and July 1726. The observations of Cotton Mather and Benjamin Colman are recorded in appendices to their execution sermons. See Mather, *A Vial Poured Out Upon the Sea* (Boston: T. Fleet, 1726), 47–48, and Colman, *It is a Fearful Thing to Fall into the Hands of the Living God* (Boston: John Philips and Thomas Hancock, 1726), 29–39. Daniel Williams has provided an excellent analysis of the Fly case in his "Puritans and Pirates: A Confrontation between Cotton Mather and William Fly in 1726," *Early American Literature* 22 (1987): 233–51.

22. Daniel Williams, "Rogues, Rascals, and Scoundrels: The Underworld Literature of Early America," *American Studies* 24 (1983), 10.

23. Robert Ritchie, *Captain Kidd and the War Against the Pirates* (Cambridge: Harvard University Press, 1986) and Marcus Rediker, *Between the Devil and the Deep Blue Sea: Merchant Seamen, Pirates and the Anglo-American Maritime World, 1700–1750* (New York: Cambridge University Press, 1993).

24. Cohen, *Pillars of Salt,* 16–20.

25. There is no summary of these developments in the capital statutes of Massachusetts Bay Colony. Edwin Powers discusses the revisions of the capital jurisdiction under the second charter (1692) in his *Crime and Punishment in Early Massachusetts* (Boston: Beacon Press, 1966), 303–5. Beyond that, the historian must look at the records of specific capital statutes that were passed and repealed in the eighteenth century. See the *Acts and Resolves of the Province of Massachusetts Bay, 1692–1780,* 5 vols. (Boston: Wright and Potter, 1869). Similar records would need to be consulted to trace development in other New England colonies.

26. Frank McLynn, *Crime and Punishment in Eighteenth-Century England* (New York: Routledge, 1989), 257–76; Douglas Hay, "Property, Authority, and Criminal Law," in *Albion's Fatal Tree: Crime and Society in Eighteenth-Century England,* ed. Douglas Hay, et al. (London: Allen Lane, 1975); Peter Linebaugh, *The London Hanged: Crime and Civil Society in the Eighteenth Century* (New York: Cambridge University Press, 1992); Clive Emsley, *Crime and Society in England, 1750–1900* (New York: Longman, 1996); Eli Faber, "The Evil that Men Do: Crime and Transgression in Colonial Massachusetts," (Ph.D. diss., Columbia University, 1974); Linda Kealey, "Patterns of Punishment: Massachusetts in the Eighteenth Century," *American Journal of Legal History* 30 (1986): 163–86; and Daniel Cohen, "A Fellowship of Thieves: Property Criminals in Eighteenth-Century Massachusetts," *Journal of Social History* 22 (1988): 65–92.

27. For the details of Hugh Henderson's burglary spree, see the records of the Supreme Judicial Court, Case Nos. 44640 and 44647 held at the Massachusetts State Archives and the *Boston Evening Post* (September 18, 1738). Henderson's last dying speech was published as an appendix to John Campbell's execution sermon, *After Souls by Death are Separated from their Bodies, they Come to Judgment* (Boston: S. Kneeland and T. Green, 1738), 34–36.

28. For James Morgan's last dying speech, see Increase Mather, *A Sermon Occasioned by the Execution of a Man Found Guilty of Murder,* 42–44. The conversion narrative and last dying speech of Esther Rodgers were published as an

appendix to John Rogers, *Holiness the Way to Blessedness* (Boston: B. Green and J. Allen, 1701).

29. Samuel Moody was a frontier preacher widely known for his aggressively evangelical preaching and was a close friend of both George Whitefield and Jonathan Edwards. See *Sibley's Harvard Graduates,* ed. J. L. Sibley and C. K. Shipton, 4 vols. (Boston: Massachusetts Historical Society, 1873–1970), 4:356–65. His conversion narrative is entitled *Summary Account of the Life and Death of Joseph Quasson, Indian* (Boston, 1726).

30. Owen Syllavan is the pseudonym of the author of the twelve-page pamphlet entitled *A Short Account of the Life of John ***, Alias Owen Syllavan* (Boston, 1756).

31. Cohen, *Pillars of Salt,* 249–50 and 12.

32. For the Simpson and Kenney executions, see the preface to William Shurtleff, *A Sermon Preached December 27, 1739* (Boston: J Draper, 1740); for Bramble, see Joshua Hempstead, *Diary* (New London: New London Historical Society, 1901), 619; and for Sheehan, see the *Essex Gazette* (January 21, 1772).

33. Charles Chauncy, *The Horrid Nature and Enormous Guilt of Murder* (Boston: T. Fleet, 1754), 22; Sylvanus Conant, *The Blood of Abel and the Blood of Jesus Considered and Improved in a Sermon* (Boston: T. Fleet, 1763), 30; and Moses Baldwin, *The Ungodly Condemned in Judgment* (Boston: Kneeland and Adams, 1771), 24.

34. On William Fly, see the *Boston Newsletter* (July 14, 1726), and George Dow and John Edmonds, *Pirates of the New England Coast, 1630–1730* (Mineola, N.Y.: Dover Publications, 1996), 328–37. On Thomas Carter, see the *Boston Newsletter* (May 20, 1751). On "Negro Mark," see the *Proceedings of the Massachusetts Historical Society* (March 1883): 122–46. Gibbeting became far more common in England in the late eighteenth century after Parliament passed the Murder Act (1752). The Act assumed that gibbeting the corpse of an executed murderer would improve deterrence. See Gattrell, *The Hanging Tree,* 266–69.

35. Hearn, *Legal Executions,* 156–66. The one exception to this general rule is the case of Moses Dunbar, who was executed in Connecticut for high treason in 1777. The eight persons who were executed during the American Revolution for non-wartime crimes were John Dennis (murder, 1777); William Brooks, James Buchanan, Ezra Ross, and Bathsheba Spooner (murder, 1778); Robert Young (rape, 1779); Barnett Davenport (murder, 1780) and Michael Lobidal (murder, 1781).

36. John Brooke, "To the Quiet of the People: Revolutionary Settlements and Civil Unrest in Western Massachusetts," *William and Mary Quarterly* 3d. Ser., 46:3 (July 1989): 425–62; Jacqueline Carr, "A Change 'As Remarkable as the Revolution Itself': Boston's Demographics, 1780–1800," *New England Quarterly* 73 (2000): 583–602.

37. On the crimes of Bly and Rose specifically, see the records of the Superior Court of the Judicature, case no. 160576, held at the Massachusetts State Archives and the *Hampshire Gazette* for October 17, 1787. David Szatmary, *Shays's Rebellion: The Making of an Agrarian Insurrection* (Amherst: University of Massachusetts Press, 1980); Leonard Richards, *Shays's Rebellion: The American Revolution's Final Battle* (Philadelphia: University of Pennsylvania Press, 2002).

38. Stephen West, *A Sermon Preached at Lenox* (Pittsfield, 1787), 3; David Kling, *A Field of Divine Wonders: The New Divinity and Village Revivals of Northwestern Connecticut, 1792–1822* (University Park: University of Pennsylvania

Press, 1993); Mark Valeri, *Law and Providence in Joseph Bellamy's New England: The Origins of the New Divinity in Revolutionary America* (New York: Oxford, 1994). The last dying speech of Bly and Rose was published as "Extracts from the Last Words and Dying Speeches of John Bly and Charles Rose," *Worcester Magazine,* Second Week (January 1788).

39. Michel Foucault, *Discipline and Punish: The Birth of the Prison* (New York: Vintage Books, 1979); Louis Masur, *Rites of Execution: Capital Punishment and the Transformation of American Culture, 1776–1865* (New York: Oxford, 1989), 27; Gabriel Gottlieb, "Theater of Death: Capital Punishment in Early America, 1750–1800" (Ph.D. diss., University of Pittsburgh, 2005).

40. These impressions are based upon calculations using the trial summaries in Daniel Hearn, *Legal Executions,* 156–221.

41. On Bly and Rose, see the *Hampshire Gazette* December 19, 1787; on Godfrey, see *A Sketch of the Life of Samuel E. Godfrey* (n.p., 1818), 34.

42. Ann Taylor, "The Unhappy Stephen Arnold: An Episode of Murder and Penitence in the Early Republic," in *Through a Glass Darkly: Reflections on Personal Identity in Early America,* ed. Ronald Hoffman, Mechal Sobel, and Fredrika Teute (Chapel Hill: University of North Carolina Press, 1997). On the growing fear of crowd behavior in eighteenth-century America generally, see Pauline Maier, "Popular Uprisings and Civil Authority in Eighteenth-Century America," *William and Mary Quarterly* 3d Ser., 27:3 (Autumn 1970), 3–35.

43. Jonathan Plummer, *Dying Confession of Pomp, a Negro Man* (Newburyport, Mass.: Blunt and March, 1795) and William Bentley, *The Diary of William Bentley,* 2 vols. (Gloucester, Mass.: Smith Publishers, 1962), 2:156.

44. Philip McKey, *Voices Against Death: American Opposition to Capital Punishment, 1787–1975* (New York: Burt Franklin and Company, 1975).

45. David Daggett, *Sketches of the Life of Joseph Mountain* (New Haven: T. & S. Green, 1784). See also the *Connecticut Journal* for October 27, 1790.

46. Richard D. Brown and Irene Quenzler Brown, *The Hanging of Ephraim Wheeler: A Story of Rape, Incest, and Justice in Early America* (Cambridge: Harvard University Press, 2003); *Report of the Trial of Ephraim Wheeler* (Stockbridge, Mass.: H. Willard, 1805); Ephraim Wheeler, *Narrative of the Life of Ephraim Wheeler* (Stockbridge: H. Willard, 1806); and Samuel Shepard, *A Sermon Delivered at Lenox* (Stockbridge: H. Willard, 1806).

47. After 1800, nineteen of twenty-four published execution sermons had been preached as a part of the ritual itself. The five that were preached on the Sunday following the execution are: Thaddeus Mason Harris, *A Sermon Preached in the First Parish in Dedham* (Dedham: Herman Mann, 1801); Thomas Thacher, *The Danger of Despising Divine Counsel* (Dedham: Herman Mann, 1801); Charles Lowell, *A Discourse Delivered March 16, 1817* (Boston: John Eliot, 1817); Thomas Baldwin, *The Danger of Living without the Fear of God* (Boston: Kneeland and Adams, 1819); and Jonathan Going, *A Discourse Delivered at Worcester, December 11, 1825* (Worcester: William Manning, 1825).

48. Donald Scott, *From Office to Profession: The New England Ministry, 1750–1850* (Philadelphia: University of Pennsylvania Press, 1978); Gerald Gewalt, *The Promise of Power: The Emergence of the Legal Profession in Massachusetts, 1760–1840* (Westport, Ct.: Greenwood Press, 1979).

49. Cohen, *Pillars of Salt,* 26.

50. Cohen, *Pillars of Salt,* 31–34; Halttunen, *Murder Most Foul,* 33–90.

Chapter Two

1. David Flaherty, "Law and the Enforcement of Morals in Early America," in *Law in Early America,* ed. Donald Fleming and Bernard Bailyn (Boston: Little,Brown, 1971), 203.

2. William Ames, *The Marrow of Theology,* trans. John D. Eusden (Durham, N.C.: Labyrinth Press, 1983), 107–28. Eusden's introduction provides a very helpful analysis of Ames's influence on Anglo-American Puritanism.

3. "Of the Fall of Man, of Sin, and of the Punishment Thereof," Chapter VI of the Westminster Confession of Faith (1647 ed.) in Philip Schaff, *Creeds of Christendom,* 6th ed. (New York: Harper Brothers, 1931), 615–16.

4. I am adopting the typology that Janice Knight develops in her *Orthodoxies in Massachusetts: Re-reading American Puritanism* (Cambridge: Harvard University Press, 1994).

5. H. Sheldon Smith, *Changing Conceptions of Original Sin: A Study in American Theology since 1750* (New York: Charles Scribner and Sons, 1955), 1–9.

6. Samuel Danforth, *The Cry of Sodom Enquired Into* (Boston, 1674), 7, 13, and 25; *Records of the Court of Assistants of the Colony of Massachusetts Bay, 1673–1692,* 3 vols. (County of Suffolk, 1901–1928), 1:12–13; M. Halsey Thomas, ed., *The Diary of Samuel Sewall, 1674–1729,* 2 vols. (New York: Farrar, Straus, and Giroux, 1973), 1:23; Richard Godbeer, "The Cry of Sodom: Discourses, Intercourse, and Desire in Colonial New England," *William and Mary Quarterly* 3d. Ser. 52:2 (April 1995): 259–86; Robert Oaks, "Things Fearful to Name: Sodomy and Buggery in Seventeenth-Century New England," *Journal of Social History* 12 (1978): 268–81.

7. *Record Book of the Superior Court of the Judicature,* 2:199–200, held at the Massachusetts State Archives; *Diary of Samuel Sewall,* 1:399–400; Peter Hoffer and N. E. H. Hull, *Murdering Mothers: Infanticide in England and New England, 1558–1803* (New York: New York University Press, 1981); Else Hambleton, "The World Fill'd with a Generation of Bastards: Pregnant Brides and Unwed Mothers in Seventeenth-Century Massachusetts" (Ph.D. diss., University of Massachusetts at Amherst, 2000); N. E. H. Hull, *Female Felons: Women and Serious Crime in Colonial Massachusetts* (Chicago: University of Illinois Press, 1987).

8. Increase Mather, *The Folly of Sinning Opened and Applied in Two Sermons* (Boston, 1699), 17–18, 27, and 33.

9. Mather, *The Folly of Sinning,* 40, 48.

10. Karen Halttunen, *Murder Most Foul: The Killer and the American Gothic Imagination* (Cambridge: Harvard University Press, 1998), 7–32; Kai Ericson, *Wayward Puritans: A Study in the Sociology of Deviance* (New York: John Wiley and Sons, 1966).

11. Cotton Mather, *Call of the Gospel Apply'd* (Boston: R. Pierce, 1686), 22; Cotton Mather, *Pillars of Salt: An History of Some Criminals Executed in this Land for Capital Crimes* (Boston, 1699), 71–85; Walter Lazenby, "Exhortation as Exorcism: Mather's Sermons to Murderers," *Quarterly Journal of Speech* 57 (1971): 50–56.

12. John Williams, *Warnings to the Unclean* (Boston: B. Green and J. Allen, 1699), 21; Cotton Mather, *Tremenda: The Dreadful Sound with which the Wicked are Thunderstruck* (Boston, 1721), 26.

13. Benjamin Colman, *The Hainous Nature of the Sin of Murder* (Boston: T. Fleet and T. Green, 1713), 16–17; and Cotton Mather, *The Curbed Sinner* (Boston: J. Allen, 1713), 16–17. For the details of Wallis's crime, see Cotton Mather, *A True Relation of the Murder Committed by David Wallis on his Companion Benjamin Stolwood* (Boston: J. Allen, 1713); Supreme Judicial Court of Massachusetts, case no. 9174, held at the Massachusetts State Archives. See also the brief articles appearing in the *Boston Newsletter,* August 31, 1713, and September 28, 1713. Thomas Foxcroft, *A Lesson of Caution to Young Sinners* (Boston, 1733), 60.

14. Rhode Island Court of Trials, vol. A, 225; *Boston Newsletter,* March 28, 1715, and April 18, 1715.

15. Nathaniel Clap, *The Lord's Voice Crying to His People* (Boston: B. Green, 1715), 32–35.

16. Joshua Moodey, *An Exhortation to a Condemned Malefactor* (Boston: R. P., 1686), 87; George Francis Dow and John Edmonds, *Pirates of the New England Coast, 1630–1730* (Salem, Mass.: Marine Research Society, 1923). Cotton Mather's sermon is *Faithful Warnings to Prevent Fearful Judgment* (Boston, 1704), 42–43.

17. Halttunen, *Murder Most Foul,* 33–59.

18. Williams, *Warnings to the Unclean,* 42; Samuel Willard, *Impenitent Sinners Warned of their Misery and Summoned to Judgment* (Boston: B. Green and J. Allen, 1699), 26.

19. Willard, *Impenitent Sinners,* 48; and Mather, *Reflections on the Dreadful Case,* 17.

20. Cotton Mather, *The Curbed Sinner* (Boston: J. Allen, 1713), 15, 17.

21. Increase Mather, *A Sermon . . . Wherein it is Shewed that Excess in Wickedness Doth Bring Untimely Death* (Boston, 1674), 29; John Williams, *Warnings to the Unclean,* 19.

22. Richard Bushman, *From Puritan to Yankee: Character and Social Order in Connecticut, 1690–1765* (Cambridge: Harvard University Press, 1967); Richard Johnson, *Adjustment to Empire: The New England Colonies, 1675–1715* (Rutgers: Rutgers University Press, 1981); Harry Stout, *New England Soul: Preaching and Religious Culture in Colonial New England* (New York: Oxford, 1986), 127–47; John Corrigan, *The Prism of Piety: Catholick Congregational Clergy at the Beginning of the Enlightenment* (New York: Oxford University Press, 1991).

23. W. M. Spelman, *John Locke and the Problem of Depravity* (Oxford: Clarendon Press, 1988), 39–62.

24. John Locke, "Some Thoughts Concerning Education," in *The Educational Writings of John Locke,* ed. J. Axtell (Cambridge: Cambridge University Press, 1968), 134, 214.

25. Smith, *Changing Conceptions of Original Sin,* 10–36.

26. John Taylor, *The Scripture Doctrine of Original Sin Proposed to Free and Candid Examination* (London: M. Waugh, 1740).

27. Taylor, *The Scripture Doctrine of Original Sin.*

28. Taylor, *The Scripture Doctrine of Original Sin.*

29. Clyde Holbrook, introduction to Jonathan Edwards, *The Great Christian Doctrine of Original Sin Defended* (New Haven: Yale University Press, 1970), 1–16. Samuel Webster's treatise is entitled *A Winter Evening's Conversation on the Doctrine of Original Sin* (New Haven: Green and Russell, 1757).

30. See Smith, *Changing Conceptions of Original Sin,* ch. 3; John Corrigan, *The Hidden Balance: Religion and the Social Theories of Charles Chauncy and Jonathan Mayhew* (New York: Cambridge University Press, 1987), 86–107; Conrad Wright, *American Unitarianism, 1805–1865* (Boston: Northeastern University Press, 1989). On New Divinity understandings of original sin, see Mark Valeri, *Law and Providence in Joseph Bellamy's New England* (New York: Oxford, 1994), 76–109; and Joseph Conforti, *Samuel Hopkins and the New Divinity Movement: Calvinism, the Congregational Ministry, and Reform in New England Between the Great Awakenings* (Grand Rapids, Mich.: Eerdmans, 1981), 59–75.

31. *A Brief Account of the Life and Abominable Thefts of the Notorious Isaac Frasier* (New London, Conn.: Timothy Green, 1768); Noah Hobart, *Excessive Wickedness, the Way to Untimely Death* (New Haven: Thomas and Samuel Green, 1768).

32. For an account of the crime of Moses Paul, see *The Connecticut Courant,* December 17, 1771, and September 8, 1772. Samson Occom's execution sermon is *A Sermon Preached at the Execution of Moses Paul, an Indian* (New London, 1772), 6–7.

33. *Connecticut Courant,* January 27, 1777, and March 24, 1777; Nathan Strong, *The Reasons and Designs of Public Punishments* (Hartford, 1777), 14; Thomas Thacher, *The Danger of Despising Divine Counsel* (Dedham, 1803).

34. Richard Slotkin, "Narratives of Negro Crime in New England, 1675–1800," *American Quarterly* 25 (1971): 3–31; Donna Hunter, "Dead Men Talking: Africans and the Law in New England's Eighteenth-Century Execution Sermons and Crime Narratives" (Ph.D. diss., University of California at Berkeley, 2000); Daniel Cohen, "Social Injustice, Sexual Violence, Spiritual Transcendence: Constructions of Interracial Rape in Early American Crime Literature, 1767–1817," *William and Mary Quarterly* 3d. Ser. 56 (1999): 481–526.

35. Between 1623 and 1835, twenty-four men were executed for rape, and fifteen (63%) of them were black. While the executions of black men were spread more or less evenly across the period, there were no executions of white men for rape between 1694 and 1772. Moreover, between 1623 and 1835, six persons were executed for arson, and five of them (83%) were black. A white person was not executed for arson in New England until 1821. The frequency with which blacks were executed for rape and arson, relative to the execution of whites, probably reinforced the perception that these crimes esp. were closely associated with blackness. These statistics were derived from data included in Daniel Hearn, *Legal Executions in New England, A Comprehensive Reference, 1623–1960* (Jefferson, N.C.: McFarland, 1999), 5–222.

36. Winthrop Jordan, *White Over Black: American Attitudes Toward the Negro, 1550–1812* (Chapel Hill: University of North Carolina Press, 1968), 3–43, 154–58, and 375–402; Slotkin, "Narratives of Negro Crime," and Hunter, "Dead Men Talking."

37. The narrative of the Thomas Powers case was constructed using records of the New Haven County Superior Court, Record Group 3, Drawer No. 327 of the Connecticut State Archives.

38. See *Narrative and Confession of Thomas Powers, A Negro* (Norwich: John Trumbull, 1796); William Whitcher, *History of the Town of Haverhill, New Hampshire* (Concord, N.H.: Rumford Press, 1919), 361–62.

39. Noah Worcester, *A Sermon Delivered at Haverhill, New Hampshire* (Haverhill: N. Coverly, 1796).

40. Lynn Wilson, *History of Fairfield County* (Chicago: S. J. Clarke, 1929), 404; James Montgomery Bailey, *History of Danbury, Connecticut, 1684–1896* (New York: Burr Printing House, 1896), 116–17; Timothy Langdon, *A Sermon Preached at Danbury* (Danbury: Douglas and Nichols, 1798).

41. Aaron Hutchinson, *Iniquity Purged with Mercy and Truth* (Boston: Thomas and John Fleet, 1769), 20; Thaddeus MacCarty, *The Power and Grace of Christ Display'd to a Dying Malefactor* (Boston: Kneeland and Adams, 1768).

42. David Daggett, *Sketches of the Life of Joseph Mountain* (New Haven: T. & S. Green, 1790); James Dana, *The Intent of Capital Punishment* (New Haven: T. & S. Green, 1790).

43. Of course, interpreting arson and dominicide depends completely on the perspective of the interpreter. Modern historians interpret these crimes as instances of resistance to slavery. Destroying work implements, ruining crops, burning down storage barns, and even murdering their enslavers or members of the enslaver's family were ways in which blacks resisted the oppression of slavery, esp. under circumstances in which armed insurrection was impossible. See Lawrence Levine, *Black Culture and Black Consciousness: Afro-American Folk Thought from Slavery to Freedom* (New York: Oxford University Press, 1978), and Sterling Stuckey, *Slave Culture: Nationalist Theory and the Foundations of Black America* (New York: Oxford, 1987). On "cross-cultural murder," esp. dominicide, see Robert Asher, Lawrence Goodheart, and Alan Rogers, "Cross-cultural 'Murther' and Retribution in Colonial New England," in their *Murder on Trial, 1620–2002* (Albany: State University of New York Press, 2005), 33–60.

44. Thomas Davis, *A Rumor of Revolt: The Great Negro Plot in Colonial New York* (New York: The Free Press, 1985); Peter Hoffer, *The Great New York Conspiracy of 1741: Slavery, Crime, and Colonial Law* (Lawrence: University of Kansas Press, 2003); Fortune Price, *The Dying Confession of Fortune* (Boston: n.p., 1762).

45. Sylvanus Conant, *The Blood of Abel and the Blood of Jesus* (Boston: Edes and Gill, 1764), 35.

46. Arthur Browne, *Religious Education of Children Recommended* (Boston: S. Kneeland and T. Green, 1740), 6–7.

47. Browne, *Religious Education,* 9–10.

48. *Connecticut Gazette,* July 28, 1786, and December 28, 1786. See also Francis Caulkins, *A History of New London* (unpublished manuscript, 1852) held at the Connecticut State Historical Society.

49. Henry Channing, *God Admonishing his People of their Duty, as Parents and Masters* (New London: T. Green, 1786), 25.

50. Channing, *God Admonishing,* 6.

51. Channing, *God Admonishing,* 10–17.

52. *A Brief Sketch of the Life of Horace Carter* (Worcester: William Manning, 1825); *Massachusetts Spy* for October 12, December 14, and December 21, 1825.

53. Jonathan Going, *A Discourse Delivered at Worcester* (Worcester, 1825), 5–8.

54. Going, *Discourse,* 6, 21.

55. Jay Fleigelman, *Prodigals and Pilgrims: The American Revolution against Patriarchal Authority, 1750–1800* (Cambridge: Cambridge University Press, 1982), 59.

56. Carl Kaestle and Maris Vinovskis, *Education and Social Change in Nineteenth-Century Massachusetts* (Cambridge: Harvard University Press, 1980); Charles Glenn, *The Myth of the Common School* (Amherst: University of Massachusetts Press, 1988); Carl Kaestle, *Pillars of the Republic: Common Schools and American Society, 1780–1860* (New York: Hill and Wang, 1983); Timothy Smith, "Protestant Schooling and American Nationality, 1800–1850," *Journal of American History* 53 (1966–1967): 679–94; David Tyack, "The Kingdom of God and the Common School," *Harvard Educational Review* 36 (Fall 1966); Maris Vinovskis, "Trends in Massachusetts Education, 1826–1860," *History of Education Quarterly* 12 (Winter 1972): 501–29; Paul Mattingly, "Educational Revivals in Ante-Bellum New England," *History of Education Quarterly* 11 (Fall 1971): 39–71; Dennis Denenberg, "The Missing Link: New England's Influence on Early National Educational Policies," *New England Quarterly* 52 (June 1979).

Chapter Three

1. Increase Mather, *A Sermon Occasioned by the Execution of a Man Found Guilty of Murder* (Boston: Joseph Browning, 1686), A2. Mather and other Puritan execution preachers sometimes repeated the claim that "late repentance is seldom true" in the prefaces to their published sermons.

2. Theodore Beza articulates his theology of predestination and conversion in *A Briefe Declaration of the Chiefe Poyntes of Christian Religion,* trans. William Whittingham (London: Thomas Mann, 1575). R. T. Kendall, *Calvin and English Calvinism to 1649* (New York: Oxford, 1979), 29–38; and Charles Cohen, *God's Caress: The Psychology of Puritan Religious Experience* (New York: Oxford, 1986), 10–11.

3. William Perkins, *The Works of William Perkins,* 3 vols. (London: John Lagatt, 1631), 1:362–65; Gordon Keddie, "Unfallible Certenty of the Pardon of Sinne and Life Everlasting: The Doctrine of Assurance in the Theology of William Perkins," *Evangelical Quarterly* 48 (1976): 230–44; Mark Shaw, "Drama in the Meetinghouse: The Concept of Conversion in the Theology of William Perkins," *Westminster Theological Journal* 45 (1983): 45–57; Cohen, *God's Caress,* 79–80.

4. Thomas Hooker, *The Application of Redemption by the Effectual Work of the Word and Spirit of Christ* (London: Peter Cole, 1657); John Cotton, *A Treatise on the Covenant of Grace* (London: Peter Parker, 1671); Norman Petit, *The Heart Prepared: Grace and Conversion in Puritan Spiritual Life* (New Haven: Yale University Press, 1966).

5. Cohen, *God's Caress,* 23–134.

6. Cohen, *God's Caress,* 135–270. Ross Beales, "The Halfway Covenant and Religious Scrupulosity," *William and Mary Quarterly* 3d. Ser. 31: 465–80; Patricia Caldwell, *The Puritan Conversion Narrative: The Beginnings of American Expression* (Cambridge: Cambridge University Press, 1985); Michael McGiffert, *God's Plot: The Spirituality of Thomas Shepard's Cambridge* (Amherst: University of Massachusetts Press, 1994).

7. Joshua Moodey, *An Exhortation to a Condemned Malefactor* (Boston: R. Pierce, 1685), 70–71.

8. Increase Mather, *The Folly of Sinning, Opened and Applied* (Boston: B. Green and J. Allen, 1699), 44–45.

9. Increase Mather, *Sermon Occasioned by the Execution of a Man Found Guilty of Murder* (Boston: Joseph Browning, 1686), 40–41.

10. Cotton Mather, *Speedy Repentance Urged* (Boston: Samuel Green, 1690), 65.

11. John Williams, *Warnings to the Unclean* (Boston: B. Green and J. Allen, 1699), 15.

12. Cotton Mather, *Pillars of Salt: An History of Some Criminals Executed in this Land for Capital Crimes* (Boston: B. Green and J. Allen, 1699), A2.

13. Samuel Danforth, *The Cry of Sodom Enquired Into* (Boston: Marmaduke Johnson, 1674), 9.

14. Williams, *Warnings to the Unclean,* 18.

15. Mary Douglas, *Purity and Danger: An Analysis of the Concepts of Pollution and Taboo* (London: Routledge, 1966).

16. Increase Mather, *A Sermon . . . Wherein it is Shewed that Excess in Wickedness Doth Bring Untimely Death* (Boston: R. Pierce, 1685), 22, 33.

17. Cotton Mather, *The Call of the Gospel Applyed* (Boston: R. Pierce, 1686), 46–54.

18. William McLoughlin, "Pietism and the American Character," *American Quarterly* 17 (Summer 1965): 163–86; F. Ernest Stoeffler, *Continental Pietism and Early American Christianity* (Grand Rapids, Mich.: Eerdmans, 1976); Sydney Ahlstrom, "From Puritanism to Evangelicalism," in *The Evangelicals: What They Believe, Who They Are, Where They are Changing,* ed. David Wells and John Woodbridge (Nashville: Abingdom Press, 1975); Janice Knight, *Orthodoxies in Massachusetts: Re-Reading American Puritanism* (Cambridge: Harvard University Press, 1994); Richard Lovelace, *The American Pietism of Cotton Mather: Origins of American Evangelicalism* (Grand Rapids: Christian University Press, 1979); N. Ray Hiner, "Preparing for the Harvest: The Concept of New Birth and the Theory of Religious Education on the Eve of the Great Awakening," *Fides et Historia* 9 (Fall 1976): 8–25; and Jerald Brauer, "Conversion: From Puritanism to Revivalism," *Journal of Religion* 58 (1978): 227–43.

19. William Ames, *Marrow of Theology,* trans. John D. Eusden (Boston: Pilgrim Press, 1968), esp. 24–29; Michael Malone, "The Doctrine of Predestination in the Thought of William Perkins and Richard Hooker," *Anglican Theological Review* 52 (1970): 103–17; and Mark Dever, *Richard Sibbes: Puritanism and Calvinism in Late Elizabethan and Early Stuart England* (Macon, Ga: Mercer University Press, 2000).

20. Introduction to Jonathan Edwards, *A Treatise on Religious Affections,* ed. John E. Smith (New Haven: Yale University Press, 1959).

21. Harry Stout, *The New England Soul: Preaching and Religious Culture in Colonial New England* (New Haven: Yale University Press, 1986), 99–101; Michael Schuldiner, "Solomon Stoddard and the Process of Conversion," *Early American Literature* 17:3 (Winter 1983): 215–26; David Laurence, "Jonathan Edwards, Solomon Stoddard and the Preparationist Model of Conversion," *Harvard Theological Review* 72 (1979): 267–83. On Stoddard's opponents, see Paul Lucas, *Valley of Discord: Church and Society Along the Connecticut River, 1636–1725* (Hanover, N.H.: University Press of New England, 1976).

22. John Rogers, *Death the Certain Wages of Sin to the Impenitent* (Boston: B. Green and J. Allen, 1701), 21; *Life the Sure Reward of Grace to the Penitent*

(Boston: B. Green and J. Allen, 1701), 99; and *Holiness the Way to Blessedness* (Boston: B. Green and J. Allen, 1701), 117.

23. Nathaniel Clap, *The Lord's Voice Crying to His People* (Boston: B. Green, 1715), 98.

24. Cotton Mather, *Valley of Hinnom* (Boston: J. Allen, 1717), 32; and Samuel Checkley, *Murder a Great and Crying Sin* (Boston: T. Fleet, 1733), 25–26.

25. Samuel Moodey, *A Faithful Narrative of the Wicked Life and Remarkable Conversion of Patience Boston, alias Samson* (Boston: S. Kneeland and T. Green, 1738), 11.

26. Cotton Mather, *Valley of Hinnom,* 38–39; Benjamin Colman, *It is a Fearful Thing to Fall Into the Hands of the Living God* (Boston: John Phillips and Thomas Hancock, 1726), 24; Cotton Mather, *Tremenda: The Dreadful Sound with which the Wicked are to be Thunderstruck* (Boston: B. Green, 1721), 22.

27. Hugh Henderson, *The Confession and Dying Warning of Hugh Henderson* (Boston: n.p., 1737), 1.

28. Henderson, *The Confession and Dying Warning of Hugh Henderson.*

29. Thomas Foxcroft, *Lessons of Caution to Young Sinners* (Boston: S. Kneeland and T. Green, 1738), 58; and Mather Byles, *The Prayer and Plea of David* (Boston: Samuel Kneeland, 1751), 12.

30. John Webb, *The Greatness of Sin Improv'd by the Penitent as an Argument with God for a Pardon* (Boston: S. Kneeland and T. Green, 1734), 27–28.

31. John Corrigan, *The Hidden Balance: Religion and the Social Theories of Charles Chauncy and Jonathan Mayhew* (New York: Cambridge University Press, 1987); John Corrigan, *The Prism of Piety: Catholick Congregational Clergy and the Beginning of the Enlightenment* (New York: Oxford University Press, 1991); Conrad Wright, *American Unitarianism, 1805–1865* (Boston: Northeastern University Press, 1989); Mark Valeri, *Law and Providence in Joseph Bellamy's New England* (New York: Oxford University Press, 1994); Joseph Conforti, *Samuel Hopkins and the New Divinity Movement: Calvinism, the Congregational Ministry, and Reform in New England Between the Awakenings* (Grand Rapids: Eerdmans, 1981); and Edmund Morgan, *A Gentle Puritan: A Life of Ezra Stiles, 1727–1795* (Chapel Hill: University of North Carolina Press, 1974).

32. Luke 23:39–43 (King James Version).

33. William Smith, *The Convict's Visitor* (Newport: Peter Edes, 1791).

34. Nathan Strong, *A Sermon Preached at Hartford . . . at the Execution of Richard Doane* (Hartford: Elisha Babcock, 1797), 14–15, 20. Hartford County Superior Court Files, September Term, 1796; and the *American Weekly Mercury* for June 12, 1797.

35. James Diman, *A Sermon Preached at Salem* (Salem: Ebenezer Hall, 1772), 16.

36. Thaddeus MacCarty, *The Guilt of Innocent Blood Put Away* (Worcester: Isaiah Thomas, 1778), 28, 40. For more on Spooner's case, see *Independent Chronicle* of July 9, 1778; and Peleg Chandler, *American Criminal Trials,* 2 vols. (Boston: Little and Brown, 1841–44), 2:1–58 and 2:375–83.

37. Moses Cook Welch, *The Gospel Preached to All Men* (Windham: John Byrne, 1805), 16, 31; *New York Spectacle* of October 2, 1805; *Hampshire Gazette* of November 27, 1805.

38. James Dana, *Men's Sins Not Chargeable on God, but on Themselves* (New Haven: T. & S. Green, 1783). Dana's sermon and that of John Marsh refer-

enced in the following note are not execution sermons in the strictest sense of the word, but funeral sermons, because Beadle committed suicide shortly after committing his crime. Nonetheless, because the deaths occasioning these sermons were the result of capital criminal activity, they have been included here.

39. John Marsh, *The Great Sin and Danger of Striving with God* (Hartford: Hudson and Goodwin, 1783), 22, 24, 17.

40. Walter Chapin, *A Sermon Delivered at Woodstock* (Windsor: A. & W. Spooner, 1818), 11.

41. Leland Howard, *A Sermon Delivered at Woodstock* (Windsor: A. & W. Spooner, 1818), 9.

42. Samuel Godfrey, *Sketch of the Life of Samuel E. Godfrey* (n.p., 1818), 32.

43. Charles Shively, *A History of the Conception of Death in America, 1650–1860* (New York: Garland Publishing Company, 1988); Margaret Coffin, *Death in Early America* (New York: Thomas Nelson, 1976).

Chapter Four

1. Edmund Morgan, *Puritan Political Ideas, 1558–1794* (Indianapolis: Bobbs-Merrill Company, 1965).

2. John Putnam Demos, *A Little Commonwealth: Family Life in Plymouth Colony* (New York: Oxford University Press, 1970); Edmund Morgan, *The Puritan Family: Religion and Domestic Relations in Seventeenth-Century New England* (New York: Harper and Row, 1966).

3. Laurel Thatcher Ulrich, *Good Wives: Image and Reality in the Lives of Women in Northern New England, 1650–1750* (New York: Knopf, 1981); Marilyn Westerkamp, *Women and Religion in Early America, 1600–1850: The Puritan and Evangelical Traditions* (New York: Routledge, 1999).

4. John Calvin, *Institutes of the Christian Religion,* ed. John T. McNeill (Philadelphia: Westminster Press, 1960), 1490. On the calling of ministers in Puritan New England, see David Hall, *The Faithful Shepherd: A History of the New England Ministry in the Seventeenth Century* (Chapel Hill: University of North Carolina Press, 1972).

5. Timothy Breen, *The Character of a Good Ruler: A Study of Puritan Political Ideas in New England, 1630–1730* (New Haven: Yale University Press, 1970), 8–12.

6. Delbert Hillers, *Covenant: The History of a Biblical Idea* (Baltimore: Johns Hopkins University Press, 1968); Perry Miller, *Errand into the Wilderness* (New York: Harper Torchbooks, 1956), 48–98; Peter de Jong, *The Covenant Idea in New England Theology: 1620–1847* (Grand Rapids: Eerdmans, 1945).

7. See Chapter IV of the Cambridge Platform in Williston Walker, *The Creeds and Platforms of Congregationalism* (Boston: The Pilgrim Press, 1960), 207–9.

8. Kenneth Lockridge, *A New England Town: The First Hundred Years* (New York: Norton, 1970); Sumner Powell, *Puritan Village: The Formation of the New England Town* (Middletown, Ct.: Wesleyan University Press, 1963); Paige Smith, *As a City Upon a Hill: The Town in American History* (New York: Knopf, 1966); Michael Zuckerman, *Peaceable Kingdoms: New England Towns in the Eighteenth Century* (New York: Knopf, 1970); Bruce Daniels, *The Connecticut Town: Growth and Development, 1635–1790* (Middletown: Wesleyan University Press, 1979); David Wier, *Early New England: A Covenanted Society* (Grand Rapids: Eerdmans, 2005).

9. Richard Bushman, *From Puritan to Yankee: Character and the Social Order of Connecticut, 1690–1765* (Cambridge: Harvard University Press, 1967), 3–21; Francis Bremer, *The Puritan Experiment: New England Society from Bradford to Edwards* (Hanover, N.H.: University Press of New England, 1995), esp. 86–93.

10. Romans 13:1–7 (Geneva Bible).

11. Ralph Keen, "The Limits of Power and Obedience in the Later Calvin," *Calvin Theological Journal* 27 (1992): 252–76; Richard Muller, "Calvin, Beza, and the Exegetical History of Romans 13:1–7," in *Identity of Geneva* (Westport, Ct.: Greenwood Press, 1998), 39–56; Nathan Hatch, *The Sacred Cause of Liberty: Republican Thought and the Millennium in Revolutionary New England* (New Haven: Yale University Press, 1977).

12. Increase Mather, *A Sermon . . . wherein it is Shewed that Excess in Wickedness doth Bring Untimely Death* (Boston: Joseph Browning, 1685), 15.

13. Increase Mather, *A Sermon Occasioned by the Execution of a Man* (Boston: Joseph Browning, 1686), 8, 14–15, 18–19.

14. Benjamin Colman, *The Hainous Nature of the Sin of Murder* (Boston: J. Allen, 1713), 8–9.

15. Colman, *Hainous Nature,* 10–11, 14.

16. Benjamin Colman, *The Divine Compassions Declar'd and Magnified* (Boston: T. Fleet and T. Green, 1717), 25–26.

17. Samuel Checkley, *Murder a Great and Crying Sin* (Boston: T. Fleet, 1733), 14–15.

18. Viola Barnes, *The Dominion of New England* (New Haven: Yale University Press, 1923); Guy Miller, "Rebellion in Zion: The Overthrow of the Dominion of New England," *Historian* 30:3 (1968): 439–59; Richard Johnson, *Adjustment to Empire: The New England Colonies, 1675–1715* (New Brunswick: Rutgers University Press, 1981); Philip Haffenden, *New England in the English Nation, 1689–1713* (Oxford: Clarendon Press, 1974); David Lovejoy, *The Glorious Revolution in America* (New York: Harper and Row, 1972); Theodore Lewis, "A Revolutionary Tradition, 1689–1774: There was a Revolution Here as Well as in England," *New England Quarterly* 46:3 (1973): 424–38.

19. At least two scholars suggest that New Englanders understood the tyrannical administration of the Andros regime as a divine punishment for the region's faltering spiritual state. In other words, opposition to Andros took the form of a jeremiad. See Barnes, 250–51; and Perry Miller, *The New England Mind: The Eighteenth Century* (Cambridge: Harvard University Press, 1953), 179. Breen disagrees. He argues that, with the exception of Cotton Mather, the majority of New England commentators opposed the Dominion governor on purely constitutional and pragmatic grounds. See Breen, 152–54 and 199–202.

20. Ian Harris, *The Mind of John Locke: A Study of Political Theory in its Intellectual Setting* (New York: Oxford, 1994); John Locke, *Second Treatise of Government,* ed. Sterling Lamprecht (New York: Appleton-Century-Crofts, 1965), 5–7; Richard Ashcraft, "Locke's State of Nature: Historical Fact or Moral Fiction," *American Political Science Review* 62:3 (September 1968): 898–915; John Simmons, "Locke's State of Nature," in *The Social Contract Theorists: Critical Essays on Hobbes, Locke, and Rousseau,* ed. Christopher Morris (Lanham, Md.: Rowan and Littlefield, 1999), 97–120.

21. See Locke, 10–11, 61–62.

22. Locke defines "property" principally in terms of material possessions, esp. land that has been improved by one's labor. It is important to realize,

however, that Locke also means intangible "property" such as the right to life and liberty. See Locke, *Second Treatise of Government,* 63–85, 142–64.

23. Robert Kraynak, "John Locke: From Absolutism to Toleration," *American Political Science Review* 74 (March 1980): 53–69; Jeremy Waldron, "Locke: Toleration and the Rationality of Persecution," in *Justifying Toleration,* ed. Susan Mendes (Cambridge: Cambridge University Press, 1988), 61–88.

24. Lawrence Leder, *Liberty and Authority: Early American Political Ideology, 1689–1763* (Chicago: Quadrangle Books, 1968), 37–60.

25. Alice Baldwin, *The New England Clergy and the American Revolution* (Durham: Duke University Press, 1928); Steven Dworetz, *The Unvarnished Doctrine: Locke, Liberalism, and the American Revolution* (Durham: Duke University Press, 1990), 135–83.

26. Chauncy Graham, *God will Trouble the Troublers of his People* (New York: H. Gaine, 1759), 4, 7–9.

27. Graham, *God will Trouble,* 11–12.

28. Graham, *God will Trouble,* 12–13.

29. Noah Hobart, *Excessive Wickedness the Way to an Untimely Death* (New Haven: Thomas and Samuel Green, 1768), n.p. When he refers to the state of nature in his execution sermon, Hobart is drawing on English philosopher Thomas Hobbes. In his famous *Leviathan,* Hobbes posits a much more pessimistic view of humanity's natural state than that of Locke, calling it a "war of each against all."

30. Ezra Ripley, *Love to Our Neighbor, Explained and Urged* (Boston: Samuel Hall, 1800), n.p.

31. Timothy Pitkin, *A Sermon Preached at Litchfield* (Hartford: Green and Watson, 1769), 5.

32. Charles Chauncy, *The Horrid Nature and Enormous Guilt of Murder* (Boston: T. Fleet, 1754), 16.

33. Increase Mather, *Sermon Occasioned by the Execution,* 5; Joshua Moodey, *An Exhortation to a Condemned Malefactor* (Boston: R. P., 1686), 64; and Samuel Checkley, *Murder a Great and Crying Sin* (Boston: T. Fleet, 1733), 8, 34. Aaron Hutchinson, *Iniquity Purged by Mercy and Truth* (Boston: Thomas and John Fleet, 1769), 13–15.

35. Hutchinson, *Iniquity Purged,* 15.

36. William Breitenbach, "The Consistent Calvinism of the New Divinity Movement," *William and Mary Quarterly* 3d Ser., 41 (1984): 241–64; Edmund Morgan, "The American Revolution Considered as an Intellectual Movement," in *Paths of American Thought,* ed. Arthur Schlesinger and Morton White, (Boston: Houghton Mifflin, 1963).

37. Jonathan Edwards, *The Nature of True Virtue* (Ann Arbor: University of Michigan Press, 1960).

38. Joseph Conforti, *Samuel Hopkins and the New Divinity Movement: Calvinism, the Congregational Ministry, and Reform in New England between the Great Awakenings* (Grand Rapids: Eerdmans, 1981), 121; Oliver Ellsbree, "Samuel Hopkins and the Doctrine of Benevolence," *New England Quarterly* 8 (1935): 534–50; Joseph Haroutunian, *Piety Versus Moralism: The Passing of the New England Theology* (New York: Holt, 1932). Several recent biographies of major figures also shed considerable light on the movement as a whole, e.g., Robert Ferm, *Jonathan Edwards the Younger, 1745–1801: A Colonial Pastor* (Grand Rap-

ids: Eerdmans, 1976); John Fitzmier, *New England's Moral Legislator: Timothy Dwight, 1752–1817* (Bloomington: Indiana University Press, 1998).

39. Jonathan Sassi, *A Republic of Righteousness: The Public Christianity of the Post-Revolutionary New England Clergy* (New York: Oxford University Press, 2001), 52–83.

40. Stout, *The New England Soul,* 259–311.

41. *Connecticut Courant,* January 27, 1777, and March 24, 1777; *Norwich Packet,* March 24, 1777. Bradley Chapin, *The American Law of Treason: Revolutionary and Early National Origins* (Seattle: University of Washington Press, 1964).

42. Nathan Strong, *The Reasons and Designs of Public Punishments* (Hartford: Ebenezer Watson, 1777), 5.

43. Strong, *The Reasons and Designs,* 7–8.

44. Strong, *The Reasons and Designs,* 9.

45. Strong, *The Reasons and Designs,* 15–17.

46. *Narrative of the Life of Joseph Mountain, a Negro* (New Haven: T. and S. Green, 1790); *Connecticut Journal,* June 2, 1790, and October 27, 1790.

47. James Dana, *The Intent of Capital Punishment* (New Haven: T. and S. Green, 1790), 5.

48. Dana, *The Intent of Capital Punishment,* 6–9.

49. Noah Worcester, *A Sermon Delivered at Haverhill, New Hampshire* (Haverhill: N. Coverly, 1796), 17–19.

50. Fitzmier, *New England's Moral Legislator,* 158–82.

Chapter Five

1. Two important histories of American criminal justice make similar points. See Samuel Walker, *Popular Justice: A History of American Criminal Justice* (New York: Oxford University Press, 1998), esp. 37–44; and Lawrence Friedman, *Crime and Punishment in American History* (New York: Basic Books, 1993), esp. 61–82. Both of these scholars cite the work of Gordon Wood on the relationship between the Revolutionary War and the cultural transformations that followed. See his book *The Radicalism of the American Revolution* (New York: Knopf, 1991).

2. For more on the cultural and religious difference between New England and the middle Atlantic colonies in early America, see Digby Balzell, *Puritan Boston and Quaker Philadelphia: Two Protestant Ethics and the Spirit of Class Authority and Leadership* (New York: The Free Press, 1979). Balzell's work suffers from the same shortcoming that plagued the work of his ideological mentor, Max Weber. In constructing the ideal types of the "Puritan ethic" and the "Quaker ethic," he overstates the opposition between them. Nonetheless, if treated with care, his typology remains a useful paradigm.

3. Baron de Montesquieu, *The Spirit of the Laws,* trans. Anne Cohler, Basia Carolyn Miller, and Harold Stone (New York: Cambridge University Press, 1989), 82–83.

4. Montesquieu, 189.

5. Montesquieu, 191.

6. Paul Spurlin's work *Montesquieu in America, 1760–1801* (University: University of Louisiana Press, 1940) is a dated but important study of the baron's

influence in early national America. Ann Kohler explores Montesquieu's impact on the American legal tradition in *Montesquieu's Comparative Politics and the Spirit of American Constitutionalism* (Lawrence: University of Kansas Press, 1988). The text of Jefferson's bill is most conveniently available in *The Papers of Thomas Jefferson,* ed. Julian Boyd (Princeton: Princeton University Press, 1950), 2:492–507. Douglas Wilson has written two very important articles germane to any consideration of Jefferson on crime and punishment. For the influence of French Enlightenment thinkers on his intellectual development, see Wilson's "Thomas Jefferson's Library and the French Connection," *Eighteenth-Century Studies* 26:4 (Summer 1993): 669–85. For a limited discussion of his early ruminations on crime and punishment, see Wilson's "Thomas Jefferson's Early Notebooks," *William and Mary Quarterly* 3d. Ser. 42:4 (October 1985): 433–52.

7. Cesare Beccaria, *On Crime and Punishments* ed. David Young (Indianapolis: Hackett Publishing Company, 1986), 8–10. It should be clear by now that Beccaria's understanding of the social contract differs from that of his Enlightenment contemporaries who held that persons submitted to the social contract voluntarily.

8. See William Paley, *The Principles of Moral and Political Philosophy* (New York: Garland Publishers, 1978), and Jeremy Bentham, *Rationale of Punishment,* ed. Heinrich Oppenheimer (Montclair, N.J.: Patterson Smith, 1975). See also Beccaria, 48–53. For an excellent but brief treatment of Beccaria's opposition to capital punishment, see Marcello Maestro, "A Pioneer in the Abolition of Capital Punishment: Cesare Beccaria," *Journal of the History of Ideas* 34:3 (Autumn 1973): 463–68. For Maestro's more comprehensive study of the same subject, see his *Cesare Beccaria and the Origins of Penal Reform* (Philadelphia: Temple University Press, 1973). On the relationship between Beccaria and other late eighteenth-century criminal justice reformers, see Coleman Phillipson's study, *Three Criminal Law Reformers: Beccaria, Bentham and Romilly* (London: J. M. Dent and Sons, 1923).

9. Beccaria, 48–53.

10. Paul Spurlin investigated the availability and influence of Beccaria's *Essay* in his article "Beccaria's *Essay on Crimes and Punishments* in Eighteenth-Century America," *Studies on Voltaire and the Eighteenth Century* 27 (1963): 1489–504.

11. William Offnut explores Quaker influence on the criminal law of the Middle Atlantic colonies in his recent study *Of Good Laws and Good Men: Law and Society in the Delaware Valley, 1680–1710* (Urbana: University of Illinois Press, 1995). See also Paul Cromwell, "Quaker Reforms in American Criminal Justice: The Penitentiary and Beyond," *Criminal Justice History* 10 (1989): 77–94.

12. For a detailed study of the Walnut Street jail, see Negley Teeters, *The Cradle of the Penitentiary: The Walnut Street Jail at Philadelphia, 1773–1835* (Philadelphia: Temple University Publications, 1955). Michael Meranze locates the development of the penitential ideal in the larger historical context of Revolutionary and Early National Philadelphia. See his *Laboratories of Virtue: Punishment, Revolution, and Authority in Philadelphia, 1760–1835* (Chapel Hill: University of North Carolina Press, 1996).

13. Caleb Lownes, *An Account of the Alteration and Present State of the Penal Laws of Pennsylvania* (Lexington: J. Bradford, 1794). For a similar enthusias-

tic eyewitness review of the Walnut Street jail, see Robert Turnbull, *A Visit to the Philadelphia Prison* (Philadelphia: Budd and Bartram, 1796). The jail impressed even foreign visitors to Philadelphia, as witnessed by François-Alexandre-Frédéric La Rochefoucauld-Liancourt, *On the Prisons of Philadelphia* (Philadelphia: Moreau de Saint-Mery, 1796).

14. On the development of penitentiaries generally, see Adam Jay Hirsch, *The Rise of the Penitentiary: Prisons and Punishment in Early America* (New Haven: Yale University Press, 1992). Of these pioneering states, only New York has a comprehensive history of the rise of the penitentiary: see David Lewis, *From Newgate to Dannemora: The Rise of the Penitentiary in New York, 1796–1848* (Ithaca: Cornell University Press, 1965).

15. On the role of the Quakers in nineteenth-century American prison reform, see Paul Cromwell, "The Holy Experiment: An Examination of the Influence of the Society of Friends upon the Development and Evolution of American Correctional Philosophy" (Ph.D. diss., Florida State University, 1986). In England, too, Quakers were the leading voices in prison reform and the building of penitentiaries. See Robert Alan Cooper, "The English Quakers and Prison Reform, 1809–1823," *Quaker History: The Bulletin of Friends Historical Association* 68:1 (Spring 1979): 3–19.

16. The quote here comes from the *Statutes at Large of Pennsylvania,* 26 vols. (Harrisburg: C. M. Busch, 1911), 12:280. David Brion Davis discusses the reform of state penal codes in his classic essay "The Movement to Abolish Capital Punishment in America, 1787–1861," *American Historical Review* 63 (1957): 22–46. With the exception of Virginia, where willful murder was the only capital crime (if the accused were white), the American South continued to have an expansive capital jurisdiction throughout the nineteenth century.

17. The details of this case have been extracted from John Watson, *Annals of Philadelphia and Pennsylvania* (Philadelphia: Carey and Hart, 1843), ch. 89; and the *Pennsylvania Archives,* 12 vols. (Philadelphia: Joseph Sevrens, 1852), 7:24, 39, and 55. The case has received some scholarly attention in Peter Messer, "'A Species of Treason and Not the Least Dangerous Kind': The Treason Trials of Abraham Carlisle and John Roberts," *Pennsylvania Magazine of History and Biography* 123 (1999): 303–32.

18. On the early history and persecution of English Quakers, see Hugh Barbour, *The Quakers in Puritan England* (New Haven: Yale University Press, 1964), and more recently Adrian Davies, *The Quakers in English Society, 1655–1725* (New York: Oxford University Press, 2000). Concerning legal issues in the treatment of Quakers by the Stuart monarchs, see Craig Horle, *The Quakers and the English Legal System, 1660–1688* (Urbana: University of Illinois Press, 1988).

19. See Howard Brinton, *Friends for Three Hundred Years: The History and Beliefs of the Society of Friends* (Wallingford, Pa.: Pendle Hill Publications, 1995).

20. Robert Shalhope has provided two very useful surveys of the issues involved in the historiographic debate over the term. See "Toward a Republican Synthesis: The Emergence of an Understanding of Republicanism in American Historiography," *William and Mary Quarterly* 3d Ser., 29:1 (January 1972): 49–80; and "Republicanism and Early American Historiography," *William and Mary Quarterly* 3d. Ser., 39:2 (April 1982): 334–54. Two other scholars have provided more recent surveys of the debate. See Joyce Appleby, "Republicanism

in the History and Historiography of the United States," *American Quarterly* (Autumn 1985): 461–73; and Daniel Rodgers, "Republicanism: The Career of a Concept," *The Journal of American History* 79:1 (June 1992): 11–38. In developing this definition of republicanism as a social ideology, I am relying greatly on Gordon Wood's classic study, *The Creation of the American Republic, 1776–1787* (Chapel Hill: University of North Carolina Press, 1969), esp. 48–53.

21. The distinction between republicanism and liberalism in early national America is the subject of considerable historiographic debate. The best recent treatment of these issues is Joyce Appleby, *Republicanism and Liberalism in the Historical Imagination* (Cambridge: Harvard University Press, 1992). See also Wood, 53–70. Republican authors of the period often referred to this public-spirited disposition as "virtue." As we noted in Chapter Four, New England clergy who were influenced by the Edwardsean tradition equated political virtue with their theological and ethical principle of "disinterested benevolence." On the notion of virtue in republican thought, see James Kloppenberg, "The Virtues of Liberalism: Christianity, Republicanism, and Ethics in Early American Political Discourse," *The Journal of American History* 74:1 (June 1987): 9–33.

22. Wood, 70–75.

23. Cited in Bernard Bailyn, *The Ideological Origins of the American Revolution* (Cambridge: Harvard University Press, 1967), 230.

24. For a comprehensive biography, see David Freeman Hawk, *Benjamin Rush: Revolutionary Gadfly* (Indianapolis: Bobbs Merill, 1971).

25. Scottish moral philosopher Thomas Reid (1710–1796) is widely regarded to be the first systematic faculty psychologist. His *Inquiry into the Human Mind on the Principle of Common Sense* (1764) and esp. his *Essays on the Intellectual Powers of Man* (1785) lay out the basic theoretical principles on which faculty psychologists would build for the next century. On Reid and his influence in the Anglo-American empirical tradition, see Philip de Bary, *Thomas Reid and Skepticism: His Reliabilist Response* (New York: Routledge, 2002); William Rowe, *Thomas Reid on Freedom and Morality* (Ithaca, N.Y.: Cornell University Press, 1991); Peter Jones, *The Science of Man in the Scottish Enlightenment: Hume, Reid, and their Contemporaries* (Edinburgh: University of Edinburgh Press, 1989).

26. See John Wright, "Metaphysics and Physiology: Mind, Body and the Animal Economy in Eighteenth Century Scotland," in *Studies in the Philosophy of the Scottish Enlightenment,* ed. M. A. Stewart (Oxford: Oxford University Press, 1990). See also Neal Wood, "Tabula Rasa, Social Environmentalism, and the 'English Paradigm,'" *Journal of the History of Ideas* 53 (1992): 647–68; and Lisbeth Haakonssen, *Medicine and Morals in the Enlightenment* (Amsterdam: Rodophi, 1997).

27. Benjamin Rush, *An Enquiry into the Influence of Physical Causes Upon the Moral Faculty* (Philadelphia: Charles Cist, 1786), quoted at 23–25.

28. Benjamin Rush, *An Enquiry into the Effects of Public Punishments upon Criminals and Upon Society* (Philadelphia: Joseph James, 1787). Rush's essay has been made available conveniently in *Essays: Literary, Moral, and Philosophical,* ed. Michael Meranze (Schenectady, N.Y.: Union College Press, 1988). The quote appears on page 80 of Meranze's volume.

29. Rush, 81–86.

30. Rush, 93.

31. Benjamin Rush, "An Enquiry into the Justice and Policy of Punishing Murder by Death," *American Museum* 4 (July 1788).

32. Philochorus [Robert Annan], "Observations on Capital Punishment: Being a Reply to an Essay on the Same Subject," *American Museum* 4 (November & December 1788).

33. Rush made his accusations in semi-private correspondence with a leading Unitarian minister in Boston, namely Jeremy Belknap (1744–1798). See Rush to Belknap, August 19, 1788, in Lyman Butterfield, ed., *The Letters of Benjamin Rush,* 2 vols. (Princeton: Princeton University Press, 1951), 1:419; and Rush to Belknap, October 7, 1788, *Letters,* 1:490. Annan included his attack on Rush in the discourse itself. See Philochorus [Robert Annan], "Observations," 444–48.

34. For an excellent description and analysis of this debate, see Louis Masur, *Rites of Execution: Capital Punishment and the Transformation of American Culture, 1776–1865* (New York: Oxford, 1989), esp. ch. 3. The high quality of Masur's analysis makes it unnecessary to reconstruct that debate here. For example, Rush gathered together his contributions to *The American Museum* and published them as *Considerations on the Injustice and Impolicy of Punishing Murder by Death* (Philadelphia: Matthew Carey, 1792). Virtually the same materials appeared again in his *An Enquiry into the Consistency of the Punishment of Murder by Death, with Reason and Revelation* (Philadelphia: [Joseph James], 1797).

35. This brief biography of Bradford follows the one provided in The Justice Management Division, *The 200th Anniversary of the Office of Attorney General* (Washington, D.C.: The United States Department of Justice, 1991). For the best recent treatment of the Whiskey Rebellion, see Thomas Slaughter, *The Whiskey Rebellion* (New York: Oxford University Press, 1986).

36. William Bradford, *An Enquiry into How Far the Punishment of Death is Necessary in Pennsylvania* (Philadelphia: T. Dobson, 1793), 5. In the same volume as Bradford's treatise was published Caleb Lowne's *Account of the Alteration and Present State of the Penal Laws of Pennsylvania, Containing also an Account of the Gaol and Penitentiary House of Philadelphia and the Management Thereof.* The Quaker's account amounts to a how-to manual for penal reform and penitentiary administration.

37. Bradford, 14, 20. As we have already noted above, the Pennsylvania legislature heeded Bradford's advice in 1794 when it restricted the state's capital jurisdiction to willful murder and high treason.

38. The baron claimed that "in all or nearly all the states of Europe penalties have decreased or increased in proportion as one has approached or departed from liberty." See Montesquieu, 82. See also Bradford, 36.

39. Bradford, 21.

40. Bradford, 43–46.

41. M. E., *Essays on the Injustice and Impolicy of Inflicting Capital Punishment* (Philadelphia: The Democratic Press, 1809).

42. Thomas Thacher, *The Danger of Despising the Divine Counsel* (Dedham, 1801), 24–25.

43. Thacher, 25–26.

44. Jonathan Going, *A Discourse Delivered at Worcester* (Worcester: William Manning, 1825), 11.

45. Masur, 96.

46. Jacob Cassat, *Journal of the Thirty-Fourth House of Representatives of the Commonwealth of Pennsylvania* (Harrisburg: John Weistling, 1823–1824), 577. Albert Post long ago suggested that the public disorder occasioned by the execution of John Lescher in October of 1822 motivated the Pennsylvania legislature to investigate the possibility of privatization. See "Early Efforts to Abolish Capital Punishment in Pennsylvania," *Pennsylvania Magazine of History and Biography* 68 (1944): 33–53. On the subject of public executions in Pennsylvania generally, see Negley Teeters, "Public Executions in Pennsylvania: 1682–1834," in *Crime and Justice in American History: The Colonies and Early Republic,* ed. Eric Monkkonen (Westport, Ct.: Meckler, 1990). Also see Cassat, 706–9.

47. Francis Bacon [Francis Parkman], "Capital Punishment," *The Christian Examiner* (March 1832), 28–29.

48. Masur, ch. 3, should be consulted as a helpful starting point for understanding the origins of private executions in Early National America. I am left with the impression that he minimizes the theological dimensions of the debate over privatization, preferring to focus only on the political.

Works Cited

Books and Journal Articles

Acts and Resolves of the Province of Massachusetts Bay, 1692–1780. 5 vols. Boston: Wright and Potter, 1869.

Allen, David Grayson. *In English Ways: The Movements of Societies and the Transferal of English Local Law and Customs to Massachusetts Bay in the Seventeenth Century*. Chapel Hill: University of North Carolina Press, 1981.

Ames, William. *The Marrow of Theology,* trans. John D. Eusden. Durham, N.C.: Labyrinth Press, 1983.

Amory, Thomas. *Life of James Sullivan with Selections from his Writings*. Boston: Phillips, Sampson, and Company, 1859.

Appleby, Joyce. *Republicanism and Liberalism in the Historical Imagination*. Cambridge: Harvard University Press, 1992.

———. "Republicanism in the History and Historiography of the United States." *American Quarterly* (Autumn 1985).

Ashcraft, Richard. "Locke's State of Nature: Historical Fact or Moral Fiction." *American Political Science Review* 62:3 (September 1968).

Asher, Robert, Lawrence Goodheart, and Alan Rogers. "Cross-cultural 'Murther' and Retribution in Colonial New England." In their *Murder on Trial, 1620–2002*. Albany: State University of New York Press, 2005.

Bailey, James Montgomery. *History of Danbury, Connecticut, 1684–1896*. New York: Burr Printing House, 1896.

Bailyn, Bernard. *The Ideological Origins of the American Revolution*. Cambridge: Harvard University Press, 1967.

Baldwin, Alice. *The New England Clergy and the American Revolution*. Durham: Duke University Press, 1928.

Baldwin, Moses. *The Ungodly Condemned in Judgment*. Boston: Kneeland and Adams, 1771.

Baldwin, Thomas. *The Danger of Living without the Fear of God*. Boston: Kneeland and Adams, 1819.

Balzell, Digby. *Puritan Boston and Quaker Philadelphia: Two Protestant Ethics and the Spirit of Class Authority and Leadership*. New York: The Free Press, 1979.

Barbour, Hugh. *The Quakers in Puritan England.* New Haven: Yale University Press, 1964.

Barnes, Viola. *The Dominion of New England.* New Haven: Yale University Press, 1923.

Beccaria, Cesare. *On Crime and Punishments,* ed. David Young. Indianapolis: Hackett Publishing Company, 1986.

Bentham, Jeremy. *Rationale of Punishment,* ed. Heinrich Oppenheimer. Montclair, N.J.: Patterson Smith, 1975.

Bentley, William. *The Diary of William Bentley.* 2 vols. Gloucester, Mass.: Smith Publishers, 1962.

"Biographical Sketches of the Thacher Family, from their First Settlement in New England." *New England Magazine* 7:1 (July 1834).

Bosco, Ronald. "Early American Gallows Literature: An Annotated Checklist." *Resources for American Literary Studies* 8 (1978).

———. "Lectures at the Pillory: The Early American Execution Sermon." *American Quarterly* 30 (1978).

———. *Sermons for Days of Fast, Prayer, and Humiliation and Execution Sermons, The Puritan Sermon in America.* Vol. 1. Delmar, N.Y.: Scholars' Facsimiles and Reprints, 1978.

Breen, Timothy. *The Character of a Good Ruler: A Study of Puritan Political Ideas in New England, 1630–1730.* New Haven: Yale University Press, 1970.

Breitenbach, William. "The Consistent Calvinism of the New Divinity Movement." *William and Mary Quarterly* 3d Ser., 41 (1984).

Bremer, Francis. *The Puritan Experiment: New England Society from Bradford to Edwards.* Hanover, N.H.: University Press of New England, 1995.

A Brief Account of the Life and Abominable Thefts of the Notorious Isaac Frasier. New London, Conn.: Timothy Green, 1768.

A Brief Sketch of the Life of Horace Carter. Worcester: William Manning, 1825.

Brooke, Frances. *The History of Lady Julia Mandeville.* N.p., 1763.

Brooke, John. "To the Quiet of the People: Revolutionary Settlements and Civil Unrest in Western Massachusetts." *William and Mary Quarterly* 3d. Ser. 46:3 (July 1989).

Brown, Richard D., and Irene Quenzler Brown. *The Hanging of Ephraim Wheeler: A Story of Rape, Incest, and Justice in Early America.* Cambridge: Harvard University Press, 2003.

Browne, Arthur. *Religious Education of Children Recommended.* Boston: S. Kneeland and T. Green, 1740.

Bushman, Richard. *From Puritan to Yankee: Character and Social Order in Connecticut, 1690–1765.* Cambridge: Harvard University Press, 1967.

Butler, Jon. *Becoming America: The Revolution Before 1776.* Cambridge: Harvard University Press, 2000.

Calvin, John. *Institutes of the Christian Religion,* ed. John T. McNeill. Philadelphia: Westminster Press, 1960.

Campbell, John. *After Souls by Death are Separated from their Bodies, they Come to Judgment.* Boston: S. Kneeland and T. Green, 1738.

Carr, Jacqueline. "A Change 'As Remarkable as the Revolution Itself': Boston's Demographics, 1780–1800." *New England Quarterly* 73 (2000).

Cassat, Jacob. *Journal of the Thirty-Fourth House of Representatives of the Commonwealth of Pennsylvania.* Harrisburg: John Weistling, 1823–1824.

Caulkins, Francis. *A History of New London*. Unpublished manuscript (1852) held at the Connecticut State Historical Society.

Channing, Henry. *God Admonishing his People of their Duty, as Parents and Masters*. New London: T. Green, 1786.

Chapin, Bradley. *The American Law of Treason: Revolutionary and Early National Origins*. Seattle: University of Washington Press, 1964.

Chauncy, Charles. *The Horrid Nature and Enormous Guilt of Murder*. Boston: T. Fleet, 1754.

Checkley, Samuel. *Murder a Great and Crying Sin*. Boston: T. Fleet, 1733.

Clap, Nathaniel. *The Lord's Voice Crying to His People*. Boston: B. Green, 1715.

Cockburn, J. S. *Crime in England, 1550–1800*. Princeton, N.J.: Princeton University Press, 1977.

Cohen, Daniel. "A Fellowship of Thieves: Property Criminals in Eighteenth-Century Massachusetts." *Journal of Social History* 22 (1988).

———. *Pillars of Salt, Monuments of Grace: New England Crime Literature and the Origins of American Popular Culture, 1674–1860*. New York: Oxford University Press, 1993.

———. "Social Injustice, Sexual Violence, Spiritual Transcendence: Constructions of Interracial Rape in Early American Crime Literature, 1767–1817." *William and Mary Quarterly* 3d. Ser. 56:3 (1999).

Colman, Benjamin. *The Divine Compassions Declar'd and Magnified*. Boston: T. Fleet and T. Green, 1717.

———. *The Hainous Nature of the Sin of Murder*. Boston: T. Fleet and T. Green, 1713.

———. *It is a Fearful Thing to Fall into the Hands of the Living God*. Boston: John Philips and Thomas Hancock, 1726.

Conant, Sylvanus. *The Blood of Abel and the Blood of Jesus Considered and Improved in a Sermon*. Boston: T. Fleet, 1763.

———. *The Blood of Abel and the Blood of Jesus*. Boston: Edes and Gill, 1764.

Conforti, Joseph. *Samuel Hopkins and the New Divinity Movement: Calvinism, the Congregational Ministry, and Reform in New England between the Great Awakenings*. Grand Rapids: Eerdmans, 1981.

Cook, Louis. *History of Norfolk County, Massachusetts, 1622–1918*. 2 vols. New York: S. J. Clarke Publishing Company, 1918.

Cooper, David. *The Lesson of the Scaffold: The Public Execution Controversy in Victorian England*. Athens, Ohio: The Ohio University Press, 1974.

Cooper, Robert Alan. "The English Quakers and Prison Reform, 1809–1823." *Quaker History: The Bulletin of Friends Historical Association* 68:1 (Spring 1979).

Corrigan, John. *The Hidden Balance: Religion and the Social Theories of Charles Chauncy and Jonathan Mayhew*. New York: Cambridge University Press, 1987.

———. *The Prism of Piety: Catholick Congregational Clergy at the Beginning of the Enlightenment*. New York: Oxford University Press, 1991.

Crawford, Mary Caroline. *The Romance of Old New England Rooftrees*. Boston: L.C. Page and Company, 1902.

Cromwell, Paul. "The Holy Experiment: An Examination of the Influence of the Society of Friends upon the Development and Evolution of American Correctional Philosophy." Ph.D. diss., Florida State University, 1986.

———. "Quaker Reforms in American Criminal Justice: The Penitentiary and Beyond." *Criminal Justice History* 10 (1989).

Daggett, David. *Sketches of the Life of Joseph Mountain*. New Haven: T. & S. Green, 1784.

Dale, Elizabeth. "Conflicts of Law: Reconsidering the Influence of Religion on Law in Massachusetts Bay." *Numen* 43 (1996).

Dalzell, George. *Benefit of Clergy in America*. Winston-Salem, N.C.: J. F. Blair, 1955.

Dana, James. *The Intent of Capital Punishment*. New Haven: T. & S. Green, 1790.

Danforth, Samuel. *The Cry of Sodom Enquired Into*. Boston: Marmaduke Johnson, 1674.

Daniels, Bruce. *The Connecticut Town: Growth and Development, 1635–1790*. Middletown: Wesleyan University Press, 1979.

Davies, Adrian. *The Quakers in English Society, 1655–1725*. New York: Oxford University Press, 2000.

Davis, David Brion. "The Movement to Abolish Capital Punishment in America, 1787–1861." *American Historical Review* 63 (1957).

Davis, Thomas. *A Rumor of Revolt: The Great Negro Plot in Colonial New York*. New York: The Free Press, 1985.

DeCoursey Fales, *The Fales Family of Bristol Rhode Island*. N.p., 1919.

de Jong, Peter. *The Covenant Idea in New England Theology: 1620–1847*. Grand Rapids: Eerdmans, 1945.

Demos, John Putnam. *A Little Commonwealth: Family Life in Plymouth Colony*. New York: Oxford University Press, 1970.

Denenberg, Dennis. "The Missing Link: New England's Influence on Early National Educational Policies." *New England Quarterly* 52 (June 1979).

The Diary of Samuel Sewall, 1674–1729, ed. M. Halsey Thomas. 2 vols. New York: Farrar, Straus, and Giroux, 1973.

Dow, George Francis, and John Edmonds. *Pirates of the New England Coast, 1630–1730*. Salem, Mass.: Marine Research Society, 1923.

Dworetz, Steven. *The Unvarnished Doctrine: Locke, Liberalism, and the American Revolution*. Durham: Duke University Press, 1990.

Edwards, Jonathan. *The Nature of True Virtue*. Ann Arbor: University of Michigan Press, 1960.

Ellsbree, Oliver. "Samuel Hopkins and the Doctrine of Benevolence." *New England Quarterly* 8 (1935).

Emsley, Clive. *Crime and Society in England, 1750–1900*. New York: Longman, 1996.

Ericson, Kai. *Wayward Puritans: A Study in the Sociology of Deviance*. New York: John Wiley and Sons, 1966.

Faber, Eli. "The Evil that Men Do: Crime and Transgression in Colonial Massachusetts." Ph.D. diss., Columbia University, 1974.

———. "Puritan Criminals: The Economic, Social, and Intellectual Background to Crime in Seventeenth-Century Massachusetts." *Perspectives in American History* 11 (1977–1978).

Fairbanks, Ebenezer. *The Solemn Declaration of the Late Unfortunate Jason Fairbanks*. Dedham, Mass.: H. Mann, 1801.

Fairbanks, Lorenzo. *Genealogy of the Fairbanks Family, 1633–1897*. Washington, D.C., 1897.

Faithful Warnings to Prevent Fearful Judgment. Boston, 1704.

Fales, DeCoursey. *The Fales Family of Bristol, Rhode Island*. New York: privately printd, 1919.

Ferdinand, Theodore. "Criminal Justice: From Colonial Intimacy to Bureaucratic Formality." In *The Handbook of Contemporary Urban Life,* ed. David Street, et al. San Francisco: Jossey-Bass, 1978.

Ferm, Robert. *Jonathan Edwards the Younger, 1745–1801: A Colonial Pastor*. Grand Rapids: Eerdmans, 1976.

Fitzmier, John. *New England's Moral Legislator: Timothy Dwight, 1752–1817*. Bloomington: Indiana University Press, 1998.

Flaherty, David. "Law and the Enforcement of Morals in Early America." In *Law in Early America,* ed. Donald Fleming and Bernard Bailyn. Boston: Little, Brown, 1971.

Fleigelman, Jay. *Prodigals and Pilgrims: The American Revolution against Patriarchal Authority, 1750–1800*. Cambridge: Cambridge University Press, 1982.

Foucault, Michel. *Discipline and Punish: The Birth of the Prison*. New York: Vintage Books, 1979.

Foxcroft, Thomas. *A Lesson of Caution to Young Sinners*. Boston, 1733.

Freeman, Dale. "'Melancholy Catastrophe!' The Story of Jason Fairbanks and Elizabeth Fales." *Historical Journal of Massachusetts* 26:1 (Winter 1998).

Friedman, Lawrence. *Crime and Punishment in American History*. New York: Basic Books, 1993.

Gattrell, V. A. C. *The Hanging Tree: Execution and the English People. 1770–1868*. New York: Oxford University Press, 1994.

"The General Lawes and Liberties of the Massachusetts Colony." In *Colonial Laws of Massachusetts,* ed. William Whitmore. Boston: City Council of Boston, 1890.

Gewalt, Gerald. *The Promise of Power: The Emergence of the Legal Profession in Massachusetts, 1760–1840*. Westport, Ct.: Greenwood Press, 1979.

Gildrie, Richard. "The Ceremonial Puritan Days of Humiliation and Thanksgiving." *New England Historical and Genealogical Record* 136 (1982).

Glenn, Charles. *The Myth of the Common School*. Amherst: University of Massachusetts Press, 1988.

Godbeer, Richard. "The Cry of Sodom: Discourses, Intercourse, and Desire in Colonial New England." *William and Mary Quarterly* 3d. Ser. 52:2 (April 1995).

Going, Jonathan. *A Discourse Delivered at Worcester*. Worcester: William Manning, 1825.

Gottlieb, Gabriel. "Theater of Death: Capital Punishment in Early America, 1750–1800." Ph.D. diss., University of Pittsburgh, 2005.

Graham, Chauncy. *God will Trouble the Troublers of his People*. New York: H. Gaine, 1759.

Haakonssen, Lisbeth. *Medicine and Morals in the Enlightenment*. Amsterdam: Rodophi, 1997.

Haffenden, Philip. *New England in the English Nation, 1689–1713*. Oxford: Clarendon Press, 1974.

Hall, David. *The Faithful Shepherd: A History of the New England Ministry in the Seventeenth Century*. Chapel Hill: University of North Carolina Press, 1972.

———. *Worlds of Wonder, Days of Judgment: Popular Religious Belief in Early New England*. Cambridge: Harvard University Press, 1989.

Halttunen, Karen. *Murder Most Foul: The Killer and the American Gothic Imagination.* Cambridge: Harvard University Press, 1998.

Hambleton, Else. "The World Fill'd with a Generation of Bastards: Pregnant Brides and Unwed Mothers in Seventeenth-Century Massachusetts." Ph.D. diss., University of Massachusetts at Amherst, 2000.

Hanson, Robert Brand, ed., *Diary of Nathaniel Ames, 1758–1822.* 2 vols. Camden, Maine: Picton Publishers, 1998.

Haroutunian, Joseph. *Piety Versus Moralism: The Passing of the New England Theology.* New York: Holt, 1932.

Harris, Ian. *The Mind of John Locke: A Study of Political Theory in its Intellectual Setting.* New York: Oxford, 1994.

Harris, Thaddeus Mason. *A Sermon Preached in the First Parish in Dedham.* Dedham: Herman Mann, 1801.

Haskins, George. *Law and Liberty in Early Massachusetts: A Study in Tradition and Design.* New York: Macmillan, 1960.

Hatch, Nathan. *The Sacred Cause of Liberty: Republican Thought and the Millennium in Revolutionary New England.* New Haven: Yale University Press, 1977.

Hawk, David Freeman. *Benjamin Rush: Revolutionary Gadfly.* Indianapolis: Bobbs Merill, 1971.

Hay, Douglas. "Property, Authority, and Criminal Law." In *Albion's Fatal Tree: Crime and Society in Eighteenth-Century England,* ed. Douglas Hay, et al. London: Allen Lane, 1975.

Hearn, Daniel. *Legal Executions in New England: A Comprehensive Reference, 1623–1960.* Jefferson, N.C.: McFarland, 1999.

Hempstead, Joshua. *Diary.* New London: New London Historical Society, 1901.

Hillers, Delbert. *Covenant: The History of a Biblical Idea.* Baltimore: Johns Hopkins University Press, 1968.

Hirsch, Adam Jay. *The Rise of the Penitentiary: Prisons and Punishment in Early America.* New Haven: Yale University Press, 1992.

Hobart, Noah. *Excessive Wickedness the Way to an Untimely Death.* New Haven: Thomas and Samuel Green, 1768.

Hoffer, Peter. *The Great New York Conspiracy of 1741: Slavery, Crime, and Colonial Law.* Lawrence: University of Kansas Press, 2003.

Hoffer, Peter, and N. E. H. Hull. *Murdering Mothers: Infanticide in England and New England, 1558–1803.* New York: New York University Press, 1981.

Hogarth, William. *Idle 'Prentice Executed at Tyburn.* N.p., 1747.

Holbrook, Clyde. Introduction to Jonathan Edwards, *The Great Christian Doctrine of Original Sin Defended.* New Haven: Yale University Press, 1970.

Horle, Craig. *The Quakers and the English Legal System, 1660–1688.* Urbana: University of Illinois Press, 1988.

Hull, N. E. H. *Female Felons: Women and Serious Crime in Colonial Massachusetts.* Chicago: University of Illinois Press, 1987.

Hunter, Donna. "Dead Men Talking: Africans and the Law in New England's Eighteenth-Century Execution Sermons and Crime Narratives." Ph.D. diss., University of California at Berkeley, 2000.

Hutchinson, Aaron. *Iniquity Purged by Mercy and Truth.* Boston: Thomas and John Fleet, 1769.

"John Dutton to George Larkin, March 25, 1686." In *The Puritans: A Sourcebook of their Writings,* ed. Perry Miller and Thomas Johnson. 2 vols. New York: Harper and Row, 1963.

Johnson, Richard. *Adjustment to Empire: The New England Colonies, 1675–1715.* Rutgers: Rutgers University Press, 1981.

Jones, Peter. *The Science of Man in the Scottish Enlightenment: Hume, Reid, and their Contemporaries*. Edinburgh: University of Edinburgh Press, 1989.

Jordan, Winthrop. *White Over Black: American Attitudes Toward the Negro, 1550–1812*. Chapel Hill: University of North Carolina Press, 1968.

The Justice Management Division. *The 200th Anniversary of the Office of Attorney General*. Washington, D.C.: The United States Department of Justice, 1991.

Kaestle, Carl. *Pillars of the Republic: Common Schools and American Society, 1780–1860*. New York: Hill and Wang, 1983.

Kaestle, Carl, and Maris Vinovskis. *Education and Social Change in Nineteenth-Century Massachusetts*. Cambridge: Harvard University Press, 1980.

Kealey, Linda. "Patterns of Punishment: Massachusetts in the Eighteenth Century." *American Journal of Legal History* 30 (1986).

Keen, Ralph. "The Limits of Power and Obedience in the Later Calvin." *Calvin Theological Journal* 27 (1992).

Kennedy, Lawrence. *Planning the City Upon a Hill. Boston Since 1630*. Amherst: University of Massachusetts Press, 1992.

Kling, David. *A Field of Divine Wonders: The New Divinity and Village Revivals of Northwestern Connecticut, 1792–1822*. University Park: University of Pennsylvania Press, 1993.

Kloppenberg, James. "The Virtues of Liberalism: Christianity, Republicanism, and Ethics in Early American Political Discourse." *The Journal of American History* 74:1 (June 1987).

Knerr, Harry. "The Election Sermon: Primer for Revolutionaries." *Speech Monographs* 29 (1962).

Knight, Janice. *Orthodoxies in Massachusetts: Re-reading American Puritanism*. Cambridge: Harvard University Press, 1994.

Kohler, Ann. *Montesquieu's Comparative Politics and the Spirit of American Constitutionalism*. Lawrence: University of Kansas Press, 1988.

Kraynak, Robert. "John Locke: From Absolutism to Toleration." *American Political Science Review* 74 (March 1980).

Lake, Peter, and Michael Questier. *The Antichrist's Lewd Hat: Protestants, Papists, and Players in Post-Reformation England*. New Haven: Yale University Press, 2002.

Langdon, Timothy. *A Sermon Preached at Danbury*. Danbury: Douglas and Nichols, 1798.

La Rochefoucauld-Liancourt, François-Alexandre-Frédéric. *On the Prisons of Philadelphia*. Philadelphia: Moreau de Saint-Mery, 1796.

Lazenby, Walter. "Exhortation as Exorcism: Mather's Sermons to Murderers." *Quarterly Journal of Speech* 57 (1971).

Leder, Lawrence. *Liberty and Authority: Early American Political Ideology, 1689–1763*. Chicago: Quadrangle Books, 1968.

The Letters of Benjamin Rush. Ed. Lyman Butterfield. 2 vols. Princeton: Princeton University Press, 1951.

Levine, Lawrence. *Black Culture and Black Consciousness: Afro-American Folk Thought from Slavery to Freedom*. New York: Oxford University Press, 1978.

Lewis, David. *From Newgate to Dannemora: The Rise of the Penitentiary in New York, 1796–1848*. Ithaca: Cornell University Press, 1965.

Lewis, Theodore. "A Revolutionary Tradition, 1689–1774: There was a Revolution Here as Well as in England." *New England Quarterly* 46:3 (1973).

Linebaugh, Peter. *The London Hanged: Crime and Civil Society in the Eighteenth Century*. New York: Cambridge University Press, 1992.

Locke, John. *Second Treatise of Government,* ed. Sterling Lamprecht. New York: Appleton-Century-Crofts, 1965.

———. "Some Thoughts Concerning Education." In *The Educational Writings of John Locke,* ed. J. Axtell. Cambridge: Cambridge University Press, 1968.

Lockridge, Kenneth. *Literacy in Colonial New England: An Enquiry into the Social Context of Literacy in the Early Modern West*. New York: Norton, 1974.

———. *A New England Town: The First Hundred Years, Dedham, Massachusetts, 1636–1736*. New York: W.W. Norton and Company, 1970.

Lovejoy, David. *The Glorious Revolution in America*. New York: Harper and Row, 1972.

Lowell, Charles. *A Discourse Delivered March 16, 1817*. Boston: John Eliot, 1817.

Lownes, Caleb. *An Account of the Alteration and Present State of the Penal Laws of Pennsylvania*. Lexington: J. Bradford, 1794.

———. *Account of the Alteration and Present State of the Penal Laws of Pennsylvania, Containing also an Account of the Gaol and Penitentiary House of Philadelphia and the Management Thereof*. Philadelphia: T. Dobson, 1793.

MacCarty, Thaddeus. *The Power and Grace of Christ Display'd to a Dying Malefactor*. Boston: Kneeland and Adams, 1768.

Maestro, Marcello. *Cesare Beccaria and the Origins of Penal Reform* (Philadelphia: Temple University Press, 1973).

———. "A Pioneer in the Abolition of Capital Punishment: Cesare Beccaria." *Journal of the History of Ideas* 34:3 (Autumn 1973).

Maier, Pauline. "Popular Uprisings and Civil Authority in Eighteenth-Century America." *William and Mary Quarterly* 3d Ser., 27:3 (Autumn 1970).

Mandeville, Bernard. *An Enquiry into the Causes of the Frequent Executions at Tyburn*. London, 1725.

Masur, Louis. *Rites of Execution: Capital Punishment and the Transformation of American Culture, 1776–1865*. New York: Oxford, 1989.

Mather, Cotton. *Call of the Gospel Apply'd*. Boston: R. Pierce, 1686.

———. *The Curbed Sinner*. Boston: J. Allen, 1713.

———. *The Diary of Cotton Mather*. 2 vols. New York: Frederick Ungar, 1957.

———. *Pillars of Salt: An History of Some Criminals Executed in this Land for Capital Crimes*. Boston: B. Green and J. Allen, 1699.

———. *Speedy Repentance Urged*. Boston: Samuel Green, 1690.

———. *Tremenda: The Dreadful Sound with which the Wicked are Thunderstruck*. Boston: Bartholomew Green, 1721.

———. *A True Relation of the Murder Committed by David Wallis on his Companion Benjamin Stolwood*. Boston: J. Allen, 1713.

———. *A Vial Poured Out Upon the Sea*. Boston: T. Fleet, 1726.

Mather, Increase. *The Folly of Sinning Opened and Applied in Two Sermons*. Boston, 1699.

———. *A Sermon Occasioned by the Execution of a Man Found Guilty of Murder*. Boston: Joseph Browning, 1686.

———. *A Sermon . . . Wherein it is Shewed that Excess in Wickedness Doth Bring Untimely Death*. Boston, 1674.

Mattingly, Paul. "Educational Revivals in Ante-Bellum New England." *History of Education Quarterly* 11 (Fall 1971).

McKey, Philip. *Voices Against Death: American Opposition to Capital Punishment, 1787–1975*. New York: Burt Franklin and Company, 1975.

McLynn, Frank. *Crime and Punishment in Eighteenth-Century England*. New York: Routledge, 1989.

McManus, Edgar. *Law and Liberty in Early New England: Criminal Justice and Due Process, 1620–1692*. Amherst: University of Massachusetts Press, 1993.

M. E. *Essays on the Injustice and Impolicy of Inflicting Capital Punishment*. Philadelphia: The Democratic Press, 1809.

Meranze, Michael. *Laboratories of Virtue: Punishment, Revolution, and Authority in Philadelphia, 1760–1835*. Chapel Hill: University of North Carolina Press, 1996.

Messer, Peter. "'A Species of Treason and Not the Least Dangerous Kind': The Treason Trials of Abraham Carlisle and John Roberts." *Pennsylvania Magazine of History and Biography* 123 (1999).

Miller, Guy. "Rebellion in Zion: The Overthrow of the Dominion of New England." *Historian* 30:3 (1968).

Miller, Perry. *Errand into the Wilderness*. New York: Harper Torchbooks, 1956.

———. *The New England Mind: From Colony to Province*. Cambridge: Harvard University Press, 1953.

Minnick, Wayne. "The New England Execution Sermon, 1674–1800." *Speech Monographs* 35 (1968).

Montesquieu, Baron de. *The Spirit of the Laws,* trans. Anne Cohler, Basia Carolyn Miller, and Harold Stone. New York: Cambridge University Press, 1989.

Moodey, Joshua. *An Exhortation to a Condemned Malefactor*. Boston: R. P., 1686.

Moody, Samuel. *Summary Account of the Life and Death of Joseph Quasson, Indian*. Boston, 1726.

Morgan, Edmund. "The American Revolution Considered as an Intellectual Movement." In *Paths of American Thought,* ed. Arthur Schlesinger and Morton White. Boston: Houghton Mifflin, 1963.

———. *The Puritan Family: Religion and Domestic Relations in Seventeenth-Century New England*. New York: Harper and Row, 1966.

———. *Puritan Political Ideas, 1558–1794*. Indianapolis: Bobbs-Merrill Company, 1965.

Morrison, Samuel Eliot. *Harrison Gray Otis, 1765–1848: The Urbane Federalist*. Boston: Houghton Mifflin, 1969.

A Mournful Tragedy. Dedham, 1801. Early American Imprints, 2d Ser. no. 964.

Muller, Richard. "Calvin, Beza, and the Exegetical History of Romans 13:1–7." In *Identity of Geneva*. Westport, Ct.: Greenwood Press, 1998.

Murrin, John. "Magistrates, Sinners, and a Precarious Liberty: Trial by Jury in Seventeenth-Century New England." In *Saints and Revolutionaries: Essays in Early American History,* ed. David Hall. New York: Norton, 1984.

Narrative and Confession of Thomas Powers, A Negro. Norwich: John Trumbull, 1796.

Narrative of the Life of Joseph Mountain, a Negro. New Haven: T. and S. Green, 1790.

New Haven County Superior Court, Record Group 3, Drawer No. 327 of the Connecticut State Archives.

Oaks, Robert. "Things Fearful to Name: Sodomy and Buggery in Seventeenth-Century New England." *Journal of Social History* 12 (1978).

Offnut, William. *Of Good Laws and Good Men: Law and Society in the Delaware Valley, 1680–1710*. Urbana: University of Illinois Press, 1995.

"Of the Fall of Man, of Sin, and of the Punishment Thereof." In Philip Schaff, *Creeds of Christendom*. 6th ed. New York: Harper Brothers, 1931.

Paley, William. *The Principles of Moral and Political Philosophy*. New York: Garland Publishers, 1978.

The Papers of Thomas Jefferson, ed. Julian Boyd. Princeton: Princeton University Press, 1950.

Pennsylvania Archives. 12 vols. Philadelphia: Joseph Sevrens, 1852.

Phillipson, Coleman. *Three Criminal Law Reformers: Beccaria, Bentham and Romilly*. London: J. M. Dent and Sons, 1923.

Philochorus [Robert Annan]. "Observations on Capital Punishment: Being a Reply to an Essay on the Same Subject." *American Museum* 4 (November & December 1788).

Pitkin, Timothy. *A Sermon Preached at Litchfield*. Hartford: Green and Watson, 1769.

Plummer, Jonathan. *Dying Confession of Pomp, a Negro Man*. Newburyport, Conn.: Blunt and March, 1795.

A Poem on Jason Fairbanks who is to be Executed this Day. Dedham, 1801. Early American Imprints, 2d Ser. no. 1161.

Pope, Robert. "The Myth of Declension," *Religion in American History: Interpretive Essays*. New York: Prentice Hall, 1978.

Post, Albert. "Early Efforts to Abolish Capital Punishment in Pennsylvania." *Pennsylvania Magazine of History and Biography* 68 (1944).

Potter, Harry. *Hanging in Judgment: Religion and the Death Penalty in England*. New York: Continuum, 1993.

Powell, Sumner. *Puritan Village: The Formation of the New England Town*. Middletown, Ct.: Wesleyan University Press, 1963.

Powers, Edwin. *Crime and Punishment in Early Massachusetts, 1620–1692*. Boston: Beacon Press, 1966.

Price, Fortune. *The Dying Confession of Fortune*. Boston, 1762.

Proceedings of the Massachusetts Historical Society, March 1883. Held at the Massachusetts Historical Society.

Record Book of the Superior Court of the Judicature 2:199–200. Held at the Massachusetts State Archives.

Records of the Court of Assistants of the Colony of Massachusetts Bay, 1673–1692. 3 vols. County of Suffolk, 1901–1928.

Records of the Quarterly Courts of Essex County, Mass., vol. 1. Held at the Massachusetts Historical Society.

Rediker, Marcus. *Between the Devil and the Deep Blue Sea: Merchant Seamen, Pirates and the Anglo-American Maritime World, 1700–1750*. New York: Cambridge University Press, 1993.

Reid, Thomas. *Essays on the Intellectual Powers of Man*. N.p., 1785.

———. *Inquiry into the Human Mind on the Principle of Common Sense*. N.p., 1764.

Report of the Trial of Ephraim Wheeler. Stockbridge, Mass.: H. Willard, 1805.

Report of the Trial of Jason Fairbanks on an Indictment for the Murder of Elizabeth Fales. Boston: Russell and Cutler, 1801.

Rhode Island Court of Trials, vol. A, 225.

Richards, Leonard. *Shays's Rebellion: The American Revolution's Final Battle.* Philadelphia: University of Pennsylvania Press, 2002.

Richardson, Samuel. *Familiar Letters on Important Occasions,* ed. Brian Downs. New York: Dodd, Mead, and Co., 1928.

Ripley, Ezra. *Love to Our Neighbor, Explained and Urged.* Boston: Samuel Hall, 1800.

Ritchie, Robert. *Captain Kidd and the War Against the Pirates.* Cambridge: Harvard University Press, 1986.

Rodgers, Daniel. "Republicanism: The Career of a Concept." *The Journal of American History* 79:1 (June 1992).

Rogers, John. *Death the Certain Wages of Sin for the Impenitent, Life the Sure Reward of Grace to the Penitent, together with the Only Way for Youth to Avoid the Former and Attain the Latter.* Boston, 1701.

———. *Holiness the Way to Blessedness.* Boston: B. Green and J. Allen, 1701.

Rowe, William. *Thomas Reid on Freedom and Morality.* Ithaca, N.Y.: Cornell University Press, 1991.

Rush, Benjamin. *Considerations on the Injustice and Impolicy of Punishing Murder by Death.* Philadelphia: Matthew Carey, 1792.

———. *An Enquiry into the Consistency of the Punishment of Murder by Death, with Reason and Revelation.* Philadelphia: [Joseph James], 1797.

———. *An Enquiry into the Effects of Public Punishments upon Criminals and Upon Society.* Philadelphia: Joseph James, 1787. Rush's essay is in *Essays: Literary, Moral, and Philosophical,* ed. Michael Meranze. Schenectady, N.Y.: Union College Press, 1988.

———. *An Enquiry into the Influence of Physical Causes Upon the Moral Faculty.* Philadelphia: Charles Cist, 1786.

———. "An Enquiry into the Justice and Policy of Punishing Murder by Death." *American Museum* 4 (July 1788).

Sassi, Jonathan. *A Republic of Righteousness: The Public Christianity of the Post-Revolutionary New England Clergy.* New York: Oxford University Press, 2001.

Scott, Donald. *From Office to Profession: The New England Ministry, 1750–1850.* Philadelphia: University of Pennsylvania Press, 1978.

A Sermon Preached at the Execution of Moses Paul, an Indian. New London, 1772.

Sewall, Samuel. *The Diary of Samuel Sewall,* ed. M. Halsey Thomas. 2 vols. New York: Farrar, Straus, and Giroux, 1973.

Shalhope, Robert. "Republicanism and Early American Historiography." *William and Mary Quarterly* 3d. Ser. 39:2 (April 1982).

———. "Toward a Republican Synthesis: The Emergence of an Understanding of Republicanism in American Historiography." *William and Mary Quarterly* 3d Ser., 29:1 (January 1972).

Sharpe, J. A. "'Last Dying Speeches': Religion, Ideology, and Public Execution in Seventeenth-Century England." *Past and Present* 107 (May 1985).

Shepard, Samuel. *A Sermon Delivered at Lenox.* Stockbridge: H. Willard, 1806.

*A Short Account of the Life of John ***, Alias Owen Syllavan.* Boston, 1756.

Shurtleff, William. *A Sermon Preached December 27, 1739.* Boston: J Draper, 1740.

Sibley's Harvard Graduates, ed. J. L. Sibley and C. K. Shipton. 4 vols. Boston: Massachusetts Historical Society, 1873–1970.

Simmons, John. "Locke's State of Nature." In *The Social Contract Theorists: Critical Essays on Hobbes, Locke, and Rousseau,* ed. Christopher Morris. Lanham, Md.: Rowan and Littlefield, 1999.

A Sketch of the Life of Samuel E. Godfrey. N.p., 1818.

Slaughter, Thomas. *The Whiskey Rebellion*. New York: Oxford University Press, 1986.

Slotkin, Richard. "Narratives of Negro Crime in New England, 1675–1800." *American Quarterly* 25 (1971).

Smith, H. Sheldon. *Changing Conceptions of Original Sin: A Study in American Theology since 1750*. New York: Charles Scribner and Sons, 1955.

Smith, James Morton. "The Federalist Saints vs. the Devils of Sedition." *New England Quarterly* 28:2 (June 1955).

Smith, Paige. *As a City Upon a Hill: The Town in American History*. New York: Knopf, 1966.

Smith, Timothy. "Protestant Schooling and American Nationality, 1800–1850." *Journal of American History* 53 (1966–1967).

Spelman, W. M. *John Locke and the Problem of Depravity*. Oxford: Clarendon Press, 1988.

Spurlin, Paul. "Beccaria's *Essay on Crimes and Punishments* in Eighteenth-Century America." *Studies on Voltaire and the Eighteenth Century* 27 (1963).

———. *Montesquieu in America, 1760–1801*. University: University of Louisiana Press, 1940.

Statutes at Large of Pennsylvania. 26 vols. Harrisburg: C. M. Busch, 1911.

A Story of Rape, Incest, and Justice in Early America. Cambridge: Harvard University Press, 2003.

Stout, Harry. *New England Soul: Preaching and Religious Culture in Colonial New England*. New York: Oxford, 1986.

Strong, Nathan. *The Reasons and Designs of Public Punishments*. Hartford, 1777.

Stuckey, Sterling. *Slave Culture: Nationalist Theory and the Foundations of Black America*. New York: Oxford, 1987.

Superior Court of the Judicature, case no. 160576. Held at the Massachusetts State Archives.

Supreme Judicial Court, Case Nos. 44640 and 44647. Held at the Massachusetts State Archives New Haven Colony Records.

Supreme Judicial Court of Massachusetts, case no. 9174. Held at the Massachusetts State Archives.

Szatmary, David. *Shays's Rebellion: The Making of an Agrarian Insurrection*. Amherst: University of Massachusetts Press, 1980.

Taylor, John. *The Scripture Doctrine of Original Sin Proposed to Free and Candid Examination*. London: M. Waugh, 1740.

———. "The Unhappy Stephen Arnold: An Episode of Murder and Penitence in the Early Republic." In *Through a Glass Darkly: Reflections on Personal Identity in Early America,* ed. Ronald Hoffman, Mechal Sobel, and Fredrika Teute. Chapel Hill: University of North Carolina Press, 1997.

Teeters, Negley. *The Cradle of the Penitentiary: The Walnut Street Jail at Philadelphia, 1773–1835*. Philadelphia: Temple University Publications, 1955.

———. "Public Executions in Pennsylvania: 1682–1834." In *Crime and Justice in American History: The Colonies and Early Republic,* ed. Eric Monkkonen. Westport, Ct.: Meckler, 1990.

Thacher, Thomas. *The Danger of Despising Divine Counsel.* Dedham: Herman Mann, 1801.

Toulouse, Teresa. *The Art of Prophesying: New England Sermons and the Shaping of Belief.* Athens: University of Georgia Press, 1987.

Turnbull, Robert. *A Visit to the Philadelphia Prison.* Philadelphia: Budd and Bartram, 1796.

Tyack, David. "The Kingdom of God and the Common School." *Harvard Educational Review* 36 (Fall 1966).

Ulrich, Laurel Thatcher. *Good Wives: Image and Reality in the Lives of Women in Northern New England, 1650–1750.* New York: Knopf, 1981.

Valeri, Mark. *Law and Providence in Joseph Bellamy's New England: The Origins of the New Divinity in Revolutionary America.* New York: Oxford, 1994.

Vinovskis, Maris. "Trends in Massachusetts Education, 1826–1860." *History of Education Quarterly* 12 (Winter 1972).

Waldron, Jeremy. "Locke: Toleration and the Rationality of Persecution." In *Justifying Toleration,* ed. Susan Mendes. Cambridge: Cambridge University Press, 1988.

Walker, Samuel. *Popular Justice: A History of American Criminal Justice.* New York: Oxford University Press, 1998.

Walker, Williston. *The Creeds and Platforms of Congregationalism.* Boston: The Pilgrim Press, 1960.

Watson, John. *Annals of Philadelphia and Pennsylvania.* Philadelphia: Carey and Hart, 1843.

Webster, Samuel. *A Winter Evening's Conversation on the Doctrine of Original Sin.* New Haven: Green and Russell, 1757.

West, Stephen. *A Sermon Preached at Lenox.* Pittsfield, 1787.

Westerkamp, Marilyn. *Women and Religion in Early America, 1600–1850: The Puritan and Evangelical Traditions.* New York: Routledge, 1999.

Wheeler, Ephraim. *Narrative of the Life of Ephraim Wheeler.* Stockbridge: H. Willard, 1806.

Whitcher, William. *History of the Town of Haverhill, New Hampshire.* Concord, N.H.: Rumford Press, 1919.

Wier, David. *Early New England: A Covenanted Society.* Grand Rapids: Eerdmans, 2005.

Willard, Samuel. *Impenitent Sinners Warned of their Misery and Summoned to Judgment.* Boston: B. Green and J. Allen, 1699.

Williams, Daniel. "'Behold a Tragic Scene Strangely Changed into a Theater of Mercy': The Structure and Significance of Criminal Conversion Narratives in Early New England." *American Quarterly* 38 (1986).

———. "Puritans and Pirates: A Confrontation between Cotton Mather and William Fly in 1726." *Early American Literature* 22 (1987).

———. "Rogues, Rascals, and Scoundrels: The Underworld Literature of Early America." *American Studies* 24 (1983).

Williams, John. *Warnings to the Unclean.* Boston: B. Green and J. Allen, 1699.

Wilson, Douglas. "Thomas Jefferson's Early Notebooks." *William and Mary Quarterly* 3d. Ser. 42:4 (October 1985).

Wilson, Lynn. *History of Fairfield County.* Chicago: S. J. Clarke, 1929.

Winthrop, John. *The Journal of John Winthrop, 1630–1649,* ed. Richard S. Dunn, et al. Cambridge: Harvard University Press, 1996.

Wood, Gordon. *The Creation of the American Republic, 1776–1787*. Chapel Hill: University of North Carolina Press, 1969.

———. *The Radicalism of the American Revolution*. New York: Knopf, 1991.

———. "Thomas Jefferson's Library and the French Connection." *Eighteenth-Century Studies* 26:4 (Summer 1993).

Wood, Neal. "Tabula Rasa, Social Environmentalism, and the 'English Paradigm.'" *Journal of the History of Ideas* 53 (1992).

Worcester, Noah. *A Sermon Delivered at Haverhill, New Hampshire*. Haverhill: N. Coverly, 1796.

Worthington, Erastus. *The History of Dedham from its Settlement . . . to 1827*. Boston: Dutton and Wentworth, 1827.

Wright, Conrad. *American Unitarianism, 1805–1865*. Boston: Northeastern University Press, 1989.

Wright, John. "Metaphysics and Physiology: Mind, Body and the Animal Economy in Eighteenth Century Scotland." *Studies in the Philosophy of the Scottish Enlightenment*, ed. M. A. Stewart. Oxford: Oxford University Press, 1990.

Zuckerman, Michael. *Peaceable Kingdoms: New England Towns in the Eighteenth Century*. New York: Knopf, 1970.

Periodicals

Boston Evening Post
Boston Gazette
Boston Newsletter
Christian Examiner
Columbian Minerva
Columbian Sentinel
Commercial Advertiser
Connecticut Courant
Connecticut Gazette
Connecticut Journal
Essex Gazette
Hampshire Gazette
Independent Chronicle
Massachusetts Spy
Norwich Packet
Worcester Magazine

Index